174130

The Business Establishment

Institute of Industrial Relations

University of California, Berkeley

The
Business
Establishment

Edited by Earl F. Cheit

University of California, Berkeley

John Wiley & Sons, Inc.

New York · London · Sydney

83739

658
C 515

Library of Congress Catalog Card Number: 64-23831
Printed in the United States of America

Contributors

ROBERT L. HEILBRONER, Lecturer, Graduate Faculty, New School for Social Research. Author of *The Worldly Philosophers, The Future as History, The Great Ascent.*

JOHN WILLIAM WARD, Professor of History and American Studies, Amherst College. Author of *Andrew Jackson: Symbol for an Age.*

HENRY NASH SMITH, Professor of English, University of California, Berkeley. Author of the prizewinning study *Virgin Land: The American West as Symbol and Myth.*

RICHARD HOFSTADTER, DeWitt Clinton Professor of American History, Columbia University. Author of Pulitzer prizewinning *Age of Reform* and *Anti-Intellectualism in American Life.*

EARL F. CHEIT, Professor of Business Administration, University of California, Berkeley. Author of *Injury and Recovery in the Course of Employment,* co-author, *Economic and Social Security.*

PAUL A. SAMUELSON, Professor of Economics, Massachusetts Institute of Technology. Past President American Economics Association. Author of *Economics: An Introductory Analysis, Foundations of Economic Analysis.*

PHILIPPE DE WOOT, Faculty of Economics, and Director of Research, Management Training Center, University of Louvain, Belgium.

GILBERT M. SAUVAGE, Professor of Economics, European Institute of Business Administration, Fontainebleau, France; and Director, Paris Honours Program, Institute of European Studies, Paris.

Preface

"It is a libel upon human nature," Alfred North Whitehead told a Harvard audience in 1928, "to conceive that zest for life is the product of pedestrian purposes directed toward the narrow routine of material comforts." He was defending the youthful Harvard Business School. To critics who might assert that universities should be concerned more with removing the taint of trade from young men and less with instilling in them a zest for business, he declaimed: "The justification for a university is that it preserves the connection between knowledge and the zest of life." It was in this spirit that I asked five distinguished authors from fields other than business to join me in conducting a workshop that would bring the humanities, politics, and history to bear on the establishment of business and its practitioners.

Each author was free to choose his own way of confronting the issues assigned him, and these essays on the social and political environment of business are the result. Their common assumption is the importance of preserving the connection between the intellectual adventure and the business adventure.

I am grateful to the Ford Foundation, which made an exception to the more usual format of its highly successful summer workshop program and granted assistance to this experimental venture. For the first time a group of business school faculty members teaching in the new and growing field dealing with the external world of business were brought together. At the workshop, held on the Berkeley campus of the University of California in January 1964, each author presented his essay to the group, which spent a week in seminars and critical exchange of teaching and research materials.

Two of the presentations by workshop participants spurred interest and discussion, which convinced the authors that they should be included here. I am pleased, therefore, to give the last words in this book to Professor Philippe de Woot, Faculty of Economics and Director of Research, Management Training Center, University of Louvain, Belgium, and to Professor Gilbert M. Sauvage, European Institute of Business Administration, Fontainebleau, France.

If the contributions of other workshop participants cannot be singled out for mention, they are nevertheless reflected in the final version of each essay, as well as in yet to be published work of the participants themselves. On behalf of the authors, I want to thank each participant, and to clear them of responsibility. They are: Professor Harry T. Allan, Oregon State University; Professor Robert L. Blomstrom, Arizona State University; Professor J. Boddewyn, University of Portland; Professor Wayne G. Broehl, Jr., Dartmouth College; Professor Harvey C. Bunke, State University of Iowa; Professor John C. Chitwood, Jr., University of Missouri at Kansas City; Professor Paul W. Cook, Jr., Harvard University; Dean William C. Frederick, University of Pittsburgh; Professor Cornelius Gillam, University of Pennsylvania; Professor Earl Goddard, University of Colorado; Professor J. M. Hund, Emory University; Professor Van Dusen Kennedy, University of California, Berkeley; Professor Herman E. Krooss, New York University; Professor John A. Larson, Northwestern University; Professor Sumner Marcus, University of Washington; Dean Joseph W. McGuire, University of Kansas; Professor Lynn H. Peters, San Diego State College; Professor Thaddeus Spratlen, Western Washington State College; Dean Dow Votaw, University of California, Berkeley; Dean Clarence C. Walton, Columbia University; and Professor Jacob Weissman, Hofstra University.

I am especially grateful to Mrs. Laurent Frantz for her assistance in the preparation of my essay and in the editing of the entire volume. I wish to thank Mrs. Barbara Palmer, who typed the manuscript and helped prepare it for publication, and to acknowledge the helpfulness of other staff members of the Institute of Industrial Relations and the School of Business Administration in facilitating the project.

Footnote acknowledgment is made in the text for several quotations from published works. I am indebted to the Harvard University Press for permission to quote from *The American*

Business Creed; to the University of Chicago Press for permission to quote from *Capitalism and Freedom;* to the McGraw-Hill Book Company for permission to quote from several of its McKinsey lectures; and to *Fortune* Magazine for the quotations from the article "Individualism Comes of Age."

EARL F. CHEIT

Berkeley, California
August, 1964

Contents

xi

1

The View from the Top

Reflections on a Changing
Business Ideology

Robert L. Heilbroner

I

This essay is a critical study of the ideology of the big business-man in America in the mid 1960's. More specifically, it is an investigation into the ways in which the commanding executives of some of our largest corporations see the economic world, into the justifications and rationalizations they offer to themselves about "the way things are," and, beyond that, into the adequacy of their conception of society viewed against the pressures and dysfunctions—the "challenges"—of our times.

The study of ideologies—by which I mean the various ways in which the privileges and disprivileges of any society are justified to those who enjoy or suffer them—always provides insights into the social order. But our purpose in singling out the ideology of the big businessman is not merely to explore for its own sake the contemporary version of a problem of perennial interest. It is rather to focus attention on the ideology of our own times, because to an even greater extent than is traditionally the case this ideology has a crucially important role to play in determining the course of the future.

To be sure, the beliefs of the businessman have always exerted a strong influence on the American nation. Yet in one striking respect the business creed today occupies a different position than in the past. Formerly, it was only one among a number of com-

peting ideologies. As a result, however ultimately triumphant
were business ideas, they nevertheless had to bear the criticisms
of alternative formulations of society: they had to coexist with
important currents of antibusiness ideology from which many
intellectuals and many parts of the labor movement drew their
strength.

Today these separate currents of ideological conviction have
largely disappeared within the United States. In part undermined by the sheer economic success of America, in part by the
terrible disillusionment with the Soviet Union, the antibusiness
party of ideas has suffered a crushing defeat. A militant labor
movement directly challenging many of the basic institutions of
the business world has virtually ceased to exist. Intellectual
voices of dissent advocating wholesale social change are no longer
heard. Thus, an unusual ideological consensus prevails and
claims at least the acquiescence, if not the enthusiasm, of previously hostile groups.

This is not to say that business feels itself to be the beneficiary
of an uncontested ideological acceptance. On the contrary, the
businessman constantly feels beset by "hostile" groups, be they
labor, government, or academic. However, if we compare the
degree of ideological encroachment mounted by these groups
with that of, say, the European left wing or the American labor
movement or intellectual establishment of the 1930's, it seems fair
to state that the challenge to the business ideology is severely
limited.[1] For the striking characteristic of our contemporary
ideological climate is that the "dissident" groups, labor, government, or academic, *all seek to accommodate their proposals for
social change to the limits of adaptability of the prevailing business order.* There is no attempt to press for goals that might
exceed the powers of adjustment of that order. Indeed, all these
groups recoil from such a test.

As a result, the business ideology has come to assume an un-
commonly responsible role. In the absence of any large-scale
projections of a different social order, it tends to define society
more consensually than in the past. To put it differently, be-

[1] This is not to maintain that the actual power of business enterprise is
unchallenged. Of that more later.

cause the consensus is uncontested, it establishes the limits of the social and economic flexibility of which our society is apt to be easily capable. Thus, it falls to the lot of the business ideology, as the only socioeconomic doctrine of consequence, to provide for nonbusiness groups and, in particular, for the intellectual community the sense of mission and destiny that in the past usually emanated from rival ideologies.

On the business ideology, then, much depends. But what is this business ideology? From the innumerable voices of the business world, how shall we select those that can properly serve as paradigms for our purpose?

One method of selection used in a number of previous investigations into business thought [2] has been to undertake a systematic content analysis of representative business writings, such as the material issued by the National Association of Manufacturers, the Committee for Economic Development, or the United States Chamber of Commerce. The difficulty here, aside from the prodigious demands on one's patience, is that these views represent an imprecisely defined constituency. The numerous cooks who have had a hand in the broth, including professional economists and publicists, large and small business spokesmen, and more and less persuasive members of committees, make the attribution of these views to any particular segment of the business community a dubious one and render it difficult to state with assurance that any particular businessman "believes in" this or that statement.[3]

Fortunately, however, another and much more clearly attributable source lies at hand. Beginning in 1956, a series of lectures, sponsored by the McKinsey Foundation for Management Research and held at the Graduate School of Business of Columbia University, has successfully served, in the words of the initial

2 Cf. especially Francis X. Sutton, Seymour E. Harris, Carl Kaysen, and James Tobin, *The American Business Creed*, Harvard University Press, Cambridge, Mass., 1956, and James W. Prothro, *The Dollar Decade*, Louisiana State University Press, Baton Rouge, 1954.

3 This is not so much the case with the Committee for Economic Development, thanks to its admirable tradition of signed reports and outspoken individual dissents.

lecturer, Ralph J. Cordiner, President of General Electric, "to coax us businessmen out of our offices and into the arena of public thought where our managerial philosophies can be put to the test of examination by men trained in other disciplines." [4] In chronological order the succeeding speakers have been: the late T. V. Houser, Chairman of the Board of Sears Roebuck; Crawford H. Greenewalt, President of du Pont; Roger M. Blough, Chairman of the Board of U. S. Steel; Frederick R. Kappel, President of A. T. & T.; and Thomas J. Watson, Jr., Chairman of the Board of IBM.[5]

Thus, we have an exposition of the views of the main executives in some of the leading corporations in the United States. Although the lectures were oriented in the first instance toward problems of internal organization and corporate management proper, all of them dwell to a considerable extent on the relation between the speaker's business and "the outside world." In addition, since the lectures were originally delivered to an academic and business audience, which subsequently questioned the speaker, the lecturers were afforded a chance to discover unsatisfactory formulations before their remarks were finally edited and published. As a result, the McKinsey lectures provide us with an unusual opportunity to examine the ideas of a group of big business executives, each of whom has accepted the task of presenting his corporate philosophy to a critical audience as clearly and forcefully as possible. Accordingly, although the sample is small, we shall boldly take these lectures as representing "the view from the top." What does the view reveal?

II

Before we examine the McKinsey lectures in detail, let us cast a glance over them as a whole. Ideologies do not consist

---

[4] Ralph J. Cordiner, *New Frontiers for Professional Managers*, McGraw-Hill, New York, 1956, pp. vi–vii.

[5] Another lecture, *Executive Decision-Making* by Marion B. Folsom, Director of the Eastman Kodak Company and formerly Secretary of the Department of Health, Education and Welfare, is omitted, since it is almost exclusively devoted to problems of staff organization, etc.

alone in explicit statements or implicit promises but manifest themselves equally clearly in the tone of voice in which the statements are made and the attitude in which the premises are held. It is not only content but also *style* that interests us as we begin to investigate the ideology of our big businessmen and, in particular, the contrast between their ideology and that of the past or of other business groups in the present.

No one examining the views of the leaders of American enterprise in the late nineteenth or early twentieth century can fail to miss the prevailing ideological style of their times. A supreme self-confidence, not to say arrogance, oozes from their speeches. To read the words of a typical late nineteenth-century or early twentieth-century captain of industry is to enter a universe of ideological security as unfamiliar as it is often amusing. It is hard to imagine a businessman saying today, as John D. Rockefeller did in innocence and earnest, that "God gave me my money." Even the most conservative present-day spokesman would choke over the famous remark of George F. Baer, President of the Reading Company, that "the rights and interests of the laboring man will be protected and cared for . . . by the Christian men to whom God in his infinite wisdom has given the control of the property interests of the country."

We recall the past, however, not to smile at it but to bring back to mind a tone of utterance now remarkable by its absence. It will hardly come as a surprise that the McKinsey lecturers no longer believe in the divine right or origin of property. But beyond that, it is clear that an approach very unlike that of the late nineteenth or early twentieth century pervades their declarations. A tentative, cautious—even apologetic—style characterizes their words. To quote the opening paragraph of the first of the McKinsey speakers, Ralph J. Cordiner:

Many thoughtful persons have observed that the United States has evolved a wholly new form of capitalism, variously called democratic capitalism, mass capitalism, or—more aptly—people's capitalism. As the first nation in the world to break through the ancient barriers of scarcity into an economy of abundance, we have a unique experience that we ourselves need fully to understand and to communicate to the rest of the world. But somehow we have not yet been able to do it well—to describe this new people's capitalism, and all that it means to the spiritual and cultural life of the people, as well as to their material well-being.[6]

Forgetting for a moment its content, we can see that a world of difference divides the manner of this curiously reflective and even plaintive statement from that of the unselfconscious pronouncements of a Rockefeller or the bombast of a Baer. And this difference is not merely a matter of increased sophistication, although it is surely that in part. It reflects instead, as we shall see later, an altered conceptual ground on which the new ideology is built.

In addition, the tone and style of the ideology of the modern corporate managers can also be contrasted with those of a more recent (indeed, still contemporary) strain of business thought typified by the publications of the National Association of Manufacturers. In this more traditional ideology we continue to find some of the certitude of the past, no longer justified, it is true, by reference to the Deity but buttressed by an ultimate referent almost as powerful—human nature. "Without the existence of private property," we read in *The American Individual Enterprise System,* prepared by the NAM as a definitive study of capitalism, "most individuals will not work, unless by coercion, beyond the amount necessary to take care of their immediate wants. Under these conditions their output is almost certain to be disappointing, because coercion is not conducive to productive efficiency." [7]

This traditional view of the business system grounds itself in the reassuring conviction that certain human characteristics make capitalism a natural terminal state of social organization, provided only that human nature is left alone—a conviction that makes it possible to speak in the assertive, even dogmatic fashion characteristic of very conservative groups.

6 Cordiner, *op. cit.,* p. 1.

7 National Association of Manufacturers, *The American Individual Enterprise System,* I, McGraw-Hill, New York, 1946, p. 6.

Again, we contrast the tone of the McKinsey lecturers, in this case by instancing one of the most conservative speakers, Roger M. Blough:

> We may not and do not forget that the majority of men now live in a world of compulsion and that both a society of compulsion and a free society are capable of increasing a nation's material strength, although I believe a free society will do it more adequately, and that either the voluntary or the compulsory society will produce men of resolute purpose.[8]

What is missing from this statement is the sense of the untroubled superiority, the unshakeable certitude, of the traditional philosophy of business. The traumas of the 1930's, the altered structures and new pressures of the 1950's and 1960's, have left their mark. A new tone of pragmatism and of careful deliberation distinguishes the declarations of the McKinsey speakers, and this careful tone serves as a hallmark of their style of thought quite as much as the more assertive tone serves to identify an older or more conservative strain of ideology. We shall notice the contrast in style frequently as we proceed. But a style is still only an introduction to an ideology. Now, what of the substance?

III

The six McKinsey lecturers do not—to anticipate an important point to which we shall return—present a single monolithic view of the business process. Yet, reading these lectures with their striking differences in personality and considerable differences in philosophy, we become aware that there is, withal, a common denominator of basic opinions discernible in all. It is this that we shall first seek to represent. At the risk of a certain Procrustean tactic and at the cost of a necessary amount of substantiating quotation, let us begin, then, with five propositions that give identity—at least an identity of concern—to the ideology of the McKinsey group.

---

[8] Roger M. Blough, *Free Man and the Corporation*, McGraw-Hill, New York, 1959, p. 4.

1. *The New Ideology Stresses the Distinction between "Modern" and "Old-fashioned" Capitalism*

The concept of a discontinuous break between the old "exploitative, harsh capitalism" and the new "responsible, socially aware" capitalism is a common thread that runs through many of our speakers' basic formulations. This is not surprising, for, as the authors of a recent study of business ideology, *The American Business Creed,* emphasize, an essential point of divergence between the old and the new creeds lies in their varying treatments of history: "In the typical classical expression, the American System has been homogenous in time and space. . . . By contrast, the managerial strand emphasizes the fundamental transformation of the past fifty years, and sees in the present economic system a radical break with the past." [9]

We are already familiar with the first McKinsey lecturer's endorsement of this idea, and his theme is echoed by many following speakers. Theodore V. Houser tells us that "the historic complaint that big business, as the producing arm of capitalism, exploited the many for the profit of the few and deprived the workers of the products of their own labor had a valid basis in the facts of European capitalism, but lacks substance when applied to American capitalism today." [10] Crawford Greenewalt, although doubting the factual validity for much of the bad reputation of business in the nineteenth century, nevertheless reminds us that, "The 1890 business titan, heading up his own works, was exposed but little to the sobering thought that, while he would pass along, the institution would endure." [11] And Thomas J. Watson, Jr., writes: "For centuries the businessman has been a favorite whipping boy, and the reasons are plain to see. Businessmen acquired wealth. With wealth, they gained power. And

[9] Sutton et al., *op. cit.,* p. 35.

[10] Theodore V. Houser, *Big Business and Human Values,* McGraw-Hill, New York, 1957, p. ix.

[11] Crawford H. Greenewalt, *The Uncommon Man,* McGraw-Hill, New York, 1959, pp. 83–84.

until this century, much of that power was employed almost solely in their own interests." [12]

In what ways the new American capitalism is different from its predecessor will emerge presently. But it is worth noting the considerable distance between an ideology that grounds itself in the immutable primordium of human nature and one that deliberately sets out to base itself on a newly developed system. The older ideology was, in a sense, beyond criticism inasmuch as it sought only to describe the result of modes of behavior that were age-old and thus beyond evolution. The new ideology *per contra* specifically seeks its justification in a social system that has been worked out only in the relatively recent past. Thus, many of the troublesome historic facts for which the older ideology had to apologize, often with indifferent success, can be discarded to begin with. Insofar as the system is new, the problems and guilts of the 1890 business titan no longer need be denied nor justified. What is needed instead is to find a new rationale to describe the new reality, and for this rationale we turn to the second proposition of the McKinsey lecturers.

2. *The Identifying Mark of the New Capitalism Is Professional Responsibility*

"We all know that special power imposes special responsibilities on those who hold it," writes Thomas Watson, introducing a theme that again contrasts with a basic aspect of the traditional ideology. In the older view business was not charged with any particular economic responsibilities, because the behavior of the business firm was essentially enforced by the anonymous forces of the market. In contrast, the emerging ideology, although continuing to pay its respects to competition, recognizes the accretion of economic power in the hands of the large corporation and then justifies this power by its responsible use.

"Bigness itself is a relatively new phenomenon in our society," continues Watson. "Even if nothing else had changed the vast concentrations of power in our society would demand that busi-

[12] Thomas J. Watson, Jr., *A Business and Its Beliefs*, McGraw-Hill, New York, 1963, p. 91.

nessmen reconsider their responsibilities for the broader public welfare." [13]

What catches our eye here is the explicit admission that corporate management *can* act in interests other than those of classical theory, that is, in at least partial disregard of the traditional dictates of profit making. T. V. Houser expands this point: "How much discretion does the management of a company have in its relations with stockholders?" [14] he frankly inquires and then goes on to ask what are its responsibilities *vis-à-vis* employees, customers, suppliers, community, government? In like fashion Cordiner also discusses the corporation's discretionary distributive power:

> The important principle I should like to express here, in relations with customers, share owners, employees, suppliers, educational institutions, charitable activities, government and the general public, is that all activities must be guided by the recognition of common purposes and of the contribution that each group makes toward their achievement. Now, the modern corporation, particularly one which has such deep roots in the United States society as General Electric, is taking an increasingly enlightened view as to what such institutions as education actually provide, and what are the Company's consequent obligations. . . . With this . . . balanced view of the claims and contributions of all who affect the Company's obligations, we have a sound guide toward meeting our responsibilities to society. [15]

The sign of responsibility is, in the words of another major corporation executive (not a McKinsey lecturer), "to maintain an equitable and working balance among the claims of the various directly interested groups—stockholders, employees, customers, and the public at large." [16] This equitable balance, in turn, is to be secured, because the management of our large corporations is increasingly to be considered a *professional* group. As the editors of *Fortune* magazine put it, ". . . the manager is becoming

13 *Ibid.*, p. 80.

14 Houser, *op. cit.*, p. 31.

15 Cordiner, *op. cit.*, pp. 19–20.

16 The Editors of *Fortune, The Permanent Revolution*, Prentice-Hall, Englewood Cliffs, N. J., 1951, p. 80. (The executive is Frank Abrams of Standard Oil of New Jersey.)

a professional in the sense that like all professional men he has a responsibility to society as a whole." [17] The theme, although not the explicit discussion, of professionalism runs through our McKinsey lectures as well. Note, for instance, the title of Cordiner's lecture: *New Frontiers for Professional Managers.*

The responsibility of the trained professional manager is thus a key element in assuring the equitable operation of the new capitalism. But, meanwhile, what of the structural characteristics of the new system itself? With what changed realities must management cope? The McKinsey lecturers pay special attention to one of them.

3. The Need for Large-scale Organizations Is Explicitly Recognized

Together with the acknowledgment of corporate power, this concern comes as another sharp departure from the classic ideology. As the authors of *The American Business Creed* paraphrase the older point of view:

The typical American business enterprise is small, and there are many throughout the nation. . . . The word "business" should make one think, not of a giant, impersonal corporation with offices in lower Manhattan, but of the machine shop an enterprising friend has started in his backyard. . . . Statistics are mobilized to show: seventy per cent of all manufacturing establishments have fewer than twenty employees . . . , there are 34,000 companies in the oil industry, the National Association of Manufacturers is predominantly composed of small firms.[18]

Such traditional emphasis on the supposed atomistic character of American industry is by no means entirely missing from the McKinsey lectures. Roger Blough, for example, points to the fact that we now have 886,000 corporations, where ten years ago we had only 615,000, and forty years ago only 320,000. Nevertheless, the emphasis is not on the small firm but on the large one. Thus, Blough declares: "The American public has gradually become accustomed to larger and larger groups and has be-

[17] *Ibid.,* p. 79.
[18] Sutton et al., *op. cit.,* pp. 58–59.

come convinced that big production groups are outstanding in reliability and in the quality of their products and services and are necessary to perform America's larger production tasks in research, in production, and in the procurement of raw materials." [19]

Cordiner gives a yet more basic justification for large size:

Whenever a society industrializes, one of the most important characteristics is a great increase in the scale of its undertakings. The drive toward more complex technologies, toward more massive use and guidance of the forces of nature, toward mass production and mass distribution, necessarily results in the development of large-scale economic organizations. England has them, Russia has them, Germany has them, other industrial nations have them, and the United States has them. Their size is generally related to the size and technical capacity of the national economy in which they operate. Without these large-scale economic enterprises, a nation is today a second-rate power and its people suffer both lower standards of living and greater vulnerability to attack by aggressive nations.[20]

This unvarnished admission of an inescapable technological dynamic of growth in the size of firms stands in contrast to the rationale of the past, which either ignored entirely the emergence of giant enterprises or attributed it to the particular business virtues of particular entrepreneurs.

Equally frank is an admission of a change in the nature of the competitive process. Blough speaks here, in general, for the group:

With respect to pricing and marketing, no longer is there the competition of a peddler with a pack of pots and pans on his back and a different price to each customer, nor the "perfect competition" sometimes suggested in textbooks. Today's competition is the competition of pricing policies, of quality, of consumer surveys, of mass advertising, and of mass distribution devices, of research, and of production practices and conditions of employment. This kind of competition is the only kind that is workable in a society like ours, which requires large productive groups constantly moving forward to bring improved stand-

19 Blough, *op. cit.*, p. 15.
20 Cordiner, *op. cit.*, pp. 2–3, cf. also p. 79.

ards of living. The advantages to the consumer resulting from this naturally evolved competition are far greater than could ever be possible under the theory of "perfect competition." [21]

Despite these qualifications all speakers continue to cite and praise the force of competition as the appropriate major regulative power of the system—a power that no producer can brook for long. "Even though individuals may differ greatly on what is adequate or persuasive evidence of competition between corporate groups," Blough says, "the general aim to maintain competition is agreed to be basic from a social point of view in a free society." And further: "Thus competition is a cleansing agent; competition provides the most searching discipline a free society can secure." [22]

However, this new structure of large-scale organization with its adapted forms of competition is only one aspect of the changed institutional nature of capitalism to which our ideologists call attention. Another change, although less externally apparent, is of no less significance. It is a change in the motivations that presumably drive the system, or, as we find it in the McKinsey series:

4. A New Ideological Stress on Human Values

In the older ideology a relatively simple view of human values underlay the business process. As William Feather, a publishing executive and regular contributor to *Nation's Business*, wrote in 1926: "The one-hundred per cent American believes in the doctrine of selfishness, although he is often ashamed to admit it. . . . The American idea is that every man is out to promote his own interest, and he has discovered that the best way to do this is to make himself useful to others. . . . It is inconceivable to a one-hundred per cent American that anyone except a nut should give something for nothing." [23]

This one-dimensional view of motivation has given way in the ideology we are examining to a conscious recognition of the com-

[21] Blough, *op. cit.*, pp. 10–11.
[22] *Ibid.*, pp. 16, 26.
[23] Prothro, *op. cit.*, p. 43.

plexity of motives that impel men—and, perhaps most especially, talented men—and with an entirely new concern about the impact of the business environment on the character and creativity of its employees. A new rhetoric of "employee relations" suffuses the McKinsey lectures, occasionally lending an almost clinical air to its descriptions of corporate relationships with its employees. "While improvements in earnings may be a motivating force," writes Blough, speaking of his labor force, "it may also be that the main motivation is what we refer to generally as 'working conditions,' such as status in the group or seniority or enhancement of personal dignity. But joining a labor union may also be a response to a deep-seated psychological impulse. . . ." [24]

Cordiner reports similar findings from a research survey into employees' motivations, which also revealed that money was only one of many stimuli. Then, after a discussion of stock option and other incentive plans, he turns to the upper echelons and adds:

> While I have concentrated here on financial incentives . . . , you will realize from the points made in all three lectures that the non-material motivations are the deeper, more critical determinants. . . . General Electric is trying to develop a climate in which each individual in the enterprise can constructively translate personal aspirations that are important to him into performance and results important to our customers, owners, suppliers, distributors, and the general public.[25]

This is not to say that the importance of adequate financial motivations is overlooked or denied. At least one McKinsey lecturer, Crawford Greenewalt of du Pont, declared that a search for pecuniary reward lay at the core of management success. Yet even he was forced to defend his remarks:

> To anticipate as much rebuttal as I can, let me register this concession in advance: I do not believe that the *present* generation of management is rendered less determined or dedicated in its efforts by current tax policies. Out of every dollar I was paid by du Pont Company last year, I was able to preserve for my own use perhaps nine cents,

24 Blough, *op. cit.*, p. 59.
25 Cordiner, *op. cit.*, p. 111.

yet I work just as hard, and I hope just as effectively, as I would if my gross and net compensation were equal. I am sure that the same applies to each of my associates. . . .

My concern is not with those in management today, but with the calibre of men who will be managing our business enterprises twenty-five or fifty years from now. How can we assure competence and vigor throughout our business organizations in the face of greatly weakened financial incentives? [26]

Not every lecturer would agree even with this qualified defense of the pecuniary motive. T. V. Houser, for example, is outspoken in denying this rationale:

Executive ability is not an altogether common commodity and has a market of its own which cannot be ignored. Nevertheless, reflection may reveal that custom is the chief justification for the extreme practices in executive compensation which now prevail in some quarters. Outstanding leadership capacity is an invaluable asset to any corporation, but is a direct monetary *quid pro quo* a necessary consequence? The service of great educators, great scientists, great public servants are equally invaluable to the country. Such services are not put exclusively or even primarily on a cash basis.[27]

In addition to this more sophisticated conception of managerial incentive, we notice in our big businessmen's ideology a totally new concern—new, at least, in terms of the traditional business apologetics—which centers in the problem of conformity, of the submersion of the organization man within the corporation.

"There has been a lot of talk," writes Frederick R. Kappel, President of A. T. & T., "about how the needs and drives and processes of business organizations smother individuals. The word that pops up most often in these discussions is 'conformity,' which many people apparently see as something evil." [28]

Actually, Kappel points out, some conformity is essential for society:

[26] Greenewalt, *op. cit.*, p. 98.
[27] Houser, *op. cit.*, p. 27.
[28] Frederick R. Kappel, *Vitality in a Business Enterprise*, McGraw-Hill, New York, 1960, p. 75.

To be against all conformity is to be against order and for chaos. Certainly some individuals in business are submerged. . . . But our concern is not with conformity as such. Our concern is how to build individual vitality in those situations where some conformity is also required.

Society today depends on large organizations much more than it did in the past. In consequence there is a greater need for the kind of conformity that enables people working together to get big jobs done. I wonder if some of the current hullabaloo on this subject may not arise from the fact that many people just don't care for the idea that there have to be large organizations. . . .[29]

Roger Blough also considers the question overstressed: "There is no question that this is true to a degree—but it is also true of other non-corporate groups and it is natural and necessary. . . . It is quite misleading to regard as 'restrictive' some conformity to modes of voluntary group activity. When individuals elect to associate in an interwoven pattern of cooperation to achieve production, there are bound to be some orderly means of getting the group's objective accomplished." [30]

Greenewalt adds: "Conformity in behavior is a human necessity; conformity in patterns of thought a human danger. . . . I am inclined to think that, man for man, the large business unit represents greater opportunities for individuality and requires less in the way of conformity than other institutions—in the government service, say, or in the academic world, or in the military." [31]

Thus the organization man, in the view of these corporation executives, is an unwarranted stereotype of the new capitalism. However, it is a stereotype of which modern management, in contrast with its predecessors, is uncomfortably aware.

There remains still a final ideological aspect to the changed capitalism, in addition to the new responsibility, the new emphasis on large-scale organization and the new stress on human values:

29 *Ibid.*, p. 76.
30 Blough, *op. cit.*, p. 49.
31 Greenewalt, *op. cit.*, pp. 50–51.

5. A New Legitimacy Is Accorded to the Roles of Labor
and Government

No aspect of an ideology is more important than that which defines the relationship between the group for which it is formulated and other groups that compete with the first for power. Certainly, in the traditional ideology of business the questions of the rights of labor and the proper role of government have been matters of central importance.

It is difficult to summarize quickly the traditional attitude of business toward labor, for a considerable gulf separates the mingled insensitivity and paternalism of the late nineteenth century, the undisguised hostility of the 1930's, and the rather mixed approach of such contemporary conservative groups as the National Association of Manufacturers. It is enough for our purposes to emphasize one aspect common to all these views: Whatever its cause or cure, the "labor question" was indubitably a matter of extreme importance to the business world. Thus, the power of unions is referred to three times in Blough's lectures as "glacier-like," and he tells us, "Their strength and influence in America today can hardly be overestimated." [32]

However, what makes Blough's attack on unions (preceded by a long apologia for unionism) interesting is not its content, which merely resembles that of the prevailing conservative view toward labor, but rather its relatively isolated position within the series of lectures that we are discussing. Cordiner, it is true, also mentions "growing, unchecked union power," but he does not dilate on it. *No other speaker mentions the problem at all.* The remarkable aspect of our ideologists' attitude to the labor problem is not their forbearance toward it but rather their indifference to it—an attitude that stands in the sharpest contrast to the traditional ideological concern. It may be, of course, that the silent lecturers would have had vigorous positions on the labor question, if they had been asked. Yet, it is certainly not without significance that, of the six speakers, only two were moved to mention the matter at all in their self-selected expositions of important corporate management problems. The implication is

[32] Blough, *op. cit.*, p. 62.

that the labor problem, being subsumed under the general concern with human values, has either ceased to exist or that labor unions are now regarded with an unalarmed gaze as constituting legitimate institutions in the business world.

A more provocative matter is the relationship between the corporation and the government. Let us recall here the older ideological approach of business. "Government, as seen in the [traditional] business creed is inherently evil," write the authors of *The American Business Creed*.[33] Certainly, the classic belief accords very little legitimacy to the concept of the government as an independent economic force. In the NAM prescriptive study referred to earlier the government is essentially confined to a housekeeping and rule-enforcing function, so that the enterprise system can run undisturbed. The deliberate intervention of government as a stabilizing or growth-producing force (in some sense other than as the guardian of the competitive, profit-seeking capitalist process) would not be admissible.

Some of the older ideological orientation can be seen among our McKinsey lecturers, principally Blough and Cordiner. The latter, for instance, fears the "fantastically growing federal government . . . tending to exert more and more control over the nation's economic life," and points out at some length that "state planning has failed wherever it has been tried" and that "limited, rigid, politically disjointed state planning cannot supply a vibrant and expanding economy for the United States." Nevertheless, even he prefaces his remarks by pointing to the determination of the American people "that steadily rising levels of living, along with economic stability, are both desirable and achievable." "Make no mistake about it," he goes on to say, "this decision has been made by the people, and they are going to pursue it by one means or another. The remarkable increase in consumer credit, the sharp rise in insurance and pension funds, the intense political activity for the so-called 'government stabilizers' in the national economy—all these are significant symptoms of a deep national commitment to . . . manageable stability of

33 Sutton et al., *op. cit.*, p. 186.

income in a competitive market, and rising levels of income." [34]

Much more sharply contrasting with the classical ideology is the view represented by Watson of IBM (and less explicitly by Houser of Sears Roebuck). Writes Watson:

> Much as we may dislike it, I think we've got to realize that in our kind of society there are times when government has to step in and help people with some of their more difficult problems. . . .
>
> Programs which assist Americans by reducing the hazards of a free market system without damaging the system itself are necessary, I believe, to its survival. . . .
>
> To be sure, the rights and guarantees that the average man believes in and insists upon may interfere, to some degree, with our ability to manage our enterprises with complete freedom of action. As a result, there are businessmen who either ignore or deny these claims. They then justify their views by contending that if we were to recognize or grant them, the whole system of free enterprise would be endangered.
>
> This, it would seem to me, amounts to an open invitation to exactly the kind of government intervention that businessmen are seeking to avoid. For if we businessmen insist that free enterprise permits us to be indifferent to those things on which people put high value, then the people will quite naturally assume that free enterprise has too much freedom. [35]

Thus, the new ideology seems on the whole to present a more tolerant view of both labor and government. [36] Clearly, however, there are wide divergences here—wider perhaps than those expressed on any other of the main points of the managerial creed. The significance of these differences we shall defer for the moment, however, while we turn our attention to an intervening item on the agenda—a critique of the ideology that we have attempted to summarize above. We have seen how our six representative speakers have defined their respective philosophies. Let us now say something about the general view from "the top" itself.

[34] Cordiner, *op. cit.*, pp. 37, 89–90, 86.

[35] Watson, *op. cit.*, pp. 87, 88, 89, 90.

[36] We might note here the matter-of-fact way in which Marion Folsom, in his McKinsey lecture, discusses the problems of government and business administration, stressing their similarities rather than their differences.

IV

Surely, what first strikes the reader of these statements is the plausibility of so much that is said and, with a few exceptions, the general moderation of the tone in which it is put forth. To contrast the overall view of society and business, as it emerges from these pages, with the views of an older generation or of the current conservative business creed seems like contrasting two totally different ideational worlds: the one naive, simplistic, dogmatic; the other knowing, complex, pragmatic. Indeed, the question must rise, why do we consider these newer statements as "ideologies" at all? Why do we not place them in the same category as, let us say, the essays of any social scientist, including this one?

In stressing the ideological content of the McKinsey lectures we implicitly levy against them one of two criticisms. The first is that these statements are in fact only propaganda, that is, deliberate misrepresentations of reality designed to curry favor for those on whose behalf they are delivered. No doubt there is an element of more or less conscious falsification, of carefully calculated effect, running through many of the lectures. To take only a few instances, it is mathematically impossible for Mr. Greenewalt to preserve for his own use only nine cents out of each dollar he was paid by du Pont; this is a *marginal* tax rate (on taxable income for married persons well over the quarter-million dollar level), and the statement as it stands is simply untrue. In the same fashion we read with some skepticism Roger Blough's aforementioned description of corporate life in Pittsburgh as one in which "individuals elect to associate in an interwoven pattern of cooperation to achieve production." Again, in view of the subsequent disclosures of the electrical industry's price conspiracy and of the behavior of General Electric's Board of Directors in the face of these scandals, many of Cordiner's protestations on behalf of competition and "professionalism" have a hollow ring.

It is, of course, possible to dismiss a great deal of the philosophizing of our corporate managers as, in fact, nothing but a conscious attempt to put a good face on things or to deflect genu-

ine criticism by a pretense of self-criticism. Yet, at least to this
reader, it is difficult to peruse the McKinsey lectures in their
entirety and believe that they constitute a deliberate sham, a conscious posturing. On the contrary, what emerges along with the
undoubted cant and hypocrisy is a sense of often painfully sincere belief on the part of the speakers. A few transparent instances aside, many of the disingenuous circumlocutions may
indicate not a desire to fool the public but rather an attempt,
however artless, to find convincing ways of expressing what the
speaker feels to be profoundly true. Indeed, it is of the very
essence of an ideology that it sets forth views that, however self-
serving or biased they may seem to the outsider, are perfectly
self-evident and honest from the vantage point of the expositor.

In addition, there is a certain amount of objective evidence
that the executives of large corporations are dissatisfied with the
traditional view of things and are trying to reformulate an ideology better attuned to reality. In the rise of innumerable management "institutes" and special training programs for practicing
executives as well as in the visible influence of business schools
on management thought, there are signs of an effort to improve
the quality of business philosophy. This is particularly the case
in the training programs in many of the larger companies (including at least three of those on the McKinsey series) where
top and middle executives are deliberately exposed to ideas that
are often openly critical of the business ideology. Needless to
say, it is assumed that these executives will not experience a
crisis of faith in this exposure but rather will emerge more capable of articulating their own ideology in terms acceptable to a
nonbusiness audience. Nevertheless, some of the criticism may
well penetrate, and, in my own experience with management
groups, a considerable sympathy with a "liberal" line of thought
is noticeable among many of the executives of such education-
oriented companies.

It is possible, however, to apply a criticism other than the am-
biguous touchstone of "sincerity" to the pronouncements that
we are studying. Assuming the best intentions on the part of the
speaker, we can nevertheless note the selectivity that governs the
pronouncements he makes. Thus, we can seek to demonstrate

the ideological, as contrasted with the "scientific," nature of the various managerial views not by trying to establish deliberate sins of commission on the part of their protagonists but rather by pointing out their sins of omission. We can, in other words, call attention to important and easily visible aspects of the social situation that they have excluded from their consideration. In this way, we can test the presence of ideological bias not by inquiring into the motivation of what is said but by noticing what is not.

V

Once again we will find it convenient to proceed by following the five categories under which we have grouped the main ideological emphases of the lecturers.

1. The "Newness" of Capitalism

We have noted the importance of the strand of thought that marks off a "new," "socially conscious" capitalism from the older, now admittedly "bad" system. It is not difficult to identify many features in the social landscape that objectively support this general reorientation of thought. The moderation in the attitude of big business toward labor, the growth and acceptance of certain welfare measures, the increased understanding of the countercyclical powers of the government, the self-consciousness of the big corporation—all these frequently cited examples of the newness of capitalism are undeniable realities. Still more important is the rise in the level of income, particularly among the middle income groups. It is the spread of "affluence" which above all differentiates the new capitalism from the old not only by vindicating the system responsible for that affluence but also, hopefully, by ushering in an era of abundance in which the old bitternesses and mutual distrusts can give way to a new social and economic cooperation.

These changes have been of the utmost importance for capitalism, as nearly all would admit. Yet, the question remains whether an exclusive emphasis on these altered aspects of the economic system does not present an exaggerated picture of the actual evolutionary distance that has been covered. As Edward Mason writes:

> Despite such phrases as the "permanent revolution," the "managerial revolution," the "capitalist revolution," and the "new era," some doubt persists that the contemporary economy is as different as all that from the American economy of 1900. It has been pointed out that the share of industrial assets, employment, and value accounted for by the largest firms today is about the same as their share fifty years ago. . . . Moreover, a look at certain broad indexes of economic behavior does not reveal any startling or revolutionary break in long-run trends. . . . The broad look reveals very substantial elements of stability in the system.[37]

Thus, the ideological nature of the managerial description of the new capitalism reveals itself in its selective focus on certain aspects of capitalism in which change is most noticeable. Other aspects in which change is much less noticeable are correspondingly ignored. The sluggish, not to say negligible, improvement in the relative income shares of the lower echelons of society since the early 1950's is not a subject for general managerial comment. Neither is the degree of concentration of wealth, an important, and in some ways absolutely fundamental, aspect of the system nor the remarkable fact that the top 2 per cent of families in 1953 owned 29 per cent of all personal sector wealth, as compared with 33 per cent in 1922, despite the enormous rise in income and estate taxes over the period.[38] Surely, such indices of social viscosity and inertia are as worthy of emphasis as those of change.

It may well be, as Mason concludes, that the overall degree of change has nevertheless been sufficient, so that the older apologetic will not do, and a new one is needed. However, we must certainly evaluate the adequacy of the newer ideology not merely by noting the contrasts that it legitimately makes with the past but also by remarking on its unwillingness to measure all aspects of the present.

[37] Edward S. Mason, The Apologetics of Managerialism, *Journal of Business*, XXXI (1958), p. 10.

[38] Cf. Robert J. Lampman, *Changes in the Share of Wealth Held by Top Wealth-Holders, 1922–1956*, National Bureau of Economic Research, 1960, Occasional Paper 71, Table 9, p. 31.

2. *The Stress on Responsibility*

The newness of capitalism reveals itself, we recall, not only in environmental changes but also in the growth of a sense of professional responsibility on the part of the admittedly powerful corporate managers. What can we say about the ideological content of this proposition?

Insofar as responsibility means self-awareness or refers to a need to explain corporate behavior to the public, or, again, insofar as it implies a more circumspect mode of behavior than was characteristic of the past, there would be general agreement that a changed reality underlies management's assertion of its new professional role.

But the notion of responsibility also implies responsibility *to* someone. Here the managerial statement stumbles badly. Cordiner, for instance, writes: "General Electric is owned by 358,000 share owners. . . . General Electric is managed by professional managers, who are not the owners of the business but employees hired by share owners through their elected directors and the Company Officer, to manage the business in the balanced best interests of all concerned." [39]

The characterization of ownership and control in this statement is blandly deceptive at the very least. Most scholars would maintain that the majority of large corporations are run by a more or less self-perpetuating oligarchy within the boundaries established by other power groups and by their own ideologies. [40] Although it is undoubtedly true that the oligarchs are not "owners" in the traditional sense of the word, there is ample evidence that they can manipulate the property they are "hired" to run for the stockholders in such a way as to yield benefits to themselves similar to those accruing from bona fide ownership. A recent study by the National Industrial Conference Board shows that 73 per cent of 215 top executives during the period 1950–1960 gained at least $50,000 through the use of stock options, that 32 per cent

39 Cordiner, *op. cit.*, p. 42.

40 Cf. *inter alia*, A. A. Berle, Jr., *Power Without Property*, Harcourt, Brace, New York, 1959; Richard Eells, *The Government of Corporations*, The Free Press of Glencoe, New York, 1962; and Wilbert Moore, *The Conduct of the Corporation*, Random House, New York, 1963.

gained $250,000, and that 8 per cent gained at least $1,000,000.[41]

Needless to say, we do not find such statistics in the McKinsey lectures. To be sure, one does not expect a group in power to advertise the manner in which and the extent to which it uses the existing institutions for its private advantage. But the suspicion then arises that the "responsibility" of the professional manager is at least partly a responsibility to look after himself.

The troubling question thus lurking beneath the surface is the degree to which the corporate system is not only a great, responsibly run machine for the production of goods and distribution of incomes but also a great, irresponsibly run machine for the production of privilege. It is testimony to the central importance of the ideological claim of responsibility that it constitutes a main question for those who subject contemporary capitalism to critical but not unfriendly examination, such as Berle, Moore, or Eells. However, it is testimony of another sort that none of these critics can be said to have answered the question: "To whom is the corporation responsible?"

3. The Need for Large-scale Organizations

One of the most widely held tenets of the managerial ideology is the admission of the need for—indeed, the inescapable technological dynamic of—bigness in productive enterprise. This direct admission of corporate size and power represents a considerable step toward aligning the ideological picture of the system with the reality of that system as it appears to the social scientist.

It is, however, an alignment that is, as yet, far from complete. The degree of actual concentration of corporate assets or sales is not a matter for managerial comment. Nor is the question of whether the optimal size for productive efficiency accords with the actual size of existing corporations, or whether the acquisition of diversified companies can be rationalized as part of a technological impetus toward large-scale units. These are awkward matters, which the ideology does not consider.

[41] *Management Record*, National Industrial Conference Board (June 1962), p. 13.

In the same way, the effort of the new ideology to picture competition as different from the perfect competition "sometimes suggested in textbooks" may be judged as an effort to reduce the gap between ideology and reality, but much less convincing are the protestations that competition, even in its more carefully defined form, continues to exercise its "cleansing action" on the inefficient firm. In view of the behavior of U. S. Steel during the price dispute in February 1962, it is difficult to swallow Blough's sanctimonious statement that: "By contrast with labor union power, such economic power as corporate groups do achieve arises out of their economic competency, their unprivileged serving in the market place, and their survival under the discipline of that market place." [42] It should be noted further that none of the McKinsey lecturers, in praising competition, also mentions the well-nigh ubiquitous avoidance of *price* competition or the widespread presence of price-leadership patterns. In sum, although the managerial ideology is perhaps more realistic in this area than in any other, it still offers only a partial description of the existing structure of corporate size and of corporate competition.

4. The Concern with Human Values

"It is the underlying theme of personnel management," writes Kenneth Boulding, "that the disutility of work can be diminished by creating a work environment in which the worker feels accepted and with which he can identify as a group. . . . There is much of value in this approach, though there is also a danger of cant and sentimentality. Personnel management can too easily become the art of pushing people around without their knowing enough about it to dislike it. . . ." [43]

Is the widely expressed concern for human relationships within the corporation only an ideological cover for "pushing people around"? There is no reason to doubt that the corporation manager today has an increased concern for human welfare and a more sophisticated appreciation of human wants than was the

[42] Blough, *op. cit.*, p. 125.

[43] Kenneth Boulding, *Conflict and Defense,* Harper, New York, 1963, pp. 182–183.

case a few decades ago; times and ideas have changed. At the same time—and this is half explicit in the ideological statements we have examined—there are evident mixed motives in the wooing of the man on the plant floor. Greater productive efficiency, the discouragement of unionism, the inculcation of pro-company sentiment, the procurement of labor peace—these are clearly among the motives underlying management's concern for human values in addition to its announced solicitude for the individual.[44]

Much of management's talk about values, however, refers to the executive or subexecutive individual. Here the question arises concerning the candor with which management permits itself to look upon the pressures felt by these levels of personnel. The stereotype of a slavish organization man, which the ideology indignantly and no doubt correctly denies, blocks out the larger reality of a deliberate encouragement of a generalized company loyalty as a value taking precedence over community loyalty, and to some extent, even over family commitments. Corporations expect a degree of dedication on the part of their upward-aspiring employees that does not accord well with the heavy ideological emphasis on personal creativity and freedom.

We find an instance of this in the Watson lecture, which, at first, denies the presence of conformism as a general problem: "Some say that when an organization tries to get too close to its people and makes a lot of the 'team' idea, the individual gets swallowed up, loses his identity, and becomes a carbon copy of his fellow employees. So far as I can see, this is not true to any serious degree in our large organizations today. . . ."[45]

A few pages later, however, he writes about the problem of management schools within his own company:

These schools were not only to teach general management, but—most important—they were to give our managers a feeling for IBM's outlooks and its beliefs. After a time we found that the schools tended to put too much emphasis on management, not enough on beliefs. This, we felt, was putting the cart before the horse. We felt it was

[44] Cf. Loren Baritz, *Servants of Power*, Wesleyan University Press, Middleton, Conn., 1960.

[45] Watson, *op. cit.*, pp. 24–25.

vital that our managers be well grounded in our beliefs. Otherwise, we might begin to get management views at odds with the company's outlook. If this were to happen, it might possibly slow down our growth and change our basic approach to the management of our company.[46]

Given the growth of corporate size and the more or less inevitable increase in bureaucratization, these pressures for conformity are no doubt a more or less inevitable trend. Within the managerial echelons, the position of the lower and middle range executive seems to be reverting (in Andrew Hacker's phrase) from contract to status. But this change has only been partially acknowledged by management itself. What the new ideological stress on human relations seems to offer—but not to admit—is a means of rationalizing this situation in terms that make it more acceptable to the controllers and the controlled alike.

5. *New Recognition for the Roles of Government and Labor*

There is probably no area of ideological commitment of greater overall importance than that which defines the roles of the business corporation in relation to those of labor unions and the government. Our small sample of opinion contains such varying views that it is difficult to generalize with respect to the McKinsey group itself, much less the larger universe of big business for which it is here being taken as spokesman. But a few remarks may indicate areas of reality with which the expressed views have not come fairly to grips.

We have noted that only one speaker, Blough of U. S. Steel, dwelt on the labor problem, although it was mentioned in passing as a "troublesome condition" by Cordiner as well. No one would deny, of course, that U. S. Steel must contend with a powerful union. However, the repeated references to the "glacier-like" forces of the labor movement are difficult to square with statistics that clearly show the decline of unionism over the past near-decade. In this respect, the silence of four of the six speakers concerning the general subject of labor is, perhaps unwit-

[46] *Ibid.*, p. 49.

tingly, some indication of a more realistic assessment of the diminished threat offered to the business community by organized labor during the postwar era. We should, however, be cautious in describing this view as a fixed element of the new ideology; a change in economic climate may again crystallize more vigorous sentiments on the labor question.

It is still more difficult to pass judgment on the ideological selectivity of the managerial view toward the exercise of economic power by the government. On the one hand, there is the obviously altered tone in comparison with the past. On the other, there continues to be a great deal of general suspicion of government both as to purposes and powers, which passes easily into exaggeration. The "fantastically growing" extent of government ominously remarked on by Cordiner is not explained by him as almost entirely a result of defense measures. There is no attempt made to evaluate the level of government nondefense expenditure on a per capita price-adjusted basis. The possibility that strong government encouragement to growth might be favorable for the climate of capitalism is accepted by only one or possibly two speakers.

Thus, it is very difficult to assess the degree to which a larger economic role for government is, in fact, accepted or to prognosticate what would be the attitude of large corporations toward the vigorous use of government economic power in the event of a serious economic setback. In this regard we might well ponder the following, by Andrew Hacker:

A few questions may be asked about these supposed powers of the national government. Can any public agency determine the level of wages, of prices, of profits? Can it, perhaps more important, specify the level and direction of capital investment? Can any government bureau allocate raw materials or control plant location? Can it in any way guarantee full employment or the rate of economic growth? Has any suit of the Anti-Trust Division actually broken up one of our large corporations in an appreciable way? The simple answer is that measures such as these are neither possible under the laws nor do we know what the reaction to them would be.[47]

[47] Andrew Hacker, Sociology and Ideology, *The Social Theories of Talcott Parsons*, Max Black, ed., Prentice-Hall, Englewood Cliffs, N. J., 1961, p. 302.

Such an enumeration brings home the still extremely compressed area in which government economic activity is regarded
as legitimate. It is probably valid to state that a mild Keynesian
policy would be tolerated by some large corporations and even
welcomed by a few and that opposition to countercyclical policy
would be much less hostile than in the 1930's. But it is well
to emphasize that the ideological claim to a new recognition of
the government's role—mixed as that is in the business world—
is, especially in its most conservative expression, very far from an
acceptance of those government activities that might become
necessary or salutary during the next decades.

VI

It is not difficult, then, to puncture the pretensions of much
of the new business ideology, or rather, to unveil the ideological
aspects of what Cordiner calls the "living realities of the new
American economy." As with all ideologies, the view of the large
corporation executive boggles at recognizing what an outsider
sees in every social structure—the legitimizing of privilege, differential reward, and life chances brought about by the existing
institutions. Consciously or otherwise—and it is probably fruitless to debate which—the view from the top encompasses only
part of the social landscape, passing without notice or mention
over the uglier sights and less agreeable vistas.

Nevertheless it is well to bear in mind that the view as described by our six prototypes departs in significant ways from
that of the traditional ideologist. In the concept of a new capitalism, distinguished by its sense of professional responsibility,
characterized by large-scale technological units, imbued with a
concern for human values, and aware of the legitimacy of labor
and government as centers of economic power, we have an expression, however incomplete, of what capitalism means that is
markedly different from what it meant to the late nineteenth- or
early twentieth-century big businessman and considerably different from the lingering conservative depiction today. It is true,
as the authors of *The American Business Creed* point out, that
the new creed has many common values with the older ideology,

including not least a common nationalistic emphasis. Hence, we cannot claim for the new ideology a total or radical break with the past; after all, like the creed of the NAM or that of nineteenth-century capitalism, the new ideology seeks to maintain the status quo. But the image of what the status quo means is clearly different in the mind of even the most conservative of the McKinsey lecturers than in the mind of the traditional business apologist.

Can we conclude, then, that this ideology adequately fulfills the function that has fallen to the business creed? Does it mean that the business ideology, as the uncontested expression of ideological commitment in the United States, will be functionally resourceful and flexible enough, and morally inspiring enough to bring capitalism through this age of social and economic strain? These are the last and by all odds the most difficult questions to which our study leads, and the firm ice of "objective scholarship" over which we have been making our difficult way now begins to crack alarmingly. But having ventured this far, let us risk an intellectual ducking by trying to reach the far shore.

One consideration bearing on these final questions has undoubtedly already occurred to the reader. It is the wide divergence of views within our sample of ideologists, despite their common agreement on basic tenets. An enormous distance separates the idea of business prerogatives implicit in the tone of a Blough or a Cordiner and that expressed by a Houser or a Watson, the last of whom was able to write:

My own company became involved with the Antitrust Division in 1952, and we now operate under a consent decree. It never seemed to me that this action gave me grounds to criticize the government. In fact I have frequently stated that I believed the law was a force for good and that I have no quarrel with the decision in relation to IBM.[48]

It is doubtful that many of the other McKinsey lecturers would be capable of such a statement.

In addition, it is open to question how much, if any, of the lecturers' general ideological view would be acceptable to middle-sized business, which is still typically owner-operated, or to small

[48] Watson, *op. cit.*, pp. 92–93.

proprietorships—both sources of important business pressure on the legislature. Numerous indications would lead us to believe, in fact, that small or medium businessmen depart in many ways from the ideology of big business and generally espouse a more classic, conservative creed. Thus, it would be foolhardy to generalize from the evidence of the McKinsey lectures that a new, more liberal orientation exists for American business at large. At most one can say that the view from the top seems to have moved, in some particulars, toward a recognition of a changed economic and political structure, and that a relatively liberal wing of business opinion now exists with an as yet undetermined following or strength.

Yet, looking to the future, it does not seem unwarranted to point to a few salutary possibilities bearing on the future strength of the liberal wing. The first of these possibilities concerns the climate within which the business ideology is to be shaped. It would seem very natural to assume that there is little reason for a dominant group to change its ideology, if it is not seriously threatened.[49] However, when we examine the ideologically calm postwar era during which the liberal business ideology begins to appear, the opposite conclusion suggests itself. A sharp clash of ideological views may very well press all parties into a dogmatic and rigid position in which adaptative adjustments are extremely difficult. A climate of unanimity, on the other hand, in which the dominant view feels much less defensive, may encourage deviations from the orthodox view. If this tentatively advanced suggestion proves warranted, we may find that the contemporary absence of an organized counterideology, far from serving as a cause for stand-pat attitudes, may make possible a faster evolution of the dominant ideology than would otherwise be possible.

A second hopeful suggestion directs our attention to shifting background factors behind the facade of ideology and, in particular, to the increasing prominence within the nation of the military, the scientific community, the government itself, and even, perhaps, the university. These new groups constitute independent centers of power, which, to a growing degree, compete

[49] Cf. Karl Mannheim, *Ideology and Utopia*, Harvest, New York, 1949, p. 8.

with business centers of power for the formulation of national policy. To an equally significant degree they have also penetrated the business community itself. The professionalization of the corporate manager may or may not be a part of the reality of the business structure, but unquestionably business is more and more utilizing professionals from other fields in its own policy formation. It would not be surprising if business thinking were affected to some degree by the access of recruits from nonbusiness backgrounds, who, although professing no antibusiness views, are likely to exert their influence on the side of liberal rather than conservative business attitudes.

Finally, we must not overlook the change in the cultural milieu itself. The diffusion of the sharp and cynical humor of the 1950's and 1960's, the increasing sophistication of mass (or at least middle-class) talk and reading, the disdain expressed in the popular culture for the standard homilies and pieties—all this must be expected to work its effect on the ideology of business as it has already worked its effect on advertising copy and on the content of the mass magazines. The process of rationalization and intellectualization, which both Max Weber and Joseph Schumpeter referred to as the great solvents of the spirit of our age, are at work silently and ubiquitously, and, barring a cataclysm at home or abroad that might resuscitate the forces of the irrational in mass politics, they can be expected to yield their "corrosive" effects.

Thus, there seems to be at least a chance that the liberal business ideology, riding with the general currents of change of our time, will come to dominate the older ideology and prove to be the means by which many necessary adaptations are made in our social system. This prospect has important consequences, if we are to attempt to pass judgment on the functionality or dysfunctionality of the business ideology insofar as it bears on economic and social policy. Given what I believe to be the probable economic and social strains to which capitalism is apt to be subjected over the coming decades, it is difficult to hold a sanguine view of the conservative ideology as a functional guide for capitalist adjustment in the future. Indeed, were the adaptability of

the economic structure to be limited to the boundaries of maneuver established by the Blough-Cordiner end of the ideological
spectrum, the outlook—to my mind at least—would be one of a
serious inability to cope with reality.

This cannot be said so readily of the liberal wing of business
thought. Precisely how much adaptation can be achieved within
the institutions and established privileges of a capitalist order is
unknown, but a reasonably free use of the government's fiscal
powers, some gradual widening of the welfare structure, a generally undoctrinaire attitude toward foreign or domestic problems—in a word, modes of action and reaction that might be
exceedingly difficult, if the conservative view were dominant—all
are thinkable, if the pressures of the times operate as I have suggested. This does not mean that change will exceed the tolerance
of the basic structure on which capitalism is built—in particular,
private ownership of the means of production, inheritance of
wealth, or the predominance of market relationships. But it does
make possible important changes in economic relationships
within that basic structure.

And yet, even this most hopeful, although by no means certain,
prospect does not fully answer the ultimate question. Would
such a liberal business outlook inspire the dedication needed to
guide this society through the gauntlet of the future? Would it
serve as a lasting source of satisfaction and inspiration for the
whole community, including that critically important part, the
intellectual community? In a word, would the business ideology,
even at its best, suffice as the compass by which a society could
confidently set sail for great destinations?

Here one reaches to levels at which even a pretense of objectivity is no longer possible. The icy waters of a subjective judgment must be braved to complete our journey. The question
seems to ask whether big business is aware, beyond a very limited
horizon, of the nature of the challenges of contemporary history,
and if not, whether the vision it projects is capable of acting as
an illumination for a society that must cope with that history.

One of the McKinsey lecturers spelled out the gravity of this
ultimate challenge, as he saw it, in these words:

We are involved in one of the great ideological struggles of all time. We are in it so deep that it is hard to see it in perspective. But essentially it is a contest between two quite basic concepts. One is that men are capable of faith in ideas that lift their minds and hearts, ideas that raise their sights and give them hope, energy, and enthusiasm. Opposing this is the belief that the pursuit of material ends is all that life on this earth is about.[50]

The words are searching enough, but, alas, what do they say? Which side—ours or theirs—is the side of "ideas that lift minds, etc."; which is the side in which "the pursuit of material ends is all that life on this earth is about"? In the breathtaking ambiguity of this affirmation of faith—the unwitting confusion of identities meant to be so clearly polarized—lies an all too clear warning of the weakness of the business view. It is not merely one speaker's unfortunate lapse that impels this statement; one searches the McKinsey lectures in vain for a recognition of truly great issues. A few token gestures, a respectful doffing of the cap before the "challenges of our time," only serve to give greater inanity to the declarations of economic patriotism that follow. It is not moral leadership that the McKinsey lecturers finally offer us; it is a pep talk.

What is it, in the end, that deprives the business ideology of the quality of inspiration it seeks? In part, of course, it is the more or less transparent defense of privilege masquerading as philosophy, the search for sanction cloaked as a search for truth, the little evasions and whitewashings that cheapen what purports to be a fearless confrontation of great issues. And yet, these are only surface flaws. At its core, the business ideology as a spiritual creed or as an historic beacon is vitiated by something that is missing—I cannot but think fatally missing—from its deepest conception. What it lacks is a grandiose image of society, a projection of human possibilities cast in a larger mold than is offered by today's institutions.

This lack is made clear, if we think for a moment of the "visionary" glimpses of the future often provided by business spokesmen—a future of enormous affluence, leisure, etc. What is re-

[50] Kappel, *op. cit.*, p. 102.

markable, however, in all these visions is that they never fail to speak of the "workers," however rich, and the "businessmen," however enlightened, who will continue to run such a society. A future in which there were no workers or businessmen—in which, in other words, the categories of privilege and disprivilege inextricable from capitalism had become obsolete—is not seriously imaginable to the business mind. Neither is a society in which, for example, there would be no advertising, in which consumption no longer played its nervous energizing role, in which the introduction of new technology was no longer regulated by considerations of profitability, or in which incomes were administered rather than competitively sought. Such arrangements, to the businessman, are utopian. The point is, however, that their exclusion consigns the world of business ideology to the non-utopian—that is, *to the depiction of a society not sufficiently different from our own to serve as a lodestar for the distant future.*

Perhaps it is impossible to expect such a lodestar from any ideology today, much less a conservative one. Ours is an age that hesitates before millennial slogans and transcendental visions and has learned to laugh at artists' renditions of what the future might be like. Hence, the unchallenged predominance of the matter-of-fact, conserving, incrementally progressive, and, at its best, decent and sober philosophy of the businessman. The question is whether, under the thrall of such an ideology, we shall succeed in fundamentally changing a society where most men still lead lives to which those few who have escaped would not like their sons to return.

2

The Ideal of Individualism and the Reality of Organization

John William Ward

"Such was individualism in its two aspects—
all things unto all men." (Thomas Mann)

I

The purpose of this essay is to trace the history of the ideal of individualism in American culture and then to use that history in order to understand better the deep concern for the place of the individual in contemporary American society. Our society, like all modern industrial societies, is characterized by economic and social interdependence, specialization of activity, and large-scale organization—social phenomena that pose troublesome problems for traditional American attitudes toward the relation of the individual to society. One way of coming to grips with our predicament is to see how we came to it in the first place.

"The profit of studying history," George Santayana once said, "lies in something else than in a dead knowledge of what happens to have happened." [1] Yet no good historian—and the adjective will quickly exclude those who may disagree—would suggest that history will give us ready and pat answers to problems in the present. What history can do is enlarge our experience of the events that have entered into the shaping of the present in which we live and move and, thus, make us more aware, itself a virtue, and perhaps through awareness better able to act. Since my final purpose is to bring an excursion into the past to bear

[1] George Santayana, *Reason in Science*, in *The Life of Reason, or The Phases of Human Progress*, V, Scribner's, New York, 1918, pp. 52–53.

upon the present, perhaps it will serve that purpose to begin in the present.

There is an embarrassment of riches when one looks for a contemporary text from which to begin. One thinks of the fortieth anniversary issue of *Time* magazine, The Individual in America, with its cover story on Lincoln, "the greatest, the classic, the archetypical individual in the American imagination," who knew about the organization man because "in a sense he was one himself, and a good one." [2] But I have chosen as my text an article from *Fortune* magazine for two reasons: it is shorter and therefore more adaptable to my needs; but more important, it comes from a magazine that addresses itself specifically to the leaders of American business.

A few years ago—in 1951 to be precise—in the political stalemate following the end of the Second World War, the editors of *Fortune* looked about and discovered half the world on their right hand and half on their left. There seemed to be no ground to stand on between "fascist totalitarianism," the world of the right, and "paternal state socialism," the world of the left. So *Fortune* decided to establish one. In a world made cold by the winds of change, America, in its fat and warm contentment, seemed to offer too visible a target. Although what the editors of *Fortune* were after was what they themselves called a "middle of the road" solution, they packaged it handsomely under the brand name of "the permanent revolution."

The irony cuts deeper than that. The "third force" that the world needed to combat fascism and socialism was that old American tradition, "individualism." The editors faced the cliché without flinching:

Americans are fond of saying that the state exists for the individual, not the individual for the state. Despite its truistic character, this aphorism has enormous meaning. A proletarian approach, which subordinates the individual to the group or class, represents for the American, not an advance but a reaction. . . . If a really dynamic third force

2 Lincoln and Modern America: The Heritage of a Free Choice in an Organized Society, *Time*, May 10, 1963, p. 20.

is to be created . . . the principle of individualism must constitute its foundation.[3]

But the dynamic principle of a conservative revolution based on the ideal of individualism had some awkward facts to face. The editors went on to say:

In our time, individualism has clashed with the whole industrial development, mass production and the division of labor. The key to industrialization is not independence but interdependence; no individual is self-sufficient; each is involved with others in complicated relationships. Dominating all this is the modern corporation, an organization of vast powers, which exacts of its managers purely impersonal decisions. It is little wonder that men have turned to the state to protect themselves in such a world.

The world of the state was, of course, the world of fascism or socialism. Yet, if America was to maintain its conservative, permanent revolution, it had to remain true to what the editors of *Fortune* took to be the basic proposition of American society—private, individual responsibility. To turn to the state would only further compromise the integrity of the industrial American, dependent on his fellows but lonely in a world of impersonal decisions. *"The solution is to be found,"* discovered the editors, so delighted that they put their discovery in italics, *"The solution is to be found not through a growth in government, but through a growth in the stature of the individual."*

The dialectic begins to pick up speed here, and one has to watch closely.

The concept that appears to be emerging, as the answer of the modern individual to this challenge, is the concept of the *team*. It is an old concept but it is being put to new uses. As a member of a team an individual can find full opportunity for self-expression and still retain a dynamic relationship to other individuals . . . the concept of the team has the power to challenge the individual to seek his self-

[3] *Fortune* (February 1951), p. 176. The articles in this issue of *Fortune* were gathered under the general editorship of Russell Davenport to make the book, *USA: The Permanent Revolution,* Prentice-Hall, Englewood Cliffs, N. J., 1951.

expression, not along purely egoistic channels. . . . A community—big or little—is created, and through it the individual finds a higher expression of himself.

If one stops as one reads that the individual is to realize himself as part of a team, if one stops to wonder what happened to that reactionary proletarian danger of immersing the individual in a group, one will see the same thing happened to it that happened to that independent individual. The group has become community; interdependence has become team play; complicated relationships have become dynamic relationships. "Community," "team," "dynamic": these are all plus words. We respond to them positively and happily, perhaps even mindlessly. Unless we watch the verbal magic, we will not notice that the individualism put in the hat at the beginning is not the individualism that pops out at the end.

The traditional American individual, once wrapped warmly in the pleasant connotations of self-reliance and independence, reappears as that well-known fellow, the other-directed individual, trying to find out who he truly is by relating himself to others in his society.

Now, the semanticist will find a certain perverse delight in all of this, but the historian will find a text. What the editors of *Fortune* did was to run over a century of American history through a single article. The projector works so fast that we tend to see only the blurred confusion. However, rather than blame the operator we might better be thankful for seeing what we may well have been missing in the slow-motion version of history.

At the beginning when Americans spoke of individualism, they meant the kind of independence the editors of *Fortune* point to in their beginning. Individualism meant the primacy of the individual person, the denial of social restraint, freedom from involvement with others. After an awkward transition in which they tried to make this ideal apply to conditions that made it increasingly anachronistic, Americans have begun to shift the connotations of the word in precisely the fashion that the editors of *Fortune* do when they draw to their conclusion. Individual-

ism comes to mean participation in society.   One achieves a
higher expression of one's self through the organization of society.   The early version, that is, *freedom from* society, was essentially negative; the modern version, that is, *freedom to cooperate
in society*, is essentially positive.[4]

What Americans have been doing for more than a century is
gradually changing their system of values under the protection
of big, umbrella words like "individualism."   The word stays
the same; it provides comfort against the rude weather of change.
But the meaning moves, and we come out from under the umbrella in a different climate altogether.

II

The concept, individualism, appeared first in France as *"individualisme,"* after the French Revolution.   Prior to the Revolution the French word for individual, *individu,* was used to describe someone who did not belong to any of the corporate bodies
that constituted society, someone who had no social identity.[5]
After the Revolution when all corporate bodies had been abol-
ished, the word *individualisme,* used by conservatives, liberals,
and socialists alike, first appeared to describe the evil and antisocial impulses of self-interest.   This is also Edmund Burke's
charge against the French Revolution—that the political philosophy of the Revolution with its celebration of abstract rights
would lead to the point where, in his words, "the commonwealth
itself would, in a few generations, crumble away, be disconnected

[4] There is the danger of evoking emotional connotations in using words
like "positive" and "negative" as descriptive terms, but the same danger goes
with any other pair of descriptive terms that I have been able to think of.
I settled on these two, because they are also used by Isaiah Berlin in his
essay, *Two Concepts of Liberty,* Clarendon Press, Oxford, 1958, and in the
hope that the echo might remind us that our problem far transcends the
dimensions of American history.

[5] See the discussion by Robert R. Palmer, Man and Citizen: Applications
of Individualism in the French Revolution, in Milton R. Konvitz and Arthur
E. Murphy, eds., *Essays in Political Theory Presented to George H. Sabine,*
Cornell University Press, Ithaca, 1948.

into the dust and powder of individuality, and at length dispersed to all the winds of heaven." [6]

In Europe, then, individualism meant the atomization of society, a threat to the common good, the suffocating dust of equality. Notice, however, that Burke uses the word "individuality," not "individualism," and for a good and simple reason. The word was not yet available to him; it had not yet come into the English language. According to the *Oxford English Dictionary,* "individualism" made its appearance in English in 1835 with the translation of Tocqueville's justly famous *Democracy in America.* The *Oxford English Dictionary* happens to be wrong in its particulars but still generally right. It has the date of the translation of Tocqueville wrong; it should be 1840. Also, there are a few other uses of the word in English prior to the translation of Tocqueville, but the *Oxford English Dictionary* is right in the sense that "individualism" came into the English language in response to the need for a word to describe the social philosophy of America in the 1830's, the period of Jacksonian democracy. So, since the attribution is correct in the terms that count, let us begin with Tocqueville, because he clearly sets forth the original meaning of the word.[7]

[6] Edmund Burke, *Reflections on the Revolution in France,* Thomas H. D. Mahoney, ed., Bobbs-Merrill, The Library of Liberal Arts, Indianapolis, 1955, p. 109.

[7] Tocqueville published the *Democracy* in two parts, each part appearing in two volumes, in 1835 and 1840. Both parts were immediately translated into English, appearing in London also in 1835 and 1840, by Henry Reeve, public official and author who was later to become editor of the *Edinburgh Review.* The *Oxford English Dictionary* dates Reeve's translation of Tocqueville's use of "individualism" as 1835, but the usage occurred in Tocqueville's chapter, "Of Individualism in Democratic Countries," in the second part of 1840. The editor may have been misled because the first part appeared in two volumes, or he may simply have taken the earliest date of the title, *Democracy in America,* to arrive at the date 1835. The error kept him from noting the appearance of the word in English before Reeve used it. In 1839, T. G. Bradford in Boston, translating the third edition of Michael Chevalier's, *Lettres sur l'Amérique du Nord* (1838), uses "individualism" without any sign that he is self-conscious about employing a neologism. See Michael Chevalier, *Society, Manners, and Politics in the United States: Letters on North America,* John William Ward, translator and editor, Anchor, New

Tocqueville and the Novelty of Individualism

In describing the attitude that developed because of the conditions of social equality in America, Tocqueville found himself at a loss for a word to name the social philosophy of Americans. So he introduced a new one.[8] *"Individualism,"* he wrote, emphasizing the word, "is a novel expression, to which a novel idea has given birth." [9] Tocqueville's English translator, Henry Reeve, felt the same sense of something new. When he translated the word from the French, he simply dropped the French "e" from its end, rendered it as "individualism," and put a note at the bottom of his page: "I adopt the expression of the original," he explained, "however strange it may sound to the English ear . . . because I know of no English word exactly equivalent to the expression."

What Tocqueville wanted to describe by using his new word was a social philosophy that he had discovered in America concerning the relation of the individual to society. His need for a new word is the best measure we have of his sense that the

---

York, 1961, pp. 104, 356, 391. Chevalier uses the word in the same sense Tocqueville was to use it: "Under the influence of Protestantism and republicanism, social progress had been achieved by pushing the process of division to its extreme, that is, individualism; for Protestantism, republicanism, and individualism are all one. Individuals have cut themselves off from each other; each has isolated his personality in order to protect it" (p. 356).

"Individualism" also appeared in an unsigned article in the *United States Magazine and Democratic Review,* VI (1839), pp. 208–209. Here again, the American writer is unembarrassed by the word, which suggests that a further hunt would uncover previous uses of it; more importantly, he, unlike his European contemporaries, uses the word in an honorific sense. But that is to anticipate my text.

[8] More precisely, he seems to have thought that he was using a new word. In France, the concept of individualism was relatively new, but it had been in the political vocabulary at least 16 years before Tocqueville wrote. However, all—whether extreme reactionaries like Bonald or Maistre, liberals like Tocqueville, or Saint-Simonian socialists like Chevalier—used the word to mean the disintegration of society. See Koenraad W. Swart, "Individualism" in the Mid-Nineteenth Century (1826–1860), *Journal of the History of Ideas,* XXIII (1962), pp. 77–90.

[9] Alexis de Tocqueville, *Democracy in America,* Phillips Bradley, ed., II, Knopf, New York, 1948, p. 98.

future, which he thought was embodied in America, meant a radical departure from the past of Europe. But Tocqueville was not happy with the texture of the world that he saw unfolding before his eyes. What in Europe seemed odious—the notion that the individual was superior to society—was in America "a mature and calm feeling." Tocqueville was at pains to discriminate the social philosophy of individualism from sheer egoism, sheer selfishness, but he thought that Americans, in developing a social philosophy that detached the individual from his fellow men, might come to as mean a failure as if they had acted from mere thoughtless selfishness. "Selfishness," he wrote, "originates in blind instinct; individualism proceeds from erroneous judgement more than from depraved feelings; it originates as much in deficiencies of mind as in perversity of heart." The judgment is the typical European critique: Americans mean well, but they lack mind. With all the good heart in the world, Americans, thought Tocqueville, were organizing society around a notion of the individual person, which would in the long run destroy all social virtue and end in social disaster.

Yet, Tocqueville recognized that in Jacksonian America individualism was an ideal of behavior, not simply an antisocial impulse. In attributing so much power to an idea, Tocqueville was no Platonist. As much as any modern sociologist he knew that social conditions have their characteristic intellectual counterparts. In his analysis, individualism was the idea, social equality was the condition. The tendency of the American to look to himself alone was, thought Tocqueville, a function of his environment. However, as a member of the *petite noblesse* of French society Tocqueville could not face the logical consequences of social equality and individualism without considerable apprehension. His image of the good society was formed by the notion of a social hierarchy, a chain of being in which each member of the community belonged to a clearly defined place in the hierarchical order of things. "Aristocracy," he said, "had made a chain of all the members of the community, from the peasant to the king; democracy breaks that chain and severs every link of it." [10] It was this shattering separation of man from man, the rupture of all social relationships and social obligations, that defined individualism for Tocqueville:

As social conditions become more equal, the number of persons increases who, although they are neither rich nor powerful enough to exercise any great influence over their fellows, have nevertheless acquired or retained sufficient education and fortune to satisfy their own wants. They owe nothing to any man, they expect nothing from any man, they acquire the habit of always considering themselves as standing alone, and they are apt to imagine that their whole destiny is in their own hands. Thus not only does democracy make every man forget his ancestors, but it hides his descendants and separates his contemporaries from him; it throws him back forever upon himself alone and threatens in the end to confine him entirely within the solitude of his own heart.[11]

The Democratic Hero: The Autonomous Individual

There is much one might say of Tocqueville's bleak adumbration of the myth of the self-made man, but for present purposes I would like to make one simple point about it. Tocqueville deplored the consequences of individualism, but from his context it is apparent that Americans did not. What Europeans feared, Americans celebrated. What was for Tocqueville a danger, was for the American Democrat an intoxicating ideal. Whereas, to make society possible at all, Tocqueville sought countervailing tendencies against individualism, so American a spokesman as Ralph Waldo Emerson wrote in his journals in 1840, the same year in which Tocqueville published: "In all my

[10] *Ibid.*, p. 99. For the rich tradition out of which Tocqueville spoke, see Arthur O. Lovejoy, *The Great Chain of Being*, Harvard University Press, Cambridge, Mass., 1936.

[11] Bradley, *loc. cit.* By "democracy" Tocqueville generally meant, as he clearly does in the passage here, the equality of social conditions. Reeve did Tocqueville a mild disservice by translating *démocratie* directly into our word; Tocqueville even considered calling the second part of 1840, *Egalité en Amérique* to make his sense clearer, but he was not above confusing the sense of "democracy" in his own usage. George W. Pierson, *Tocqueville and Beaumont in America*, Oxford University Press, New York, 1938, p. 747 and the note on p. 748.

lectures, I have taught one doctrine, namely, the infinitude of the private man." [12]

A considerable body of assumptions lies behind so bold an assertion, but in insisting on the individual as the ultimate reality in society Emerson was a characteristic spokesman for his time. In the early nineteenth century, Americans did not like the state any more than the editors of *Fortune* do today. "The less government we have the better" was the rallying cry of Jeffersonians and Jacksonians alike. "The antidote," said Emerson, in almost the precise words that *Fortune* was to use more than a century later, "is the influence of private character, the growth of the individual." Emerson went on, in a long series of remarkable negatives, to strip this full-grown individual of every conceivable extrinsic support:

> The appearance of character makes the State unnecessary. The wise man is the State. He needs no army, fort, or navy—he loves men too well; no bribe, or feast, or palace, to draw friends to him; no vantage ground, no favorable circumstances. He needs no library, for he has not done thinking; no church, for he is a prophet; no statute-book, for he has the law-giver; no money, for he is value; no road, for he is at home where he is; no experience, for the life of the creator shoots through him. . . . He has no personal friends.[13]

The figure of this grandly isolated man, nakedly alone, without any helpful circumstance, without the accumulated knowledge and the traditions of the past, homeless, gladly bereft of friends, is a chilling ideal—unless, that is, one can share the assumption that makes it possible. Emerson and most Americans of his time could embrace this figure because of the calm belief that there was an order that existed apart from society, a natural order, which ultimately validated the rejection of the artificial order of society and the state. As Emerson put it elsewhere, "you take the way from man, not to man." [14] This centrifugal thrust was kept from spinning madly away by a deep trust in a natural

[12] Stephen E. Whicher, ed., *Selections from Ralph Waldo Emerson*, Houghton Mifflin, Boston, 1957, p. 139.

[13] Emerson, Politics (1841), *Ibid.*, pp. 249–250.

[14] Emerson, Self-Reliance (1840), *Ibid.*, p. 158.

order, which guaranteed social unity. So society emerges miraculously as the sum of all the individual rejections of society.

I have said that in this kind of assertion Emerson was a characteristically American thinker; he was. One can see the same attitude of thought, the same conception of the relation of the individual to society, in Jacksonian political thought, in economic thought, in revivalistic and evangelical Protestantism, in literature, and in the popular ideals of American society in Emerson's time—the America that we sometimes tend to forget was the object of Tocqueville's analysis.[15] The mood rises to a climax by the end of the nineteenth century in the historical interpretation of the meaning of American history in the hands of Frederick Jackson Turner and his followers in the frontier interpretation of our history, the notion that the meaning of American life lies in the movement out of society, away from others, to a new beginning.[16]

The Unforeseen Consequence of Individualism

What happened to that heroic individual, standing alone, independent of others, the editors of *Fortune* put quite well: "The key to industrialization is not independence, but interdependence." From where we stand, looking backward, it surely seems ironic that an ideal of independence and simple harmony should have been formulated by a society on the verge of complexity and conflict, the society of industrial America. Actually, the unintended consequence of the ideal of uninhibited individual action, of this negative theory of the state, of the denial of the reality

[15] See John William Ward, Individualism Today, *Yale Review*, XLIX (Spring 1960), pp. 380–392, for a slightly fuller description of this general pattern; see also the short concluding chapter of my book, *Andrew Jackson: Symbol for an Age*, Oxford University Press, New York, 1955, for the way in which popular ideals of the time centered optimistically on the energetic and self-reliant individual.

[16] Henry Nash Smith, *Virgin Land: The American West as Symbol and Myth*, Harvard University Press, Cambridge, Mass., 1950, especially the third section, The Garden of the World; it concludes with an analysis of the way in which Turner's frontier hypothesis is the culmination of a long cultural tradition in American thought, which "conferred on him the authority of one who speaks from the distilled experience of his people" (p. 251).

of society, was to accelerate the powerful energies of an acquisitive capitalism and to lead finally to where we now stand.[17] Richard Hofstadter has observed that "the same forces in American life that had made Jacksonian equalitarianism possible and had given to the equalitarian theme in the agrarian romance its most compelling appeal had also unleashed in the nation an entrepreneurial zeal probably without precedent in history." [18]

The processes of machine industry and technology, which characterize the modern world, have made organization, the rationalization of activity, specialization, and social interdependence utterly necessary. The first response of Americans to the world that they had made was to try to keep the social benefits made possible through the economies of large-scale organization and, at the same time, to invoke and maintain an ideal of individualism, which organization and its logical consequences were rendering obsolete. Whatever the consequences (we can see them easily, because we have experienced them), Jacksonian America drew its emotional energy from the belief and assumption that there existed a simple, natural order, which would emerge spontaneously and unbidden if each individual went his own separate way.

It was, of course, the very fluidity and openness of Jacksonian society that provided a material basis for the heady optimism of this ultimately anarchic ideal of individualism. For an historian looking back on early America, the social circumstances bulk large; they may properly be primary in his assessment of the age. But for those living in the age, there was also an ideal, a moral

[17] A problem that still puzzles historians of the Jacksonian period is whether the age wished somehow to recapture the simplicity of Jefferson's pastoral politics or to seize the main chance and exploit the opportunities of a rapidly growing society. Perhaps, being human, Americans of the time entertained both emotions, however incompatible. We can say without attempting to solve the puzzle that the ideal of the free and independent person, unencumbered by social restraint, could logically serve either goal. For a review of the historical literature of the period, see John William Ward, *The Age of the Common Man,* in John Higham, ed., *The Reconstruction of American History,* Harper, New York, 1962.

[18] Richard Hofstadter, *The Age of Reform: From Bryan to F.D.R.,* Knopf, New York, 1955, p. 40.

basis for their optimism, a "cosmic optimism" built on a belief in a cosmic natural order, which undergirded and validated the ideal of the free and autonomous individual.

The original ideal of individualism in Jacksonian America was a secular jeremiad, an exhortation to begin over again, sloughing off the complexities of society by returning to a natural state of grace. Somewhat ironically, it was the material expansiveness of the society that made it possible to entertain such an ideal, to believe in the possibility of constantly beginning anew, of turning away from society to create one's own future. More ironically, it was the same material expansiveness, itself accelerated by the lack of social restraint implicit in the ideal, that finally destroyed the ideal itself. There were two "natures" in American society: the normative Nature of the Jeffersonians, the Jacksonians, and the Transcendentalists; and a physical nature of coal, iron, and oil—the raw materials of the vast industrial and technological society in which we now live. The unforeseen consequence of the Jacksonian program was, as I have already said, to liberate the energies of industrial capitalism and, thus, to accelerate the creation of our modern complex world.

III

The American Democrat described by Tocqueville—the man who saw about him no one much richer or more powerful than himself, the man who had acquired the habit of considering himself as standing alone and who imagined that his whole destiny was in his own hands—found it increasingly difficult to square his beliefs with the world he found about him. Not that the effort was not made. The years after the Civil War saw the apogee of the cult of the self-made man in America, the spawning of an immensely popular literature on success, and the appearance of the Horatio Alger stories. These phenomena represent in their different ways attempts to assert the old belief that success, or, on the more uncharitable side, failure, lay in one's own character and not in society. Robert Bremner's study of the discovery of poverty in America is instructive in the problem facing the prevailing view of the relation of the individual to society.[19]

The Discovery of Society

Social-service work, generated by the pressing needs of displaced immigrants, the squalid conditions of cities whose growth outstripped the capacity for control, and the general helplessness of those at the bottom of the new industrial economy, began as one might expect it to begin. It began with an appeal to individuals to change their way of life, to better themselves, to solve their problems by an act of will. It may seem a gratuitous insult to us today, but the Association for Improving the Condition of the Poor went about its work in the New York slums by distributing free copies of Benjamin Franklin's "Way to Wealth." A people who felt that they owed nothing to society found it hard to blame society; nurtured on the belief that the individual was all, they found it difficult to see anything more than purely individual wills operating atomistically to create society. But as social-service work became increasingly organized and information on poverty and the ills that went with it was amassed and exchanged among social-service workers, the brute fact obtruded itself that poverty was a social phenomenon and not simply a function of individual character. Experience finally teaches, but the teaching, in this case, was slow and painful.

The response of social-service workers—those most dramatically exposed to the shaping forces of society—suggests a way of comprehending much of the confused thought of the late nineteenth century. It is the simple observation that people perceive reality largely from the angle of vision provided by the concepts that they derive from tradition. They will persist in seeing the world from their inherited perspective even when, from our later perspective, it seems to us to make little sense of their world. Take, for example, the idea of the self-made man and, closely associated with it, the cluster of notions that we have come to call the "gospel of wealth."

[19] Robert H. Bremner, *From the Depths: The Discovery of Poverty in the United States*, New York University Press, New York, 1956.

The Self-Made Man

The very phrase "the self-made man," with its connotation of a radical self-sufficiency, was itself a heritage from the Jacksonian period. A nice irony surrounds its birth. The phrase was fathered in a speech in 1832 by Henry Clay in behalf of a protective tariff for the infant industries of Kentucky hemp manufacturers, Clay's constituents, whom he described as "enterprising self-made men." [20] Clay seems not to have been bothered by the incongruity of self-made men seeking the paternalistic support of the state, and the discrepancy has made it easy ever since to write parodies of the idea of the self-made man. But the discrepancy should alert us to the fact that the successful man represented more than just success to his contemporaries; he presented a whole constellation of values, especially the beauty of the American way of life and the capacity of the unaided individual to make his own way in the world.

When, in 1897, Vanderbilt University unveiled a statue in honor of its benefactor, Cornelius Vanderbilt, Chauncey M. Depew gave the address which drew the popular moral:

The American Commonwealth is built upon the individual. It recognizes neither classes nor masses. . . . We have thus become a nation of self-made men. We live under just and equal laws and all avenues for a career are open. . . . Freedom of opportunity and preservation of the results of forecast, industry, thrift, and honesty have made the United States the most prosperous and wealthy country in the world. Commodore Vanderbilt is a conspicuous example of the products and possibilities of our free and elastic conditions. . . . He neither gave nor asked quarter. The same country, the same laws, the same open avenues, the same opportunities which he had before him are equally before every other man. . . . He was not the creation of luck nor chance nor circumstances.[21]

[20] See Mitford Matthews, *A Dictionary of Americanisms on Historical Principles,* University of Chicago Press, Chicago, 1951; Irvin G. Wyllie, *The Self-Made Man in America,* Rutgers University Press, New Brunswick, N. J., 1954.

[21] Sigmund Diamond, *The Reputation of the American Businessman,* Harvard University Press, Cambridge, Mass., 1955, p. 53. One of the studies done for the Research Center in Entrepreneurial History at Harvard, Mr. Diamond's book is a summary of attitudes toward major business leaders at the moment of their death; in order to compare changes in attitudes, his book

There was, of course, the one circumstance—the great, good fortune of living under the equal laws of the American Commonwealth—so that such ritualistic celebrations of the self-made man were at the same time secular hymns of nationalistic self-congratulation. One need not be too astute to suspect that these rhetorical set pieces were serving some purpose other than a fair description of reality, when a New York newspaper found the fact that J. P. Morgan was born with millions to his name was no hindrance to citing the traditional maxim. Despite the fact, the *Tribune* observed, that Morgan had "no traditions of the steerage, in him were the qualities of the self-made man, and by his own efforts he traversed relatively as many rounds of the ladder as did many other financiers who began with nothing." [22]

When evidence and conclusion part company so blatantly, one senses a strain in the culture, some imperious need that desperately needs an answer. The terms of the answer are clear enough: if you are not a success, look to yourself, not to the system, for the reason for your failure. The easy convertibility of the cult of self-help into praise for the American way of life implies that questions were being raised about that way. Chauncey Depew's remark that Commodore Vanderbilt "neither gave nor asked quarter" suggests that success involved a fierce struggle and that the road to it was not quite so broad and open as the ideal would have it. But, given the terms of the answer, those who protested were in the uncomfortable position of being un-American. Those not eminently successful, those who sought power through the organization of workingmen or security through pension systems, were told, for example, in 1883 by Mr. Norvin Green, President of the Western Union Telegraph Company, which had just defeated a costly strike by its operators, that his company was against unions "simply to protect the free will of each individual" and that pensions were "not in accordance with the genius of our Government or our country." [23]

---

ranges from 1831, the death of Stephen Girard of Philadelphia, to 1947, the death of Henry Ford.

[22] *Ibid.*, p. 82.

[23] *Report of the Committee of the Senate Upon the Relations Between Labor and Capital*, I (Washington, 1885), pp. 913, 940–941.

There were those in the society who did not have to wait for the later researches of historians to discover that the cult of the self-made man was not an accurate transcription of social reality.[24] It was in 1901 that the Right Reverend William Lawrence of Massachusetts published what soon became a famous piece, "The Relation of Wealth to Morals," in which he maintained that "in the long run, it is only to the man of morality that wealth comes." The Bishop realized that "we, like the Psalmist, occasionally see the wicked prosper, but only occasionally" because, as he triumphantly concluded, "Godliness is in league with riches." As a preacher, Bishop Lawrence told a little parable to dramatize his abstract moralizing:

As I was beginning to write this paper an Irishman with his horse and wagon drew up at my back door. Note that I say *his* horse and wagon. Twenty years ago that Irishman, then hardly twenty years old, landed in Boston, illiterate, uncouth, scarcely able to make himself understood in English. There was no symptom of brains, alertness, or ambition. He got a job to tend a few cows. Soon the American atmosphere began to take hold. He discovered that here every man has his chance.[25]

[24] F. W. Gregory and I. D. Neu, The American Industrial Elite in the 1870's: Their Social Origins, in William Miller, ed., *Men in Business,* Harvard University Press, Cambridge, Mass., 1952, pp. 193–211. Stimulated by William Miller's similar study of business leaders in the decade 1901–1910, Gregory and Neu did their study of the earlier period and concluded: "Was the typical industrial leader of the 1870's then, a 'new man,' an escapee from the slums of Europe or from the parental farm? Did he rise by his own efforts from a boyhood of poverty? Was he as innocent of education and formal training as has often been alleged? He seems to have been none of these things. American by birth, of a New England father, English in national origin, Congregational, Presbyterian, or Episcopalian in religion, urban in early environment, he was rather born and bred in an atmosphere in which business and a relatively high social standing were intimately associated with his family life. Only at about eighteen did he take his first regular job, prepared to rise from it, moreover, not by a rigorous apprenticeship begun when he was virtually a child, but by an academic education well above average for the time" (p. 204).

[25] Gail Kennedy, ed., *Democracy and the Gospel of Wealth, Problems in American Civilization,* D. C. Heath, Boston, 1949, p. 70; Lawrence's essay was first published in *World's Work,* I (January 1901), pp. 286–292.

There is no need to follow Bishop Lawrence's Irishman until
he becomes "a capitalist, and his yearly earnings represent the
income on $30,000"; the point is made succinctly. The Irishman
"made his own way" in the inspiring American atmosphere.
"Twenty years ago" would take us back to 1881, and it so happens that we have the story of another Irishman, clearly not the
Bishop's, but one who, like him, came as an immigrant to the
United States and by hard work saved money and bought himself a horse and wagon to go into the carting business in order
to set himself up as a capitalist. In 1883, a Senate committee
inquiring into the relations between labor and capital called this
Irishman, Thomas B. McGuire of New York, before them to
relate his career.

Whether because of the "American atmosphere" or not, Mc-
Guire made himself understood quite forcibly. "I embarked
something like $300 in the business, thinking I might become
something of a capitalist eventually, but I found competition so
great that it was impossible for me to do so." [26] Although he
lacked such sophisticated terminology as "favored entry into the
market" or "the economies of large-scale organization," McGuire
knew what had happened to him. He described for the committee how the railroads had their own trucking companies with
representatives aboard the trains, so that there was no business
left at the depot for independent operators like himself. Furthermore, given the size of their operations, these subsidiaries
were able to maintain their own blacksmith shops and buy feed
for their animals in large quantities at cheaper prices. With
higher operating costs and no entry into the market, McGuire
was soon, as he put it, driven to the wall. Out of work in 1883,
he was openly contemptuous of the possibility that "politicians,"
the Senators he was addressing, would do anything to redress the
conditions under which he thought the working man had no
chance at all.

The Senate committee was clearly upset, especially when, in
response to the question whether he would go to work for room
and board for himself and his family and twenty dollars a month,

[26] *Labor and Capital, op. cit.,* p. 771.

McGuire answered, "I would be willing to do better than that. If they will guarantee me food, clothing and shelter for myself and family for twenty years, I will give them my services for nothing." A few days later, Jay Gould followed Mr. McGuire to the stand before the same committee and was asked the somewhat leading question, "Of the men who conduct business enterprise and wield the power of capital in this country today, what proportion do you think are what are called 'self-made men'?" He answered, "I think they are all 'self-made men'; I do not say *self*-made exactly, for the country has grown and they have grown up with it. In this country we have no heirlooms or handing down estates. Every man has to stand here on his own individual merit." One of the senators, however, the chairman of the committee, Senator Blair of New Hampshire, could not forget McGuire. He said to Jay Gould, "We have had a man six feet high, who has driven a truck team, and who has more intellectual capacity than half, or perhaps any, of the members of Congress, offering here before this committee to agree under contract to work diligently and faithfully for the next twenty years for anybody who would give him employment and agree to maintain himself and his family."

Gould did not comment on what he thought of the intelligence of congressmen, but he did say, "Well, I know there are a great many cases of actual suffering in a large city like [New York]. . . . I have noticed, though, that generally if men are temperate and industrious they are pretty sure of success. In cases such as the one you describe I could almost always go back behind the scenes and find a cause for such a person's 'misfortunes.' " [27]

The fascinating thing about Jay Gould's response is that he is doing more than just dismissing a bit of contrary evidence. His logic implies that this country has no unequal laws, that every man stands on his own two feet; therefore, if a man is a failure, there *must* be a personal cause for what are called his "misfortunes" but are really his just deserts. Just as with Bishop Lawrence, the adverb "generally" will take care of rude exceptions, but the confidence that these can only be exceptions is an un-

[27] *Ibid.*, p. 1088.

questioned article of faith. If the self-propelled American Democrat owes nothing to anything outside his own character, then, if he is a success, he must deserve it, and if he is a failure, he deserves that too.

The Gospel of Wealth

It is hard not to be cynical about Jay Gould's reaction, especially given the character of the witness. But hypocrisy is not too useful an analytical generalization for the historian, especially when, as in Gould's case, the sentiment is so widely shared by others at the same time. It makes more sense simply to conclude that many Americans in the late nineteenth century, a moment of massive and rapid social change, were attempting to impose a cultural ideal, inherited from the past and deeply cherished, onto a present to which the ideal had little, if any, relevance.[28] The same generalization holds true for the gospel of wealth, although the gospel of wealth had an immense psychological advantage over the idea of the self-made man. It, too, incorporated the notion that the source of success was in the individual, but it yoked with that notion the idea that the man of wealth labored not for himself but for others, that he was a trustee who spent his life in the service of society. As Andrew Carnegie put it, "Individualism will continue, but the millionaire will be a trustee for the poor; intrusted for a season with a great part of the increased wealth of the community, but administering it for the community far better than it would or could have done for itself." [29]

Throughout the late nineteenth century, Andrew Carnegie was held up again and again as an exemplum of success in Amer-

[28] This raises a troublesome question, which I do not wish to avoid but which I do not know how to answer. Ideals, by definition, always transcend and go beyond actual behavior. The question, then, is how wide the discrepancy must become before we start to call them "ideologies," that is, normative codes that one cannot, with the best of intentions, realize in present action. See Karl Mannheim's discussion of "false consciousness" in *Ideology and Utopia, An Introduction to the Sociology of Knowledge*, Routledge and Kegan Paul, London, 1936, pp. 84–87.

[29] Kennedy, *op. cit.*, p. 8; Andrew Carnegie's essay, Wealth, first appeared in the *North American Review*, CXLVIII (June 1889), pp. 653–664.

ica. His story was a paradigm of the American story—democracy triumphant, to invert the title of one of his books. The poor immigrant boy arrives on the shores of the new nation, which abounds in endless opportunity. The son of a workingman, he has little opportunity for formal education and is forced by circumstance to seek work at a tender age. His first job is a lowly one, but by diligence, cleverness, and good luck he rises to the top in short order. The story had been told before the brassy age of American industrial expansion that followed the Civil War, but it came into its own with the appearance on the American scene of men like Carnegie.

In 1889, near the peak of his success, Carnegie published in the *North American Review* a statement of his social philosophy—what he called "this intense individualism"—in an essay named simply "Wealth." Ralph Henry Gabriel has pointed out the significance of the year.[30] It came in the midst of revolt by farmers against northeastern capitalism, after the terrible railroad strikes of the 1870's, and just three years after the Haymarket Riot in Chicago. As Gabriel says, one might expect Carnegie's essay to be an *apologia,* a somewhat embarrassed defense of the concentration of wealth of which he was so outstanding an example. But such was not the case. Carnegie began his essay with a sober account of the high price that society pays for its material advancement, the division between "castes," the concentration of the labor force into large factories, and the suspicions and mutual distrust between labor and capital, but only to conclude that even "accepting conditions as they exist, the situation can be surveyed and pronounced good." In Carnegie's view the concentration of wealth was inevitable, so the only question to be asked was how concentrated wealth could best be used for the good of society. His answer was the gospel of wealth—in Gabriel's words, "an elaboration of the doctrine of the free individual of the American democratic faith and . . . a result of the discovery that this tenet had important utilities in the new industrial capitalism." [31]

[30] Ralph Henry Gabriel, *The Course of American Democratic Thought: An Intellectual History Since 1815,* Ronald, New York, 1940, pp. 143–160.
[31] *Ibid.,* p. 147.

Looking back on Carnegie's career, we tend to see his wealth as a result of the great price that society was willing to pay for the organization of one of its basic industries. Historians differ on whether the price was too high or not, but they all agree that the reward was made possible by the emergence in America of a national economy and the consolidation of individual enterprises into massive collective organizations. Yet, in Carnegie's philosophy, there is none of this. His essay resolves wealth into purely personal terms, the capacity of the single individual: "The experienced in affairs always rate the MAN . . . as not only the first consideration, but such as to render the question of his capital scarcely worth considering; . . . we might as well urge the destruction of the highest existing type of man because he failed to reach our ideal as to favor the destruction of Individualism, Private Property, the Law of the Accumulation of Wealth, and the Law of Competition."

Carnegie thought there were three ways a man could dispose of his wealth. He could leave it to his family, he could bequeath it at death for public purposes, or he could administer it during his lifetime for the public good. Carnegie rejected the first two. For the first, he thought it "not well for the children that they should be so burdened"—at first glance a charming sentiment, yet congruent with Carnegie's basic notion that wealth should come to the individual because of his worth and not by an environmental accident such as birth. For the second, in addition to the fear that legacies do not generally realize their donor's wishes, Carnegie shrewdly realized that "it may fairly be said that no man is to be extolled for doing what he cannot help doing. . . . Men who leave vast sums in this way may fairly be thought men who would not have left it at all, had they been able to take it with them." Carnegie was radical enough for his time to suggest that the state, through death taxes, should confiscate up to one-half of the wealthy man's estate. He thought the disposition to do this "a cheering indication of the growth of a salutary change in public opinion."

So there remained only one way for the man of wealth to discharge the responsibility of wealth—to administer it himself during his lifetime:

This, then, is held to be the duty of the man of Wealth: First, to set an example of modest, unostentatious living, shunning display or extravagance; to provide moderately for the legitimate wants of those dependent upon him; and after doing so to consider all surplus revenues which come to him simply as trust funds, which he is called upon to administer, and strictly bound as a matter of duty to administer in the manner which, in his judgment, is best calculated to produce the most beneficial results for the community—the man of wealth thus becoming the mere agent and trustee for his poorer brethren, bringing to their service his superior wisdom, experience, and ability to administer, doing for them better than they would or could do for themselves.

As Mr. Dooley was to say, every time "Andhrew Carnaygie" gives a speech, "he gives himself away." The individualism of the early nineteenth century was built upon a belief in the equality of all men—not only social, economic, and political equality, but a rough equality in their personal capacities. Carnegie retained the freedom, the intense individualism, for the man of wealth but at the price of a thoroughgoing paternalism for his poorer brethren. Since the man of wealth is bound only by his own private judgment of what is good for society, the only check against his economic power is the assumption that he shares, even in his superior wisdom, the same values as his inferior and poorer brethren. At a moment when, as Carnegie himself testified, there was little but suspicion and mistrust on either side, it is difficult to understand the acceptance of his message.

Part of the answer may lie in Carnegie's brilliant success in weaving together nearly every major strand of the American tradition into a blanket approval of the concentration of wealth in the hands of individuals who recognized no control outside themselves. Simply to enumerate the elements of his argument is to grasp some of its force: a secularized version of the Protestant Ethic of hard work and stewardship; the idea of progress; the sanctity of private property and the competition of laissez-faire classical economics; and a vindication of the free and responsible individual.[32]

32 I have intentionally omitted one other important element in Carnegie's essay, his use of Darwinian language, such as "survival of the fittest," and imagery drawn from geology and botany to suggest that society follows some

All these minor themes play in and around Carnegie's major one, the affirmation of present conditions. Surprisingly, at least for an essay making so much of service to others, the conclusion comes to the fact that "those worthy of assistance, except in rare cases, seldom require assistance." You cannot help a man; he must help himself. You might, as Carnegie did, put libraries in his way, so his capacity for self-help could exercise itself, but "it were better for mankind that the millions of the rich were thrown into the sea than so spent as to encourage the slothful, the drunken, the unworthy." The best that can be said for Carnegie is that he was candid enough to apply this to the sons of the rich as well as his poorer brethren.

The persistent, one would like to say passionate, appeal to the intrinsic personal qualities that determine success in the literature of the self-made man and the gospel of wealth in the latter nineteenth century was probably neither cynical nor hypocritical. American society had for a long time prided itself on being equalitarian, and one of the distinguishing virtues of the American Democrat was supposed to be that his success was due to his own unaided merit. Any other source of success was somehow alien and un-American. Status in a society can be described in a number of ways, which, in turn, break down into objective (birth, wealth, authority, power) and subjective (character, intellect, personal charm) characteristics. Those who had the obvious objective attributes (wealth and power) were not content simply to enjoy their perquisites. They had to believe that they deserved those perquisites, that they had the personal qualities that merited them. As Max Weber said in a different context, "the fortunate [man] is seldom satisfied with the fact of being fortunate. Beyond this, he needs to know that he has a *right* to his good fortune. He wants to be convinced that he 'deserves' it, and above all, that he deserves it in comparison with others. He wishes to be allowed the belief that the less fortunate also merely

---

developmental pattern through a series of determined stages analogous to the evolution of the world of nature. I do so because, although "social Darwinism" is clearly found in Carnegie's essay, there is some doubt how characteristic such thought was for business leaders themselves, rather than intellectual apologists for business.

experience their due.   Good fortune thus wants to be 'legitimate' fortune." [33]

In this view, ideas are rationalizations, and there seems no sense in denying that the process of self-justification was, consciously or not, going on.   There are few at any level of society who construct images of themselves that are not rather flattering self-portraits.   But the rub comes when we realize how widely admired these self-projections were.   The successful, the men of wealth, were, in Harry Stack Sullivan's nice phrase, the "significant others" in the late nineteenth century.   The society collaborated in the work of imputing personal qualities to those who possessed the objective power, justifying them, and in so doing, justifying the society to itself.   Those who had power and prestige were felt to merit power and prestige, because to say otherwise was to say that the old ideal of individualism was dead. But, as I said at the beginning of this excursion into the idea of the self-made man and the gospel of wealth, the increasing social and economic organization of American life was putting severe strains on the ideal of the free and autonomous individual. Worse, there were those who spoke with authority, like John D. Rockefeller, who said, "Individualism has gone, never to return." [34]

IV

The context of John D. Rockefeller's blunt remark was that cooperative activity was a necessary consequence of large-scale technological production.   The editors of *Fortune* recognize this in their article, when they observe that the key to industrialization is not independence, but interdependence.   One can say, in a general sense, that somewhere toward the end of the nineteenth century, Americans began to discover the reality of society. As they did, it became increasingly difficult to insist that the individual was all in face of this growing awareness, but there was

[33] Max Weber, The Social Psychology of World Religions, in H. H. Gerth and C. Wright Mills, eds., *From Max Weber: Essays in Sociology,* Oxford University Press, New York, 1946, p. 271.

[34] Allan Nevins, *Study in Power: John D. Rockefeller, Industrialist and Philanthropist,* I, Scribner's, New York, 1953, p. 402.

another way to preserve the emotional sanctions of the ideal of
individualism.   That was to change its meaning.   A new meaning was implicit in the very technology built upon the machine,
which was subverting belief in the original ideal of individualism.

The Idea of the Machine

One can get at the matter by stopping for a moment to consider the machine itself, abstractly, as the material embodiment
of certain ideas.   This may seem a curious way of speaking.   Nor-
mally, when we speak of ideas, we think of the written or spoken
word, but second thought makes us all aware that institutions,
even the common objects surrounding our daily lives, embody
certain attitudes; they objectify ways in which we think about
our world.   The cities we live in, the factories we work in, the
buildings we dwell in—all these "speak" to us, if only we will
listen.

To think of the machine in this fashion is to quickly recognize
that the machine clearly embodies certain ideas.   A well-designed
machine is an instance of total organization, that is, a series of
interrelated means contrived to achieve a single end.   The machine consists always of particular parts that have no meaning
and no function separate from the organized entity to which they
contribute.   A machine consists of a coherent bringing together
of all parts toward the highest possible efficiency of the functioning whole, of interrelationships marshalled wholly toward a given
result.   In the ideal machine, there can be no extraneous part,
no extraneous movement; all is set, part for part, motion for
motion, toward the functioning of the whole.   The machine is,
then, at once a perfect instance of total rationalization of a field
of action and of total organization.   This is perhaps even more
quickly evident in that larger machine, the assembly line.[35]

A society that chooses to enjoy the benefits of the power that
the machine makes possible—that is, a society committed to
mechanization, a society that accepts the logic of functional interdependence and increasing rationalization of its material life—

[35] See Sigfried Giedion, *Mechanization Takes Command: A Contribution
to Anonymous History*, Oxford University Press, New York, 1948.

is also committed inexorably to increasing organization of its economic and social life, to more and more precise articulation of its interrelations. In response to the machine, or, more accurately, to attitudes implicit in the machine, not only new patterns of social life but even new values begin to emerge. To reverse Emerson's dictum, in the social world created by industrialism we take our way to man, not from man.

All this is rather abstract, so let me restate it by an historical anecdote, a homely example of the way in which what I have described analytically worked out in historical practice. The purpose of this story is simply to show in action the cast of mind embodied in the machine itself—that is, the tendency toward rationalizing the work process, the drive toward increasing organization, and, finally and most importantly, the emergence of an ethic of the organization, describing the individual in terms of functional fitness, or in more popular language, defining the individual in terms of his ability to contribute to the group.[36]

Frederick Winslow Taylor and Rational Organization

The historical anecdote concerns the work of Frederick Winslow Taylor, the man who is generally credited with being the father of "scientific management" in our country. The particular example from Taylor's work is the "shovelling experiment" he conducted in the yards of the Bethlehem Steel Company in Pennsylvania in the 1890's.[37]

[36] See, especially, Roderick Seidenberg, *Post-Historic Man: An Inquiry,* University of North Carolina Press, Chapel Hill, 1950, also available as a Beacon Press paperback. For Mr. Seidenberg, the period of history is the period of consciousness. Prehistory is the period when man responded instinctively to his environment; the dawn of reason defines the beginning of history. The brutal paradox of Mr. Seidenberg's thesis is that reason then tends to negate itself; man organizes his world to the point that intelligence has no further function, and man moves into the frictionless, mindless world of total organization in which reason atrophies, and we enter the "post-historic" phase. Clearly Mr. Seidenberg's vision is apocalyptic, yet his book is a brilliant *tour de force*, which, by carrying implications to their extreme, arouses us to an awareness we might not otherwise have.

[37] Frederick Winslow Taylor, *The Principles of Scientific Management,* Harper, New York, 1911. The best source for Taylor's thought and the views of other early leaders in the scientific management school is the publication

Taylor had been called in by the Bethlehem Steel Company as a management consultant and allowed, at first, to introduce efficiency only into the most menial tasks in the work process. The steel yard was a big one, almost two miles long by about a quarter of a mile wide, and the company employed 400 to 600 day laborers who owned their own shovels and worked in large gangs, moving material ranging from light ash and coke to heavy ore about the yard wherever needed.

Taylor first ran a series of tests to decide the optimum shovel load for a first-class worker. As he put it, "we would see a first-class shoveller go from shovelling rice coal with a load of 3½ pounds to the shovel to handling iron ore with 38 pounds to the shovel. Now is 3½ pounds the proper shovel load or is 38 pounds the proper shovel load?" There is not space to describe the series of interesting tests that Taylor devised to arrive at the proper load for a shovel, but by experiment he came to the conclusion that 21½ pounds was the ideal weight for a first-class shoveller.

As Taylor told the story, a number of things followed. First, a variety of kinds of shovels had to be designed to handle different kinds of materials. That also meant building shovel rooms in the various parts of the yard, so that a gang would have the proper tools at hand. To eliminate the waste motion of wandering about so large a yard, it meant, as Taylor said, "organizing and planning work at least a day in advance," so that when men checked in, they would be at that day's work. This meant, Taylor reported, building a labor office for a planning staff—a bureaucracy, as we would say. Large maps of the yard were then necessary to show at a glance the location of different kinds of work and the location of men. Furthermore, the installation of a telephone network was essential for more effective interior communication. Once the yard was mapped so that one could see at a glance the relationships in time and sequence between different jobs, it led, naturally enough, to the reorganization of the

---

of *Hearings Before the Special Committee of the House of Representatives to Investigate the Taylor and Other Systems of Shop Management* . . . , 3 vols. (Washington, 1912). See also F. B. Copley, *Frederick W. Taylor, Father of Scientific Management,* 2 vols., Harper, New York, 1923.

yard itself, so that materials could be delivered or dumped in a more logical sequence.

One can see readily enough what happened. Taylor's attempt to make the crudest physical act of labor efficient led inexorably to a further organization of every aspect of the production process. Logically at least, total efficiency could be attained only when the entire plant was totally organized, when all parts in the process were related in the most efficient way, one to the other. Although this homely example is fairly simple—and I have chosen it partly because its very simplicity enables quick description— there is a good deal implicit here. Let me point to just three things: first, the sheer material success of Taylor's experiment; second, the cast of mind, the historical style, dramatized by Taylor; and, third, a problem in social values implicit in the machine and in an organized society.

The Achievements of Rational Organization

First, not only those who have to meet a payroll will be interested in the concrete results of Taylor's work. The Bethlehem Steel Company previously had 400 to 600 men at work in the yard gang. After three years under Taylor's system, 140 men were doing the same volume of work. At the same time that the labor force was cut so drastically, the actual cost per ton of material moved also dropped by 50 per cent. Taylor reported that during the last six months of the three and one-half years that he was with Bethlehem, the saving to the company was at the rate of $78,000 per year *after* paying the additional costs of the planning staff, new shovels, and new overhead. At the same time wages went up 60 per cent.

These figures do more than satisfy our curiosity. We can see here in microcosm the basic character of our productive power— a standardized process leading to a reduction in unskilled labor, an expanded output with, at the same time, a decrease in unit cost, rising wages, and an increase at the managerial level of planning. These are characteristics not only of Taylor's small experiment but also of the general direction of our economy from his time to ours.

There is a moral here too. No society is willingly going to

surrender the tremendous material benefits that flow from the rationalization and organization at the heart of the industrial system. We tend to take the enormous benefits of organization too much for granted. We hear so much today about the threat of organization to personality, to social values, even, ironically, to the efficiency of our organizations themselves that we may be tempted to think that some social panacea lies in the rejection of organization; this is clearly not true. Even if we want to—and I do not believe we want to—we cannot reject the machine upon which our society is built, and the machine inexorably demands rationalization of effort and planning and their concomitant, large-scale organization.

The Ethic of Productivity

The second point involves the style of thought symbolized by the machine and set to work by Taylor. The subjective attitude—the curious combination of the drive toward productivity along with an intensely self-conscious rationalization of the means toward that end—is perhaps as important as the material success itself. Once organization is introduced at any point, the trend toward further organization is irreversible, but one will quickly recognize that organization says nothing about the goal to be pursued; it only points to the best way to achieve whatever goal one chooses to pursue. In Taylor's work there is always the unquestioned premise that efficiency and increased productivity are their own justification, ends in themselves. What Taylor did was to stand outside the work process, consider all its parts, and put it together again in its most logical order; this is what we mean by saying that he rationalized the work process. But Taylor never questioned the unstated premise that work is its own measure of value. Quite the contrary, testifying before a Congressional committee inquiring into his system, he explicitly accepted that criterion: "In my judgment," Taylor said, "the best possible measure of the height in the scale of civilization to which any people has arisen is its productivity." [38] Only in modern Western civilization could that remark have been made.

[38] *Hearings . . . to Investigate the Taylor and Other Systems, op. cit.,* III, p. 1471.

In the East—in India and China at least, until they too decided to "modernize"—in ancient Greece, and in Christian Europe until the end of the Middle Ages, it was the most obvious and axiomatic piece of orthodoxy that action was a means to the end of life, which was contemplation. In Taylor's world and in the world of modern industrialism this view is completely reversed; thought is a means to further action. Action, Work, Productivity—choose what word you will—these have become ends in themselves.

This reversal of values, the celebration of work and activity themselves, did not, of course, come about simply as a consequence of the machine. Quite the opposite. The psychological shift preceded industrialism, and perhaps it had to. The attitude of mind that Taylor represents has been in the making a long time in Western civilization. A machine-oriented civilization represents the convergence of numerous habits, ideas, and modes of living, as well as technical instruments. If we were to trace the origin of these habits back in history, we would probably follow the trail all the way back to the monasteries of the Middle Ages. At least, Werner Sombart, the German historian of capitalism, says with a certain heavy-handed irony that the Benedictine monks were our first capitalists. What he means is that it is in the monasteries of the Western world after the collapse of the Roman empire that we see the imposition of order and control on everyday life, although for supernatural ends, of course. The revolution in men's attitudes toward work in the world comes when the Reformation destroys the monasteries and turns their ascetic discipline toward work in the world with a consequent blessing of work, order, and industry.

The Functional Individual

Instead of turning back to the past I would like to turn ahead to our own present, to our own future, to a problem implicit in the growth of organization spawned by the machine. There is a third aspect to Taylor's work, which involves a problem in social values implicit in any highly organized society. It is the emergence of a social ethic in response to the movement toward organization.

Frederick Winslow Taylor got at the matter in a single sentence. In his book setting forth the principles of his system, Taylor said bluntly, "In the past the man has been first; in the future the system must be first." [39] Taylor had the great virtue of seeing clearly the consequences of what he was doing, but he was also aware, especially because of hostility toward the Taylor system, that the consequences he saw and desired ran counter to many of the cherished ideals of his culture. A society that had always put the individual person first was going to find it hard to adapt to a system that insisted that the individual had importance only as a functioning part of some larger social organization. Not the least fascinating aspect of Taylor's work is the way in which he tried to adapt the old ideal of the primary importance of the individual to a system that itself relegated the individual to a secondary order of importance. You can see this transvaluation taking place in Taylor's own words:

> Let me say that we are now but on the threshold of the coming era of true cooperation. The time is fast going by for the great personal or individual achievement of any one man standing alone and without the help of those around him. And the time is coming when all the great things will be done by the cooperation of many men in which each man performs that function for which he is best suited, each man preserves his individuality and is supreme in his particular function, and each man at the same time loses none of his originality and proper personal initiative, and yet is controlled by and must work harmoniously with many other men.[40]

Now, we may shrink from such phrases as "man . . . is controlled by" and man "*must* work harmoniously with" others, but notice that Taylor is trying to redefine the meaning of the individual in order to escape the harshness of his conclusion. In his statement the person is defined not simply by being, but by doing.

In response to the new conditions of an industrial society built upon the machine, Taylor is trying to formulate a social theory that sanctions these new conditions by defining the relation of

[39] Taylor, *op. cit.*, p. 8.

[40] Frederick Winslow Taylor, On the Art of Cutting Metals, *Transactions of the American Society of Mechanical Engineers*, XXVIII (1906), p. 128.

the individual to society just as he has defined the relation of part to whole in his system of industrial efficiency. The person achieves his individuality by discovering the function for which he is best suited and in which he can best contribute to the whole, which is greater than he is, and to which, as one part, he must contribute. To generalize very broadly, freedom in the ethic that Taylor is struggling to formulate changes from negative freedom, that is, freedom from restraint by the group, to positive freedom, that is, freedom to do that which contributes to the group.

The goal of organization means the death of the ideal of the free, primary, autonomous person standing alone, aloof from involvement with his fellows, heroically self-sufficient. The conflict is obvious enough. But suddenly there is a way out. Each individual realizes himself by performing that function for which he is best suited, as Taylor put it; or, the individual finds a "higher expression of himself" through his dynamic relationship with others, as *Fortune* put it.

So, if we smile at the editors of *Fortune*, we must smile at ourselves as well. There are many ways to accommodate change. A favorite one is man's happy ability to keep on talking one way while acting another, as in the case of the self-made men and the stewards of great wealth in the late nineteenth century. Another, as intellectuals themselves best know, is to redefine the terms of the argument, so that it turns out that you and your opponent have really been talking about the same thing all along.

Two Versions of Individualism

In American history in general, as well as in *Fortune*'s treatment in particular, we have then two meanings of "individualism." One, the original meaning, said that the individual was an individual to the degree that he was separate from society and free from the institutions and restraints of society. The other, defined in a world quite different from the equalitarian and open society of the early nineteenth century, says that an individual is an individual to the degree that he participates in society. The individual becomes himself by furthering the good of the collective group, large or small, of which he must become a func-

tioning part. But to use a word like "collective" reminds us of
the proletariat, and, as *Fortune* warns us, to submerge the individual in the group is supposed to be a philosophy of reaction
in America, a betrayal of the American proposition of individual
responsibility.

We have done our work so well in a fit of contented absent-
mindedness that many Americans will surely protest that this
second meaning is not a valid meaning of individualism. It may
not be valid for those who like a degree of logical consistency,
but it is a meaning. The editors of *Fortune* insist it is; Frederick
Winslow Taylor said so long ago; Herbert Croly in *The Promise
of American Life,* a political textbook for the liberal reforms of
both Roosevelts in this century, defines true, "constructive" individualism so; and this second meaning permeates all the pages of
John Dewey's political and social thought. Our recent immensely popular president, Mr. Eisenhower, always insisted that
"more than ever before, in our country, this is the age of the
individual. . . . There is no limit . . . to the temporal goals
we set ourselves—as free individuals joined in a team with our
fellows." [41]

V

At this point, the historian might simply conclude and go no
further. But I began by saying that I intended to bring this
long historical excursion to bear upon a present problem. The
problem is familiar enough. From all sides we hear that the
American is an organization man lost in the lonely crowd of mass
society, that the American has ceased to be a self-reliant individual, and that this is all somehow a betrayal of the American
way of life. In the popular version, about the longest perspective
brought to bear on this faceless man in a gray flannel suit is the
accusation that progressive education started the problem by
preaching something called "adjustment." But the problem is
much older than that, and a long historical process has gone
into its making. If you accept my account of the historical process, then there are three logical ways one might attack the rela-

[41] *Vital Speeches* (June 15, 1949), pp. 518–519.

tionship of the ideal of individualism to the reality of organization in modern America.

The first would be to restrict the word "individualism" to the early nineteenth century, to insist that the word has significance only in a discussion of the historical context that gave rise to it. The simplicity of this solution has a certain appeal, but one would be sanguine indeed to think that he could legislate out of existence a word with such massive emotional associations. It ignores the very terms of the problem—that is, that it *is* a problem, that American culture has a deep affective stake in the historical connotations of the concept of individualism and will not lightly surrender it on the grounds of being responsible to some intellectual demand for historical accuracy and logical consistency. Yet, it is a solution that some intellectual historians might accept.[42]

The second answer would be to decide upon reflection that the real meaning of the word *should be* the collective sense, that the individual realizes himself by committing himself to some worthy enterprise larger than himself, that the older ideal of autonomy was simply an egoistic mistake, a mistake made possible by the peculiar and special circumstances of a passing moment in our national history. Despite its identification with the positive hero of the authoritarian mind, this version of individualism is a concept not totally alien to American culture, as we have already seen. If it were totally alien to our culture, there would be no problem. In the context of the necessary organiza-

---

[42] The suggestion is not just a possibility. Curiously, historians who stand at opposite poles in their view of history have come to just such a conclusion. Arthur O. Lovejoy has taught students of ideas to use large abstractions in the plural and never in the singular, but Lovejoy's goal is to achieve analytical precision in the definition of the meaning of ideas. See, for example, "Nature" as Aesthetic Norm, or On the Discrimination of Romanticisms, both in *Essays in the History of Ideas*, Johns Hopkins, Baltimore, 1948, pp. 69–77 and 228–253, respectively. Lovejoy treats ideas largely in terms of their rational and internal dynamics. Writing from a position quite the opposite, Charles A. Beard, at the time largely under the influence of Karl Mannheim and the sociology of knowledge, said of the idea of individualism in 1931: "The task before us, then, is not to furbish up an old slogan, but to get rid of it." The Myth of Rugged Individualism, *Harper's*, CLXIV (1931), p. 22.

tion of our economic and social life, Americans have begun to develop a native definition of the individual as a member of the group. At its most innocuous level, this means simply that the individual should be able to get along with others, to adjust to the demands of living and working with others. At its most serious, it means a submersion of the individual in the group. The individual is defined by his function; one's role in the organization becomes one's real self. The rest is mere appendage. The will of God embodied in a church; the law of history embodied in a party; the good of society embodied in a corporation; or even the good of society, the national interest itself—these are not strange and unusual creeds in our time. Yet, they are creeds that are difficult for Americans to accept, even when they act in terms of them, because of the very past out of which American society has come. Again, this second solution may be acceptable to some, but not, I think, to Americans generally.

There is a third answer to the problem, which, in turn, has so many problems in it that it may not be an answer in any responsible sense of the word. It is a political answer, not in the narrow sense of the government but rather in the wider sense of the structuring of all the institutions affecting our daily lives. But to suggest it requires first a comment on the history that I have just recounted.

The paradoxical thing about the ideal of individualism in Jacksonian America, which celebrated the individual to the point of denying the reality of society, is that it was, in its very rejection of social forces, itself a social ideal. That is, only a particular kind of society could have generated an ideal that denied society. It took an outsider, a foreign observer like Tocqueville, to see that the heroically self-reliant American was possible only because of a widely shared consensus on matters that counted. The general will, which Rousseau had to hypothesize in order to make society possible at all, was in America the general experience under conditions of approximate social equality. In similar fashion, the violent swing to an opposite ideal still calling itself individualism but with radically different connotations; an ideal that makes the individual a part of society; an ideal that at its furthest reaches attributes reality to society and makes the individual simply a shadow of its will—this too is the product of our history.

All this is simply to say that the historian can describe two different systems of values both going under the name "individualism" that verge toward opposites—one toward the isolated person, the other toward society—and be descriptively correct in saying that at different moments in our history Americans have moved toward one and then the other. But the critical historian must then say that to put the question in terms of one *or* the other, of the individual *versus* society, is a false question. To put the matter in its baldest terms, to be a human being at all is a social achievement; the human animal is simply animal without society. At the same time, society, conceived as something apart from the human beings who compose it, is simply an abstraction—a convenient one so long as we remember it, a monstrous one if we forget it. Such resounding platitudes, however, leave us nowhere but in that comfortable American position, the middle of the road, unless one asks what follows. On the one hand we can ask what kind of individuals we want, and on the other what kind of organizations we want.

The first of this linked pair of questions admits no answer. To describe attributes that say that one is an individual only if one possesses particular qualities is to violate the very integrity of the individual person. Here we are at the emotional heart of the problem that troubles contemporary America—the notion that you can properly make no demands on the individual that are not his demands too. To do otherwise is to bully the actual, empirical individual, with the added insult that you are doing it to get him to be what he really wants to be, what his ideal self demands if only his ignorant actual self would recognize it. To construct a social definition of the nature of the individual and impose it on actual individuals would result, ironically, in a uniformity that tolerated no individual differences.

At this point criticism is driven back to history once again. It is true that the notion of consent—the idea that the individual must first accept emotionally and intellectually what power demands before power is legitimate—is itself an historical ideal; that is, it is relative. It has no universal, transcendental sanction behind it.   It is the achievement of a particular history, a particular culture.   There are cultures, not only in the past but also in the present, that would find such an ideal exotic or incomprehensible.   However, it is an ideal that has informed American culture throughout its history.   It is what we mean when we say that America is democratic.   A democratic society is one in which those in positions of power, public or private, are responsible for their decisions to those whom their decisions affect.   That definition forces us, then, to ask how the organizations of our modern, complex society might be made responsible to the individual and serve the ends of a democratic society.

An actual example is the best way to proceed.   In the 1930's, when the United Auto Workers were locked in a fierce struggle with the management and owners of the automobile industry, the union was powerful because the worker identified himself with the union.   As one might expect, the literature of the union movement in its militant phase provides an excellent source of illustration for what we have called the positive version of individualism.   The worker, by a disciplined and dedicated commitment to the union, to the group of which he was a part, realized his own interest—not simply his immediate self-interest, but more importantly his own identification, his sense of who he was and where he was in a society fashioned somewhat closer to his desires.   But having achieved recognition and having won his battle with management, the worker discovered that the union was itself no organic unitary thing; he discovered opponents in his own leadership.   He did not have to read Michels on the "iron law of oligarchy" to discover that the leaders of any organization develop interests that conflict with the interests of the constituent members.   The ideal of the union allowed for no such discrepancy, no such internal conflict, just as the ideal of positive individualism assumes a congruence between the ends of the group and the self-realization of the individual member.   But conflict arose.

At this point, the leadership of the UAW performed an act of considerable political intelligence.   They built into their organizational structure a Public Review Board, an impartial agency with the power of final adjudication to which the membership could appeal some decisions made by the leadership.[43] By this action, the UAW has tried to bring its organizational structure into line with the theory of democracy that holds that leaders must be responsible to the individuals whom their decisions affect. Unless that theory is to remain empty rhetoric, there must be some means by which those affected can protest and, furthermore, they must feel free to exercise those means. The UAW Review Board is one attempt to create the means; such institutional safeguards allow the individual to participate in group action without surrendering himself entirely to a point of reference lying entirely outside his own self. Obviously, a staggering number of problems still remain, but some such feature must be present in the structure of the organization before other problems can be faced at all, and some such feature is the only means of guaranteeing to the individual some importance in the bureaucratic style of life that we call the organization.

What this comes down to is the need for a certain kind of organization. Our choice is not between organization and something else. It is a choice between organizations that serve our needs and ideals and organizations that do not. / One of the humanly disturbing features of the modern world is that the individual, drawn tighter and tighter into a network of functional relations with a greater and greater number of other individuals, feels an increasing depersonalization, the sense of emotional distance that accompanies actual physical dependence. To borrow a word from biology, our relations are increasingly symbiotic. The classic example of such a relation is the embryo in the womb, dependent directly on the mother for nourishment. Today, we depend on an untold number of others to do their work, so our life may go on. These kinds of social relationships are not only necessary; they must exist (as they do) at some level of unawareness much as the functioning and organization of the nervous system in our body. But, to pursue the analogy, the social skills of specialization and organization must serve some

[43] Jack Stieber, Walter E. Oberer, and Michael Harrington, *Democracy and Public Review: An Analysis of the UAW Public Review Board,* A Report to the Center for the Study of Democratic Institutions (Santa Barbara, California, 1960).

larger end than simply intake and output. If Americans insist that society exists to serve the individual, not the individual to serve society, then we must show more imagination with the organization of our organizations in order to bring them at least within hailing distance of our professed ideals. As one looks about, one can fairly say that there is almost no evidence of such imagination at work in our society. We see, instead, cynicism masking itself in praise of the individual. Thus, *Time* magazine in its issue on The Individual in America says: "Like all freedoms, this freedom of choice is also a burden, and that is one reason why there is so much 'conformity.' . . . To expect every individual to take in all of life through a thinking man's filter—to have his own independent, personal convictions about politics, ethics, culture—is to ask the impossible. It is, in fact, to ask for a mass elite." [44]

It is. In all its outrageous innocence, this is what America has asked for from the beginning—sufficient individual character to control the realities of society. It may be impossible, but it will surely be impossible if we decide so beforehand.

[44] *Time*, May 10, 1963, p. 24.

3

The Search for
a Capitalist Hero

Businessmen
in American Fiction

Henry Nash Smith

I

Under the archaic but elegant title of entrepreneur, the businessman has been the hero of a vast international literature of economic theory.[1] He has enjoyed an equally high status in American popular culture.[2] Yet in imaginative literature he has on
the whole fared badly. Few major writers have concerned themselves with the actual operation of the business system, and when
businessmen appear in novels, they are often treated with hostility or derision. The present paper is an effort to explore and,
if possible, to account for this discrepancy.

The inquiry involves many bad or mediocre novels and only a
few that have survived the decade of their publication. It is a
historical rather than a literary undertaking. But good books
are not only better than bad ones, they are more significant even
for historical purposes. I shall therefore organize my survey of

---

[1] I owe this suggestion to Mr. Robert Heilbroner.

[2] Attitudes toward the businessman in American society are discussed at
length in Sigmund Diamond, *The Reputation of the American Businessman,*
Harvard University Press, Cambridge, Mass., 1955, and Irvin G. Wyllie, *The
Self-Made Man in America,* Rutgers University Press, New Brunswick, N. J.,
1954.

American business novels around the two best: Mark Twain's *A Connecticut Yankee in King Arthur's Court* (1889) and Theodore Dreiser's trilogy about Frank Cowperwood (or rather, the first two volumes of it, *The Financier* (1912) and *The Titan* (1914); the third volume, *The Stoic,* begun in the 1920's and left unfinished at the writer's death, is quite inferior to the others). The fictional businessman follows a reasonably clear line of development from the 1880's, when he first becomes conspicuous as a literary type, to the publication of Dreiser's *The Financier.* In the early novels the businessman is presented simply as a villain; in Dreiser's trilogy Frank Cowperwood is held up for the reader's admiration. What has changed in the interval is not the character and behavior attributed to the businessman but rather the criteria by which he is judged. Although writers since Dreiser show a greater variety of attitudes, the development of the value systems controlling the fictive world of the novel is the central theme to be noticed.

II

The early hostility of novelists to the businessman was due to the fact that they took the characteristic type to be a financier and stock-market operator on the model of Jim Fisk or Jay Gould, who were almost universally considered reprehensible. Examples are Zedekiah Hampton in H. H. Boyesen's *A Daughter of the Philistines* (1883), "Uncle" Jerry Hollowell in Charles Dudley Warner's *A Little Journey in the World* (1889), and Jacob Dryfoos in William Dean Howells's *A Hazard of New Fortunes* (1890). The very titles of these novels express the basic revulsion of their authors against the emergent financial and industrial system of the post-Civil War period. The new millionaires are Philistines (a term popularized in the late 1860's and 1870's by Matthew Arnold), and the social atmosphere that they have created is worldly in comparison with the quiet refinement of a vanishing older order. Howells's title is taken from a passage in Shakespeare's *King John* describing footloose adventurers headed for France with the English army to seek their fortunes— a crowd of rascals who "do offence and scath in Christendom."

All three fictional financiers have grown wealthy and powerful through speculation, first on a small scale in the Middle West, then in the larger arena of New York. In accord with the sentimental convention that gave virtuous characters a monopoly of culture and sensibility, all three businessmen are depicted as coarse and vulgar. The novelists' symbolic use of the West reflects the commonly held belief that the driving force in the development of American industrial capitalism had been the energy and natural resources brought into play by expansion across the continent. But the process was obviously directed from New York and Washington, and there also were spent the fortunes accumulated by the primitive giants who had emerged as victors in the unsavory struggle. New England figured as the innocent bystander among the regions, the passive custodian of a moral and cultural tradition that provided the only basis for rendering judgment upon the post-Civil War chaos.

These assumptions appear in broad outline as early as 1873 in Mark Twain's and Warner's collaborative satire, *The Gilded Age.* It is true that in Colonel Beriah Sellers, the vivid Westerner contributed to the novel by Mark Twain, speculation becomes a theme for comic "tall talk" rather than a mark of depravity. But among the materials contributed by Warner is a New England family named Montague who have no function in the plot except to provide a yardstick for measuring the barbarity and wickedness of New York, Washington, and the West.[3] Warner's description of the refined and cultivated Montague household was to be echoed for thirty years in novels about the new captains of finance. The changes in the value system of the novel can be measured by watching the image of New England grow less and less vivid until it disappears altogether, whereas the businessman is first tolerated, then analyzed with a sort of morbid fascination, and finally made a protagonist whose system of values dominates the fictive world. The revolution in values was to be consummated in the Cowperwood trilogy.

In *A Daughter of the Philistines* Boyesen introduces an anti-

[3] *The Gilded Age. A Tale of To-Day,* in *The Writings of Mark Twain,* Definitive Edition, V, Wells, New York, 1922, pp. 210–211.

type to the elderly Zedekiah Hampton in young Harold Wellingford, who marries Hampton's daughter. Wellingford is the son
of a New England professor and holds a Ph.D. in science from
Freiberg. His training enables him to frustrate the scheme of
Hampton and others to sell stock in a Colorado mine by circu-
lating false reports of its value. Wellingford speaks for tradition
in lecturing his wife on the immorality of her father's specula-
tions; and Boyesen pointedly contrasts "the beauty of the family
relations" in the household of Wellingford's father with the crude
bickering that is habitual in the Hampton palace in New York.[4]

Boyesen's plot is the most obvious way of translating traditional hostility toward the new-rich businessman into the formulas of sentimental fiction. At the end of the decade Warner
contrives a variation on the basic scheme that constitutes a tentative step toward raising the status of the businessman in fiction.
Naive as it is, Warner's maneuver is evidently a response to
social and economic change. The businessman's rapidly growing importance in the actual world suggested to novelists who
were influenced by the doctrines of literary realism that he should
be given a corresponding position in the novel. According to a
long-established convention, the only way to do this was to make
him a protagonist. But in the standard plot the protagonist was
a suitor for the hand of the heroine—archetypally, a son rather
than a father; and he was expected to be at least superficially
refined and cultivated.

Warner solves the problem by doubling the character of the
businessman. By the side of "Uncle" Jerry Hollowell in *A Little
Journey* he introduces a younger associate named Rodney Henderson, a native of New England, a college graduate with good
taste in architecture and interior decoration, and even a collector
of first editions (although not a reader of them). With this
equipment, Henderson can be a plausible suitor of the heroine.
But since he is also a successful financier, his virtues are necessarily superficial. He has been corrupted by the business world
of New York:

4 H. H. Boyesen, *A Daughter of the Philistines,* Roberts, Boston, 1883, pp.
220–221, 107.

He was of a good New Hampshire family, exceedingly respectable without being distinguished . . . Rodney, inheriting the thrift of his ancestors, had pushed out from his home, adapting **this** thrift to the modern methods of turning it to account. . . . At this period . . . he had determined to be successful, and . . . he had not determined to be unscrupulous. He would only drift with the tide that made for fortune. . . . His business morality was gauged by what other people do in similar circumstances. In short, he was a product of the period since the civil war closed, that great upheaval of patriotic feeling and sacrifice, which ended in so much expansion and so many opportunities.[5]

Hollowell and Henderson form a team. They specialize in "railroad wrecking," a process described by one of Warner's New England observers:

The "wreckers" . . . fasten upon some railway that is prosperous, pays a liberal interest on its bonds, and has a surplus. They contrive to buy, no matter at what cost, a controlling interest in it, either in its stock or its management. Then they absorb its surplus; they let it run down so that it pays no dividends, and by-and-by cannot even pay its interest; then they squeeze the bondholders, who may be glad to accept anything that is offered out of the wreck, and perhaps then they throw the property into the hands of a receiver, or consolidate it with some other road at a value enormously greater than the cost to them in stealing it. Having in one way or another sucked it dry, they look around for another road.[6]

The plot of the story is simple to the point of allegory. Contrasting the bucolic innocence of a small New England city named Branton (that is, Hartford) with the complicated wickedness of New York, which is identified with the social life of the new millionaires, Warner uproots Margaret Debree ("a fair, simple girl, stirred with noble ideals, eager for the intellectual life, tender, sympathetic, courageous" [7]) by marrying her to Henderson and thus launches her into a metropolitan milieu. Unfortunately, the moral tradition of Branton cannot shield her from the world's slow stain. She gradually accepts the tone and

[5] Charles Dudley Warner, *A Little Journey in the World*, Harper, New York, 1889, pp. 96–97.

[6] *Ibid.*, pp. 164–165.

[7] *Ibid.*, p. 366.

attitudes of the city. The Puritan girl becomes a "dead soul"
and then actually dies; neither New England refinement nor
New England morals can stand against the "spirit of worldli-
ness," the materialistic drive of a society dominated by the love
of money and the cult of success.[8]

Warner's moral judgments are voiced by the narrator and a
few of his friends who meet for conversation in comfortable
Branton parlors that are duplicates of the Montague establishment Warner had described in *The Gilded Age*. In fact, *A Little
Journey* evidently took shape in his mind as a more thoroughly
considered version of the material he had contributed to the
collaboration with Mark Twain fifteen years earlier. His ideas
are clearer in the later version, but they are virtually unchanged.
The new world of business is bad because it threatens the moral
and cultural values of New England—originally Puritan, but now
gently secularized into a cult of refinement that we have learned
to call, in George Santayana's phrase, "the Genteel Tradition."

Yet, the modest but elegant leisure of the "little parliament"
in Branton is sustained by the income from investments in the
rapidly expanding economy. Warner doubtless took a crafts-
man's pride in showing how the operations of the railroad
wreckers impoverished certain widows in Branton, but in the
process he commits himself to a *rentier* point of view that is too
parochial to serve as the basis for lofty moralizing. And he is
not prepared to contemplate any measures to protect society
against such men as Henderson. One of his spokesmen says:
"I don't see any line between absolute freedom of acquisition,
trusting to circumstances, misfortune, and death to knock things
to pieces, and absolute slavery, which is communism." [9]

Warner's reluctance to deal with the economic issues raised
by his plot is reflected in the role he assigns to the New England
observers with whom he identifies himself. Since they are not
involved in the operation of the economy, they do not feel responsible for it. The result is a rather unpleasant smugness.
The townspeople of Branton contemplate the wickedness of the

[8] *Ibid.*, pp. 383, 370–371.
[9] *Ibid.*, p. 163.

great world of Washington and New York with an implicit belief in their own rectitude.

However, Warner shows some lack of confidence in his moral position by his choice of an antitype to Henderson. He does not assign the role to another New Englander but to a young English nobleman on a visit to the United States. A prospective peer could not be expected to engage in business; his wealth is inherited, and he has leisure to devote himself to humanitarian causes such as "aid and relief societies," especially "the work for young waifs and strays." Yet in the circumstances it seems somewhat irrelevant that Lord Chisholm's life is "on a high plane," that his world is "the world of ideas, of books, of intellectual life, of passionate sympathy with the fortunes of humanity, of deepest interest in all the new thoughts struck out by the leaders who studied the profound problems of life and destiny." [10]

III

In *A Hazard of New Fortunes* (1890) Howells finds a more appropriate antitype to the businessman in Jacob Dryfoos's son Conrad, who shares his mother's piety and has had a "lifelong wish to be a minister," despite his father's determination that Conrad shall go into business.[11] It is a radical change to make the spokesmen for Christianity in the novel not New Englanders but an Indiana boy drawn into a Christian Socialist group within the Episcopal Church in New York and a wealthy young society woman whom Conrad meets in the course of his work in a settlement house for boys.

Despite this innovation, however, Howells still relies heavily on New England to provide a moral perspective on the characters and events of the story. By a subtle and sometimes devious narrative technique he conveys the mixture of conviction and uncertainty that characterized his own troubled attitude toward the economic and social changes visible in the New York of the 1880's. The opening sequence shows Basil March and his wife

[10] *Ibid.*, pp. 39, 376.

[11] William Dean Howells, *A Hazard of New Fortunes*, Dolphin, New York, n.d., p. 383.

Isabel in the process of being uprooted from Boston and plunged into the turbulence of the metropolis. Readers of Howells's earlier novels recognized the Marches as the couple who had served before as fictional portraits of the novelist and his wife. Isabel March, a Bostonian both by birth and by conviction, is sufficiently dogmatic in her moral judgments to resemble the New England spokesmen in earlier novels, but Basil, although usually agreeing with her, on occasion can view her with some irony. In this fashion Howells is able to use New England as a symbol yet at the same time to question the region's absolute moral authority.

The Dryfooses, father and son, embody with an emblematic clarity of outline the conflict between crude financial power and idealism that is the organizing principle of Howells's big and rather sprawling novel. Except for political corruption, he brings together all the important themes related to the new world of speculation and millionaires in the fiction of the later nineteenth century and subjects them to a more searching analysis than any previous writer. Jacob Dryfoos was originally a farmer near Moffitt, Indiana, but was catapulted into real-estate speculation by a boom which developed with the discovery of a natural-gas field and brought him an offer of a hundred thousand dollars for his farm. When he has quadrupled his capital by operations in real estate, he moves his family to New York and begins playing the stock market, where he is successful on a much larger scale and acquires interests in railways and mines. Howells is explicit about what happens to Dryfoos in this new environment:

> His moral decay began with his perception of the opportunity of making money quickly and abundantly, which offered itself to him after he sold his farm. . . . The money he had already made without effort and without merit bred its unholy self-love in him. . . . He came where he could watch his money breed more money, and bring greater increase of its kind in an hour of luck than the toil of hundreds of men could earn in a year. He called it speculation, stocks, the Street; and his pride, his faith in himself, mounted with his luck.[12]

[12] *Ibid.*, p. 230.

The most important contribution of the novel to the fictional representation of business and the businessman is Howells's distress over the massive poverty of the New York slums for which no remedy is in sight. He has the vague feeling that poverty is caused by the concentration of undeserved wealth in the hands of meanspirited capitalists like Dryfoos. Yet after the novel's long struggle with the question of how a man can conscientiously live in a capitalist world, it arrives at no firm answer. The ideal of sainthood represented by Conrad is shown to lead only to martyrdom; but Basil March, the ordinary decent man who is neither speculator nor saint, cannot accept the outlook of "the vast, prosperous commercial class, with unlimited money, and no ideals that money could not realize. . . ." [13] His peace of mind has been permanently dispelled by his awareness of what Howells calls "complicity," the inescapable involvement of everyone in society as a whole.

IV

Howells is more sensitive to moral nuances than Boyesen or Warner, but all three of these novels of the 1880's reveal an inchoate sense of guilt somehow related to the rapid economic expansion of the period. This feeling is almost certainly one cause of the general hostility that writers showed toward the businessman. He was a candidate for the role of scapegoat because he was an alien intruder into the fictive world. In contrast with the familiar protagonists of sentimental love stories, he seemed both crude and immoral. Yet he was acknowledged to be immensely powerful. He controlled the energies of economic, social, and political change; the future belonged to him; and no matter how many times the novelists might condemn the businessman to social rebuffs, rejection by the heroine, bankruptcy, public exposure for his crimes, or even suicide, they recognized at bottom that traditional manners and morals were doomed by the growing dominance of the business system.

This was disconcerting, because when New England could no

[13] *Ibid.*, p. 268.

longer serve as a moral base, the novelist analyzing the business system was left without a stable viewpoint from which to survey his subject. It was difficult to find the elements of an acceptable code of values within the system, yet he faced an even more difficult task if he attempted to construct a moral code not supported by some historical reality. Writers of fiction were thus, on the whole, committed to the belief that American life showed an increasing disparity between value and fact, between ideal and actual. Howells's hope that somehow, sometime, loving-kindness would yet prevail in the world has little support in the description of that world presented in *A Hazard of New Fortunes*.

But what if a writer should break with tradition and attempt to deal with the new capitalism on its own terms? In several respects Mark Twain's *A Connecticut Yankee in King Arthur's Court* (1889), published almost simultaneously with *A Hazard of New Fortunes,* is just such an effort. His undertaking was, to be sure, less deliberate than this statement implies. His rejection of literary tradition was not a conscious act but the result of his having developed within the quite different tradition of native American humor—the tall tale, the journalistic hoax, the comic burlesque. The impulse that eventually developed into *A Connecticut Yankee* was quite antiliterary—the notion of writing a burlesque of Malory's *Morte D'Arthur,* which is expressed in a dream recorded in Mark Twain's notebook in 1885.[14] The economic and political implications of the story appeared only later, as it gestated over a period of years. Yet they were not irrelevant, for a cult of medievalism, and specifically of the aristocratic ideals of chivalry, had become one of the principal weapons used by genteel critics against the growing power of business in the nineteenth century. James Russell Lowell had made his Sir Launfal a sentimental humanitarian, a knight who learned the lesson of true charity. Sidney Lanier had protested against post-Civil War commercialism in his poem "The Symphony" (1875), which proposed Chivalry as a counterforce to

14 The development of the book is treated in detail in Henry N. Smith, *Mark Twain's Fable of Progress,* Rutgers University Press, New Brunswick, N. J., 1964, Chapter 2, pp. 36–66.

the blighting influence of Trade. For most readers in the 1880's
the Knights of the Round Table had much the same status as the
antitypes of the businessman conceived by the novelists. The
very impulse to make fun of Malory was thus profoundly hostile
to the Genteel Tradition; it implied taking the side of a modern
world which everyone agreed was permeated with commercialism against the current conception of the aristocratic, noncom-
mercial Middle Ages.

Quite early in the development of Mark Twain's burlesque,
he began to give to his modern protagonist many of the traits
that had been associated with the businessman in fiction. Hank
Morgan, the Yankee, is "practical," and devoid of poetry and
sentiment. He is crude in his tastes, being for example very
fond of chromos and repelled by medieval tapestries; he has no
reverence for antiquity and tradition; and he takes a commercial
view of everything, greedily seeking opportunities to make money
and constantly using figures of speech derived from business
transactions—contracts, discounts, bookkeeping, and operations
on the market such as running a corner, selling short, and so on.
Dropped suddenly and inexplicably into sixth-century Britain,
he secures for himself the status and title of Boss, and sets about
putting Arthur's kingdom on a business basis.

The important question is how Mark Twain justifies his generally favorable attitude toward such a protagonist. The reader
familiar with earlier fictional portraits of the businessman will
be struck by the fact that almost nothing is said about the financial system of Arthur's kingdom or the means by which the
Yankee raises the capital necessary for his operations. It is true
that eventually we discover the Round Table has been trans-
formed into a stock board, but the protagonist himself does no
trading on it, and until almost the end of the story it is no more
than a bit of irreverence toward a prime symbol of chivalry. The
only influence that speculation has on the plot is to foment a
rivalry among the knights which sets off a civil war; and this
event is a great misfortune for the Yankee because it leads to
the collapse of his plans for reforming British society.

In other words, whether deliberately or not, Mark Twain
shields his hero against the charge of gaining wealth through

speculation. Thus despite Hank Morgan's indifference to culture and refinement, he is free of the graver taint of immorality that literary convention had associated with business enterprise. Furthermore, instead of causing poverty, the Yankee is determined to alleviate it. Mark Twain emphasizes the constructive functions of his nineteenth-century invader by making a distinction anticipating Thorstein Veblen's contrast between the engineer interested in production and the financier interested only in profits. The Yankee plans an industrial revolution in the backward feudal economy of sixth-century Britain by means of modern technology. He sets about building factories, workshops, mines, and systems of transportation and communication that will drastically raise the standard of living for the people as a whole. He believes that industrialization will also educate the workers. They will become enlightened through their contact with machines and will in this way become capable of participating as citizens in the republic that he hopes eventually to proclaim.

In making his protagonist a master technician and interpreting economic development as an increase in productive power rather than as a mysterious opportunity for speculators to enrich themselves, Mark Twain was taking over a rationale of capitalism familiar in economic and political discussion but previously unknown in fiction. His attitude toward industrialization throws into relief the primitive character of the economic ideas used by his literary predecessors. Even when writing in detail about financial transactions, earlier writers show no awareness that the speculative boom of the post-Civil War period was the result of an immense increase in production based on the mechanization of transportation and industry. This narrowness of horizon is particularly striking in Howells, whose Utopian romance *A Traveller from Altruria* (1894) describes an ideal future society in which machines play almost no part.

The preoccupation of the novelists with the Napoleonic battles among captains of finance indicates that they gained their impressions of the new capitalism from newspaper reports of political scandals rather than from observing actual economic changes. They were almost totally ignorant of what was really going on in the American economy. Even Mark Twain, despite his intention to exhibit an industrial and managerial genius at work, is unable to give imaginative substance to the Yankee's activities because he simply does not know enough about the technology that he ascribes to his hero.

Yet the intention is there, and it represents a bold attempt to evaluate the industrial revolution from the standpoint of the business community itself rather than from the standpoint of genteel literary and moral tradition. As the agent of technological progress, Hank Morgan takes on a kind of Promethean stature, and through three-fourths of the story the reader can believe that Mark Twain has at last found a way to create an authentic capitalist hero—one who represents the operative values of his society and performs a significant action expressing these values. But the Yankee's civilizing mission ends in failure. The causes of his defeat are not clear because the plot loses itself in a maze of complications. Toward the end of the story Mark Twain seems to be moved by an emotional reaction against his own confident ideology in the earlier chapters rather than by any consistent line of reasoning. Yet from the tangle emerges one powerful conviction—the common people cannot be enlightened as the Yankee had hoped. He has not been able to educate the superstition out of them after all; they are but "human muck," chained forever by their own prejudices and fears of authority, unable in a crisis to resist the commands of their masters, the Church and the nobles. Mark Twain's bitterness of disillusion finds expression in a horrible scene in which the Yankee and a handful of loyal followers kill twenty-five thousand knights with dynamite bombs, Gatling guns, and an electrically charged wire fence and become in turn victims of their own powers of destruction.

Although *A Connecticut Yankee* seems an anomaly in the series of realistic novels about the businessman, Mark Twain's use of a radically different fictional convention casts much light on the issues involved. The method of the fable brings out in bold relief the central myth of nineteenth-century American capitalism; it is indeed the myth of Prometheus, enemy of the reactionary and tyrannical gods of tradition, bringer of intellectual light and material well-being to the downtrodden masses. These achievements were what was usually meant by the term "progress," and the hold of the big businessman on the popular imagination depended on the belief that the achievements were *his* achievements. But the myth of Prometheus had other aspects that were not fully recognized. For example, his revolt against the tyranny of an irrational Olympian monarchy was not identical with democracy or even republicanism; he was under strong temptation to wield despotic power in behalf of mortals too dull and ignorant to recognize their own interests. Similarly, Prometheus could not be expected to pattern his own code of morals upon the mores and traditional beliefs of the mortals he strove to benefit. If he defied the established values of Olympus, could he be expected to pay deference to the idols of the tribe? From the standpoint of the common man, Prometheus must seem incomprehensible and probably shocking—a transcendent figure beyond good and evil as they were defined in the sphere of everyday life on earth.

V

Henry B. Fuller's *The Cliff-Dwellers* (1893) brings us back to the more conventional series of novels about business. Fuller's characterization of Erastus Brainard, the banker who is meant to be the dominant force in the story, recalls Boyesen's Zedekiah Hampton. Brainard is physically ugly, his tastes are gross, and in his indifference to anything except money making and parsimony he suggests a stereotype of the miser that goes back centuries in literary history. It is even hinted that Brainard was once imprisoned for some unspecified crime.[15] Nevertheless, *The Cliff-Dwellers* embodies important fresh attitudes and ideas. Fuller's device of choosing a group of characters who work in the same skyscraper office building is more appropriate than Howells's use of a magazine to link diverse characters in *A Hazard of New Fortunes*, because the skyscraper is more integral to the business system. The choice of Chicago as the setting also clarifies the problem of values in a commercial society, because

15 Henry B. Fuller, *The Cliff-Dwellers*, Harper, New York, 1893, p. 35.

Chicago is conceived as an almost pure product of economic forces, with few vestiges of tradition, either moral or cultural, to complicate matters.   Most important of all, there is no character who establishes a moral perspective.   Through much of the novel Fuller uses a young New Englander, George Ogden, to express his own judgments of Chicago and its inhabitants.   But toward the end of the book the novelist makes a striking departure from fictional conventions.   Under pressure of his wife's extravagance George embezzles funds from Brainard's bank, where he is employed, and is saved from prison only by Brainard's death.   This incident compromises Ogden as a moral focus and, in compromising him, compromises New England.   The only remaining representative of the older value system is Abbie Brainard, long-suffering daughter of Erastus Brainard, whom George Ogden marries after the death of his first wife.   This vestige of traditional machinery serves only to provide an ending for the story.

Fuller's failure to express a clear judgment of his characters may be simply the result of technical ineptitude, but his effort to exclude any kind of uncriticized glamor suggests a conscious striving for the moral neutrality usually identified with literary naturalism.   In this limited sense, *The Cliff-Dwellers* may be said to mark the liquidation of the nineteenth-century sentimental novel.   It clears the ground, so to speak, for the discovery of new criteria of value in fiction.   And the prominence of businessmen in the story, even though they are not shown carrying out financial operations on a large scale, suggests that these representatives of economic forces might become the basis for the nascent system of values.

VI

Like Henry James's *The Portrait of a Lady*, Robert Herrick's *The Gospel of Freedom* (1898) takes an American heroine to Europe and confronts her with a choice between suitors who represent conflicting outlooks on life—a businessman and his antitype.   Simeon Erard is a Jewish art critic rather venomously modeled on Bernard Berenson, a college mate of Herrick's at

Harvard.   John Foster Wilbur is a self-made midwestern industrialist and financier who, in his competence and strength, resembles James's Caspar Goodwood.

In explaining Wilbur's attraction for Adela Anthon, the heroine, Herrick breaks new ground, for he recognizes a positive value
in the businessman's character:

> [Wilbur's] every act [muses Adela] indicated freedom, a large, hope-
> ful way of life, full of plans and the realizing of plans by constant,
> swift, clever calculation.   How much more vital *that,* than the dead
> groping into one's interior self after expression or some faint repre-
> sentation of that inadequate self,—called art!   It is better to live than
> to paint . . . it is best to make life your art.[16]

But the marriage does not work, despite (or rather because of)
Wilbur's success in finance.   He becomes associated with "a group
of young capitalists" in Chicago under the leadership of a sinister
politician named Writhington.   The program looks forward to
that of Frank Cowperwood; it involves street-railway franchises
obtained through bribery.   After a time Wilbur reaches the point
of asserting that bribery is justifiable because it is necessary in
order to do business in Chicago.[17]

When Adela leaves her husband, however, she does so not
primarily in protest against his immoral business practices, but
because she has grown bored with him and with Chicago—that
is, on basically esthetic rather than moral grounds.   She perceives
that Wilbur is

> . . . the American peasant. . . . Anywhere else there would have been
> intermediate stages in the social evolution where he would have stuck,
> his descendants to go on as they proved ready and had imbibed the
> ideas of service and honour that befitted the possessors of great power.
> But Wilbur with one powerful effort had gained the heights, and he
> had no humbleness, no distrust,—nothing was too good for a clever
> man who had made his money.[18]

The phrase "American peasant" foreshadows the fictional businessmen who would be described not only by Sinclair Lewis but

---

[16] Robert Herrick, *The Gospel of Freedom,* Macmillan, New York, 1898,
p. 89.

[17] *Ibid.,* pp. 126–127.   [18] *Ibid.,* p. 180.

by Eugene O'Neill and J. P. Marquand. Yet the esthetic ideal associated with Europe is in turn subjected to destructive criticism. Adela becomes a kind of research assistant to Erard in France and Italy, but after a few months she is overcome once again by impatience with his cult of "associations and ideas," and she rejects him a second time. The good life now seems to her to be represented by a different antitype to the businessman, a young lawyer named Thornton Jennings who has devoted himself to reformist crusades. He was the spokesman for the Civic Association that denounced the bribery involved in the traction franchise and is on the point of returning to the United States to take charge of a school for Negroes in the South. She offers herself to him, but he gently rejects her; he is to marry a more deserving and less complicated woman. At the end of the book Adela thinks she may join Jennings and his bride in their work with the Negroes; in any case, she is still trying to "learn how to live." [19]

In Warner's *A Little Journey* the businessman was promoted in the hierarchy of the novel by being allowed to marry the heroine, but the immorality of his world killed her. In *The Gospel of Freedom* the businessman's immorality is of less consequence than his lack of cultivation. Herrick's *Memoirs of an American Citizen* (1905) takes the drastic step of making a businessman the protagonist and allowing him to tell the story of his life in the first person. The result of this innovation in technique is to place the reader inside the mind of a character engaged in actions that had been uniformly condemned by earlier novelists. Edward Van Harrington, Chicago meat-packing magnate, financier, and eventually United States Senator, is as powerful and ruthless as any of his fictional predecessors, but the narrative viewpoint provides a new and less hostile perspective on his career.

Of course, Herrick does not actually mean to endorse Harrington's motives or methods. The overall intention of the novel is ironic; Harrington is supposed to reveal himself as a rascal without realizing it. And Herrick is not content to rely on irony alone as a means of expressing his adverse judgment of the pro-

[19] *Ibid.*, p. 287.

tagonist. He falls back upon a vestige of sentimental conventions by introducing a sister-in-law of Harrington who vehemently denounces his bribery of public officials:

". . . you think you can break through all laws [she says on one occasion] because laws are made for small people . . . and you and your kind are Napoleons. You talk as if you were a part of God's destiny. And I say . . . , Van, you are the devil's instrument! You and those like you—and there are a good many of them—are just plain big rascals, only the laws can't get hold of you!" [20]

This is only a little more hostile than Herrick's own attitude toward Harrington. Yet the first-person point of view obliges the novelist to formulate some kind of self-justification for the narrator, and the need to explain Harrington's attitude inevitably leads to a degree of sympathy with it:

No business in this large, modern world [says the financier] could be done on her plan of life. That beautiful scheme of things which the fathers of our country drew up in the stage-coach days had proved itself inadequate in a short century. We had to get along with it the best we could. But we men who did the work of the world, who developed the country, who were the life and force of the times, could not be held back by the swaddling-clothes of any political or moral theory. Results we must have: good results; and we worked with the tools we found at hand.[21]

At the end, after his corrupt election to the United States Senate, Van Harrington looks out over the smoke and dirt of Chicago and reflects on his career:

Traffic, business, industry,—the work of the world was going forward. A huge lumber boat blocked the river at the bridge, and while the tugs pushed it slowly through the draw, I stood and gazed at the busy tracks in the railroad yards below me, at the line of high warehouses along the river. I, too, was a part of this. The thought of my brain, the labor of my body, the will within me, had gone to the making of this world. . . . Surely there was another scale, a grander one, and by this I should not be found wholly wanting! [22]

[20] Robert Herrick, *Memoirs of an American Citizen*, Daniel Aaron, ed., Harvard University Press, Cambridge, Mass., 1963, p. 192.
[21] *Ibid.*, p. 191.   [22] *Ibid.*, p. 266.

In passages like these, Herrick presents the elements of a rationale of business enterprise that contradicts the attitude embodied in literary tradition.

VII

The overt plot of Frank Norris's *The Pit* (1903), published two years before *Memoirs of an American Citizen,* resembles that of *The Gospel of Freedom;* once again, a young and desirable heroine is the moral arbiter. Laura Dearborn, like Adela Anthon, is obliged to choose between suitors representing the world of art (Sheldon Corthell, designer of stained-glass windows) and the world of business (Curtis Jadwin, self-made "strong" man and speculator). As in *The Gospel of Freedom,* the heroine marries the businessman but grows bored because he neglects her; she is tempted to leave her husband for the esthete. But Norris adopts a more conventional solution than Herrick's. In the nick of time Jadwin returns home, bankrupt and broken, and gravely in need of a wife's care. Since he has renounced his career as speculator, she cleaves to him and spurns the tempter.

Although Norris follows convention in making Laura Dearborn a New England girl, the phenomenon of Chicago can be observed altering the long-established pattern of cultural symbols. Norris says that when Laura came West shortly before the action of the novel begins, she had already realized that the "New England spirit" was "a veritable cult, a sort of religion, wherein the Old Maid was the priestess, the Spinster the officiating devotee, the thing worshipped the Great Unbeautiful, and the ritual unremitting, unrelenting Housework." [23]

What Norris is really interested in, however, is the evaluation of Jadwin's career and thus of the economic forces that provide food for society. By refusing to make his protagonist explicitly a criminal, Norris states the problem in a purer form than Herrick achieves in *Memoirs.* Jadwin does not bribe anyone; he simply undertakes to corner the wheat market by a speculative coup. His attempt is shown to be potentially destructive by the suicide of a friend who is bankrupted without Jadwin's knowl-

[23] Frank Norris, *The Pit,* Random House, New York, 1934, p. 40.

edge. But on the broader scale that Norris explores, the distress in Europe caused by the rise in the price of bread resulting from Jadwin's speculation is offset by the prosperity that the same speculation brings to wheat farmers throughout the Midwest.

The novelty in Norris's view lies in his insistence that economic processes are vast, impersonal forces, part of some inscrutable cosmic design to which individual guilt or innocence, like individual happiness or misery, is indifferent. He tries to give imaginative substance to the doctrine that the business system is controlled by natural rather than moral laws. Again and again the production and distribution of wheat are linked with images of waves, currents, resistless torrents, and so on. The Chicago Board of Trade is "a great whirlpool, a pit of roaring waters that spun and thundered, sucking in the life tides of the city, sucking them in as into the mouth of some tremendous cloaca, the maw of some colossal sewer; then vomiting them forth again, spewing them up and out, only to catch them in the return eddy and suck them in afresh." [24] When Jadwin sets out to corner the market, he is defying these superhuman forces; indeed, one of his associates declares, "you're fighting against the earth itself." [25] The rise in wheat prices caused by the attempted corner causes thousands of additional acres to be planted, until the increased supply breaks the market and defeats Jadwin.

The fascination with force and power expressed in Norris's bombastic imagery is one consequence of his effort to shift the focus of the novel from psychological processes to an external, nonhuman world of Nature. Within the sphere of human motives and behavior the same preoccupation leads the novelist to try to make his protagonist larger than life. He evidently admires Jadwin's strength and is inclined to consider him—and with him, the financial tycoon as a type—somehow more than human. This feeling is the germ of the cult of the superman which London and Dreiser would express in Nietzschean ideas and images. And although Norris is not prepared to allow Jadwin a moral status beyond good and evil corresponding to his transcendent power of body and of will, the emphasis on the

24 *Ibid.*, p. 73.
25 *Ibid.*, p. 332.

control of human affairs by "insensate" natural forces precludes the moralizing so familiar in earlier novelists of business.

VIII

Jack London's *Burning Daylight* (1910) also relies heavily on Nature, but in opposition to the business system rather than in support of it. Elam Harnish (nicknamed "Burning Daylight"), a sourdough prospector in the Yukon with incredible physical strength, "hard, practical judgment, imagination and vision, and the daring of the big gambler," buys up claims supposed worthless and becomes a town builder at the mouth of the Klondike.[26] He eventually sells out his holdings for eleven million dollars and goes to San Francisco to begin a career of speculation on an even larger scale. After being cheated by Californian and then by Eastern financiers, he determines to take revenge on the giants who control the crooked world of big business. He is highly successful in "the fierce, savage game he now played," but because he has lost contact with the elemental outdoor life of the North, he becomes flabby in body and cynical and brutal in outlook.[27] The strain of business makes him an alcoholic; he has no friends and virtually no recreations except drink. His redemption begins when a weekend trip to inspect a brickyard in Sonoma Valley makes him suddenly aware of "the beauty of the world," [28] and his regeneration continues after he falls in love with a stenographer whom he accompanies on Sunday horseback rides in the hills overlooking Oakland and Berkeley. When she maintains that his financial operations do not create anything, he begins an elaborate real-estate development in the East Bay which expands to include construction of a transportation system for commuters and other related enterprises. The girl still refuses to marry him, however, because his business activities have first claim on his interest and his energies. In the end he abruptly abandons all his projects and takes her to

---

[26] Jack London, *Burning Daylight,* Macmillan, New York, 1937, pp. 101–102.

[27] *Ibid.,* pp. 162–163, 180.

[28] *Ibid.,* p. 183.

live in a cabin in Sonoma Valley, where they emulate the peaceful existence of a Thoreauvian retired newspaperman that Harnish had encountered when he first discovered the rural paradise.

Although London's analysis of the moral issues connected with business is not subtle, as always he states his themes vigorously and explicitly. He draws upon a simplified blend of Marx and Nietzsche in order to depict his protagonist as a superman who makes cynical use of a socialist insight into capitalism for his own advantage. But Harnish's theory of society is only a more explicit development of the view presented by Herrick in his account of Van Harrington's service as a juror in the Haymarket trial:

> Little business men, shopkeepers, and such ilk took what whack they could out of the product of the worker, but, after all, it was the large business men who formed [farmed?] the workers through the little business men. . . . They were hired men for the large business men. Still again, higher up, were the big fellows. They used vast and complicated paraphernalia for the purpose, on a large scale, of getting between hundreds of thousands of workers and their products. These men were not so much mere robbers as gamblers. And, not content with their direct winnings, being essentially gamblers, they raided one another. They called this feature of the game *high finance*. . . .
>
> Thus, all unread in philosophy, Daylight preëmpted for himself the position and vocation of a twentieth-century superman. . . . *Thou shalt not steal* was only applicable to the honest worker. They, the supermen, were above such commandments. They certainly stole and were honored by their fellows according to the magnitude of their stealings.[29]

London can maintain that capitalist society is corrupt because he identifies it with "civilization" in a bipolar scheme contrasting civilization with Nature and making Nature the source of all value. His attitude owes more to the long tradition of primitivism than to radical political and economic theory. Civilization is symbolized by the City—in this novel, San Francisco, a place of physical and moral degradation—so that when Harnish receives the shock of Nature in Sonoma Valley, "As he drank in the air, the scene, and the distant song of larks, he felt like a poker-

[29] *Ibid.*, pp. 159–160.

player rising from a night-long table and coming forth from the pent atmosphere to taste the freshness of the morn." [30]   London's crude primitivism is, of course, quite irresponsible; the news-paperman turned hermit who serves as an antitype to the finan-cier does not resemble the intensely committed Thoreau so much as the genteel observers in Warner's little parliament in Branton passing judgment on the corrupt world of New York.   Nor does anything come of the socialist ideas in the novel.   When Harnish and his bride retire into the lark-resounding valley, the exploited workers are forgotten.   The basic value affirmed by the plot is not justice but a simple life of moderate physical labor.   Not sur-prisingly, in this idyllic setting the wife reverts to the type of the nineteenth-century genteel heroine.   She teaches her unculti-vated husband to like poetry, and while she works on "certain small garments," he practices on the violin.[31]

For the same reasons, London's proclamation that the business tycoon is a superman, beyond good and evil, has no more sub-stance than Norris's depiction of Curtis Jadwin as a Napoleon, a giant of will power and intellect.   In both cases the superman has to abandon his role before he becomes an acceptable hus-band and receives the fictional good-conduct medal of a wife's devotion.   London, in other words, like Norris, is guilty of a kind of dilettantism.   Both are playing with concepts and themes from which in the end they retreat in order to take refuge in the citadel of monogamous marriage and domestic felicity.   In this regard they are markedly less advanced than Herrick, who re-fused to allow either Adela Wilbur or Van Harrington to regard marriage as a solution for the problem of values in a world domi-nated by big business, and was willing to end his novels without tying up the loose ends of the narrative in a lovers' knot.

IX

Dreiser's trilogy about Frank Cowperwood contains by far the most impressive portrait of a big businessman in American fic-tion.   No later writer has brought to the subject anything like

[30] *Ibid.*, p. 183.
[31] *Ibid.*, pp. 352–354.

Dreiser's commitment, no one else has dealt with it at such length or with such intensity. Yet in characterizing Cowperwood, Dreiser has in the main simply taken over the familiar catalogue of the businessman's vices and presented them as virtues. For example, Cowperwood resembles many of his predecessors in being an unsatisfactory husband, but Dreiser makes the failure of his two marriages turn upon his sexual prowess; Cowperwood is irresistible as a lover, and he refuses to be content with one woman at a time. The moral indictment brought against the businessman by earlier novelists becomes a blueprint for Dreiser's demonstration that Cowperwood is superior to the moral and legal codes binding the average of mankind. The characterization involves ideas drawn at second hand from H. L. Mencken's *The Philosophy of Frederick Nietzsche* (1908). Cowperwood exerts the inexplicable charm of the superman because he is beyond good and evil; he has "no consciousness of what is currently known as sin." [32]

Much of the vividness of Cowperwood as a character is due to Dreiser's evident sympathy with his protagonist's scorn for "the conventional mind." [33] The novelist remarks in his own person that Addison, a powerful Chicago banker, was "ostensibly a church-member, a model citizen; he represented a point of view to which Cowperwood would never have stooped." [34] In fact, the attitudes that had earlier been associated with New England and had provided the basis for literary condemnation of the businessman in the 1880's and 1890's are associated in Dreiser's fictive world with the "silk-stocking crew" represented by Addison—men and women of established social and financial position who dominate Chicago and against whom Cowperwood must fight his way upward.[35] Virtually all Dreiser's allusions to morals carry the express or implied charge of hypocrisy. He contrasts "the cold political logic of a man like Cowperwood" with "the

---

[32] Theodore Dreiser, *The Financier*, World, Cleveland, 1946, p. 271.

[33] *Ibid.*, pp. 244–245.

[34] Theodore Dreiser, *The Titan*, World, Cleveland, 1946, p. 8.

[35] *Ibid.*, p. 291. When Dreiser compares Cowperwood with Prometheus, it is in a reference to his "attitude of Promethean defiance which had never yet brooked defeat" (*ibid.*, p. 528).

polite moralistic efforts" of the silk-stocking crowd, "who were content to preach morality and strive to win by the efforts of the unco good." And he calls the newspapers that criticize Cowperwood "those profit-appointed advocates and guardians of 'right' and 'justice.' " [36]

What has happened is that Dreiser, writing from the viewpoint of an outsider with a background of poverty, disorder, and early sorrow, takes at face value the state of affairs made explicit in Warner's *A Little Journey,* where the moral principles are affirmed by observers remote from the "real" world of business. Dreiser translates the older contrast between a virtuous, semi-rural New England and the wickedness of commercial-minded New York into a contrast between the families of established economic and social position in Chicago and aggressive newcomers like Cowperwood. He insists that traditional codes of conduct are rationalizations supporting the status of a ruling class; his admiration for Cowperwood expresses his own resentment of the silk-stocking crowd. Perceiving that the tradition supporting this class has lost its moral authority and become a mere ideology, the superman brushes it aside and makes his own rules. To put this another way, with the waning of the values linked with New England, the morally neutral enclave that apologists for business had declared to be controlled by the impersonal laws of trade has widened its boundaries to embrace the whole of Dreiser's fictive universe.

But Dreiser does not share the prevalent belief in inevitable progress resulting from the free play of economic forces. He makes little of the fact that Cowperwood's consolidation of the street-railway systems of Chicago and London benefits society by providing more efficient transportation at lower cost. Although he asserts that "God or the life force, if anything, is an equation," [37] the world of business is not a harmony maintained by an invisible hand but an anarchy of struggle. The collapse of Cowperwood's financial empire conveys the idea that such a man must sooner or later threaten the stability of society, whereupon

[36] *Ibid.,* pp. 288, 302.
[37] *Ibid.,* p. 551.

an equilibrium of forces neither good nor bad will reestablish itself.

Both the Promethean accomplishments and the ultimate failure of Cowperwood link him with that other subversive, Mark Twain's Connecticut Yankee, and back of him with Emerson's conception of Napoleon as the representative figure of the commercial nineteenth century. Cowperwood's empire, like theirs, cannot survive him. It is dissipated amid the bickerings of heirs, creditors, administrators, and courts. Even though, as Dreiser says, a Titan may "for the hour illuminate the terrors and wonders of individuality," there awaits him "the eternal equation—the pathos of the discovery that even giants are but pygmies, and that an ultimate balance must be struck." [38]

X

The dominant trend in fictional portraits of the businessman during the past thirty years has led in quite a different direction from the celebration of individualism. Within a decade of the publication of *The Financier* appeared an influential novel depicting the businessman as a helpless victim of social pressure. Cowperwood's "private law" is, "I satisfy myself." [39]   George F. Babbitt's valedictory cry is, "They've licked me!" and "I've never done a single thing I wanted to." [40]   The contrast almost seems contrived. Yet Cowperwood has had few literary descendants, whereas Babbitt, henpecked and coerced by his fellow members of the Boosters' Club, has been succeeded by a host of conformists from Dos Passos's fatuous public-relations counsel, J. Ward Moorehouse (in *U.S.A.*, 1930–36), to the organization men in the novels of Cameron Hawley and Howard Swiggett.

It is hard to believe that this sudden transformation in the fictional businessman accurately reflects a change in society itself. History, even in the twentieth century, does not move that fast. Perhaps Cowperwood should be considered an anachronistic figure representing a vanished era of moguls and robber barons,

[38] *Ibid.*, p. 551.
[39] *Ibid.*, p. 9.
[40] Sinclair Lewis, *Babbitt*, Signet, New York, 1961, pp. 316, 319.

whereas Babbitt is an emergent type. By the 1920's the business-man had evidently ceased to be viewed by the literary community as a giant, whether admirable or menacing, and had become instead something of a buffoon. If we take Sinclair Lewis's novel *Babbitt* (1922) and Eugene O'Neill's play *Marco Millions* (1927) as characteristic of the decade, we can say that the businessman was viewed in literature from a perspective similar to that of Erard in *The Gospel of Freedom* or Corthell in *The Pit*—the perspective, that is, of the artist, of the emancipated intellectual, a Bohemianism more vividly impressed by the businessman's philistinism and his ineptitude as a lover than by his power or wickedness. Given this comic stance, summed up in Mencken's jeering designation of the business community as the "booboisie," one could fill out the counts in Lewis's and O'Neill's indictment with relative ease from earlier novels. The only revision necessary in the established portrait would be a reduction in scale.

The relation between Dreiser's fictive world and Lewis's can be illustrated by the passage in which Babbitt encounters one Charles McKelvey at a dinner for alumni of the state university. McKelvey, says Lewis,

. . . built state capitols, skyscrapers, railway terminals. He was a heavy-shouldered, big-chested man, but not sluggish. There was a quiet humor in his eyes, a syrup-smooth quickness in his speech, which intimidated politicians and warned reporters; and in his presence the most intelligent scientist or the most sensitive artist felt thin-blooded, unworldly, and a little shabby. He was, particularly when he was influencing legislatures or hiring labor-spies, very easy and lovable and gorgeous. He was baronial; he was a peer in the rapidly crystallizing American aristocracy, inferior only to the haughty Old Families. . . . His power was the greater because he was not hindered by scruples, by either the vice or the virtue of the old Puritan tradition.[41]

Babbitt, who is dazzled by this godlike figure, manages to entice the McKelveys to his house once for dinner, but the evening is painful as only Lewis can make such a scene painful, and the relation comes to nothing.

McKelvey is a diminished Cowperwood, yet even so he towers

[41] *Ibid.*, p. 158.

on the horizon of Babbitt's world with a remote grandeur. The reduction in scale of Lewis's protagonist corresponds to a change in literary modes; where Dreiser is serious and, in aspiration at least, epic, Lewis is comic and mock-heroic. The difference is not accidental, for Dreiser's predecessor Norris had been even more epic than he, whereas Eugene O'Neill's Marco Polo is even more of a buffoon than Babbitt. Although Lewis has a half-concealed fondness for his bewildered realtor, he does not look up to him as Dreiser looks up to Cowperwood. (The artist who felt thinblooded and shabby in the presence of McKelvey is not really present in Lewis's fictive world.) And if O'Neill has any liking at all for Marco, it is indulgent and patronizing. The literary data indicate that the muckraking of the early 1900's and the cultural revolution following the First World War had drastically altered the American writer's conception of his own status in relation to a business community that the Van Wyck Brookses, the Waldo Franks, and the H. L. Menckens had spent so much energy and talent in attacking.

Yet the system of values supporting Lewis and O'Neill in their satiric portrayal of the businessman is rickety. The evidence can be found in the antitypes that Lewis presents—the European scientist Dr. Kurt Yavitch and the radical lawyer Seneca Doane, spokesman for the labor unions that are crushed by the Good Citizens League. They talk rather sketchily about self-fulfillment, self-knowledge, and taste in the arts, and the characterization of Yavitch suggests that Lewis intends here (as he had intended in *Main Street*) an unfavorable contrast between Europe and America. But the ideal of the good life thus hinted at is never brought into focus or made to play a part in the plot; Lewis has no clear conception of either art or science as the basis for an alternative to the outlook of the business community. Furthermore, in his Midwest the New England tradition has dwindled to the suggestion that the mansion of William Washington Eathorne, bank president and patriarch of the Old Families of Zenith, "remains virtuous and aloof, reminiscent of London, Back Bay, Rittenhouse Square." [42]

---

[42] *Ibid.*, p. 174.

The only significant effort to discover a source of value and hence a vantage point from which to pass judgment on the business system in the literature of the 1920's and 1930's was that of the radical left. The criticism of American capitalism by novelists adhering to various forms of socialism is a large subject; several books have been devoted to it, and there is obviously no opportunity here to attempt even the briefest survey. Conceivably, a novelist on the left might have shown a Cowperwood in conflict with the workers, but the hostility to the businessman in proletarian fiction precludes even this degree of respect for him. Dos Passos speaks for the decade of the depression when he ends his trilogy with the image of a young hitchhiker beside the highway trying to thumb a ride, while overhead in a Douglas airliner,

> The transcontinental passengers sit pretty, big men with bankaccounts, highlypaid jobs, who are saluted by doormen; telephonegirls say goodmorning to them. Last night after a fine dinner, drinks with friends, they left Newark. . . . The transcontinental passenger thinks contracts, profits, vacationtrips, mighty continent between Atlantic and Pacific, power, wires humming dollars, cities jammed, hills empty, the indiantrail leading into the wagonroad, the macadamed pike, the concrete skyway, trains, planes: history the billiondollar speedup,
> and in the bumpy air over the desert ranges towards Las Vegas
> sickens and vomits into the carton container the steak and mushrooms he ate in New York. No matter, silver in the pocket, greenbacks in the wallet, drafts, certified checks, plenty restaurants in L.A.[43]

XI

Recent novels of business—and there have been many of them— are in the main, as Albert Van Nostrand has pointed out in *The Denatured Novel,* imitations and adaptations of John P. Marquand's *Point of No Return* (1949).[44] The usual theme is the submergence of the individual businessman in the corporation, the System. But whereas Marquand treats this material satiri-

[43] John Dos Passos, *The Big Money* (in *U.S.A.,* 3 volumes in one), Random House, New York, n.d., pp. 560–561.

[44] Albert Van Nostrand, *The Denatured Novel,* Bobbs-Merrill, Indianapolis, 1960, p. 159.

cally, his most popular successors, such as Howard Swiggett and
Cameron Hawley, imply that the subordination of the individual
to the system is inevitable and desirable. As William H. Whyte,
Jr., remarks in *The Organization Man,* their slogan might be,
"Love that system." Thus, to quote Mr. Whyte again, the search
for a capitalist hero which reached its culmination in Frank
Cowperwood has now been supplanted by the depiction of "Society as Hero." [45] The dominant force is not an individual but
an institution, the large corporation, which could be called a
metaphor for society if these novelists were aware that the two
ideas can be distinguished from one another.

Swiggett and Hawley habitually expose a businessman protagonist to the threat of failure, then reveal that the danger was
only apparent. The protagonist is immersed in a corporation or
a broader system of business relationships; he feels panic, but a
mysterious power comes to his rescue. The fictive world is shown
to be controlled by forces beyond the knowledge or comprehen-
sion of the individual, yet in the end the determinism proves
to be not malign but benevolent.

In Swiggett's *The Durable Fire* (1957) Stephen Lowry appears
to be eccentric and refreshingly defiant of conventions when he
is hired as vice president of Continental Industries Corporation,
but when subjected to the stupid tyranny of a new president
named Cramer, he proves himself according to the rules of the
system. In an interview with the directors he steadfastly refuses
to utter even an implied criticism of Cramer. The directors,
who have already discovered that Cramer is incompetent, are
ravished by this restraint; Lowry is a team man, he cannot conceive of insubordination. They tell him they are "deeply impressed, deeply, by the way you behaved in there and by what
you would not be drawn into saying." [46] It is a singularly passive
way of proving one's capacity for executive responsibility.

[45] William H. Whyte, Jr., *The Organization Man,* Anchor, New York, n.d.,
pp. 269–276.

[46] Howard Swiggett, *The Durable Fire,* Houghton Mifflin, Boston, 1957, p.
356.

Hawley's *The Lincoln Lords* (1960) makes the business executive dependent on his wife as well as on his corporation. As the title suggests, the story has a dual protagonist, a married couple of whom the wife is clearly the more able. After an agonizing sequence in which Lincoln Lord is out of a job, he is almost miraculously put in charge of a canning factory. The climax of the plot is precipitated by a new baby food (partially predigested by enzymes) which Lord's company places on the market. When several babies become ill after eating the first cans of the food, Lord makes a radio announcement warning mothers of the danger—an act that destroys the investment in the new product and gravely injures the sales prospects of the company's entire line. It is suggested later that the illness of the children was only coincidental, but Lord tells his wife he is nevertheless glad that he made the announcement, because "Something happened last night. . . . Always before, it's been someone else's company . . . —all I ever did was what I thought they wanted me to do. But it wasn't that way last night. Coastal Foods . . . was *my* company. I've never felt that way before. I suppose that's why I've always been running away. . . ." He decides to refuse the offer of a college presidency which has tempted him. "I'm not . . . doing it because I think the company needs me," he says—"maybe it doesn't. . . . It's the other way round— I need the company." [47] There is something sacramental about this moment; the corporation, the System, has acquired the status of a father, even a divinity.

The functions of the System as a superpersonal power conferring success and happiness on the protagonist make it resemble the Providence that contrives happy endings through the most improbable means (reappearance of long-lost brothers or sisters, unexpected bequests, and so on) in nineteenth-century "sensation novels." But it is no news that virtue is rewarded in popular fiction, and there is no reason to dwell longer on this stereotyped fare.

[47] Cameron Hawley, *The Lincoln Lords,* Little-Brown, Boston, 1960, pp. 555–556.

XII

The last novel to be considered in this survey, Ayn Rand's *Atlas Shrugged* (1957), offers a violent contrast to the celebrations of togetherness and the bland managerial tone of Hawley and Swiggett. It is an apocalyptic vision of the last days of the American welfare state, laid in the 1970's, when governmental interference with free enterprise finally strangles the economic system. After creeping socialism has made the nation a wasteland, a messiah of laissez-faire named John Galt issues forth from his hiding place in the Colorado mountains to begin the work of constructing a society around the profit motive and the gold standard. In the last line of the book, "He raised his hand and over the desolate earth he traced in space the sign of the dollar."

Miss Rand builds her rather confused plot around several business and industrial executives who are struggling like Laokoön in the coils of bureaucracy. The most fully characterized is Henry ("Hank") Rearden, inventor and manufacturer of an alloy stronger and lighter than steel, who shares with John Galt the status of lover of the heroine Dagny Taggart, a businesswoman surrogate of Miss Rand in the story. The mythological title of the novel is explained by a mysterious character called Francisco d'Anconia who acts as Miss Rand's mouthpiece:

". . . if you saw Atlas, the giant who holds the world on his shoulders [he says to Rearden], if you saw that he stood, blood running down his chest, his knees buckling, his arms trembling but still trying to hold the world aloft with the last of his strength, and the greater his effort the heavier the world bore down upon his shoulders—what would you tell him to do?"

"I . . . don't know. . . . What would *you* tell him?"

"To shrug." [48]

This makes the businessman a Titan, but the reader not familiar with Miss Rand's special vision of contemporary society is likely to be puzzled by the blood running down Atlas's chest—a detail lacking in the Greek myth. In fact, it is not immediately clear why Miss Rand has chosen Atlas rather than Prometheus as the

[48] Ayn Rand, *Atlas Shrugged*, Signet, New York, 1959, p. 429.

prototype of her rebellious entrepreneurs. Presently she shows that she has not forgotten about Prometheus. D'Anconia asserts that "John Galt is Prometheus who changed his mind. After centuries of being torn by vultures in payment for having brought to men the fire of the gods, he broke his chains and he withdrew his fire—until the day when men withdraw their vultures." [49] The second myth is a commentary on the first; the vultures torturing Prometheus probably explain why Atlas is bleeding. Here again Miss Rand alters the traditional story. In her version the vultures are sent by men, not by Zeus; and since the Titan's human enemies have no weapon against him except accusations, the vultures seem to represent remorse rather than physical punishment ordered by an omnipotent tyrant. D'Anconia tells Rearden that the deadliest weapon of his enemies is "their moral code." The businessman suffers because he has not demanded "what the whole world owes you and what you should have demanded of all men before you dealt with them: a moral sanction." In accepting "an undeserved guilt," d'Anconia says, Rearden has been paying blackmail "not for your vices, but for your virtues." "You, who've created abundance where there had been nothing but wastelands and helpless, starving men before you, have been called a robber." [50] The myths of Atlas and Prometheus are blended in d'Anconia's summary: "You have been willing to carry the load of an unearned punishment—and to let it grow the heavier the greater the virtues you practiced." [51]

Miss Rand's revision of the classical myths is significant. For one thing, there is a comic disproportion between the metaphors of blood and vultures and their empirical referent, which turns out to be nothing more than the refusal of the public to grant the businessman a moral sanction for his activities. The sufferings of Atlas and Prometheus are reduced to the entrepreneur's pangs of conscience. In the second place, the substitution of Atlas for Prometheus as the dominant prototype of the businessman makes his role—in comparison, say, with Van Harrington's or Cowperwood's—strikingly passive. Even when Miss Rand in-

---

[49] *Ibid.*, p. 486.   [50] *Ibid.*, p. 428.   [51] *Ibid.*, p. 428.

vokes the figure of Prometheus, she does not have in mind his aggression against the gods but rather the punishment visited upon him for that aggression—punishment that is by implication largely self-inflicted.

It is true that the events of Miss Rand's plot do not always conform to the generalizations implicit in her mythological glosses. Dagny Taggart, in particular, is capable of vehement action to overcome the incompetence or apathy of her subordinates in the railway system of which she is operating vice president. And there are occasional outbursts of senseless violence in the manner of Mickey Spillane. In the end, however, like Rearden and numerous other executives the heroine accepts John Galt's strategy of passive resistance to the governmental bureaucracy. One by one they quietly leave their jobs and retire to the valley in the mountains, leaving the welfare state to destroy itself. Their revolution is not overt aggression but merely a shrug of the shoulders. It is implied that Galt and his chosen band will build a new society on the ruins of the old, but they have not even begun this task when, after more than a thousand pages, the novel ends. The substance of the narrative is not the actions but the sufferings of the Titans.

Thus Miss Rand's novel might be said to reveal the fantasy life of an unusually disturbed businessman caught in the dilemma analyzed by Francis X. Sutton and his collaborators in *The American Business Creed:*

> Possibly the most fundamental source of strain in the business role is an inconsistency in the ethical norms by which American society expects business behavior to be governed. On the one hand, self-interested actions by businessmen are tolerated in law and approved in social mores. On the other hand, self-interest is considered to be an unworthy goal of action which conflicts with ethical norms to which society attaches great importance.

The norms in question, described as "the universalistic ethic of our society," are explained more fully as follows:

> . . . it is expected that, in taking actions which affect others, an individual will assume some moral responsibility for their welfare, quite apart from his feelings toward them.

Furthermore,

Unvarnished self-interest is not an admissible explanation of action; to be socially approved, the actions of an individual must be interpretable as contributing something to society.[52]

"The managerial strand of business ideology" attempts to soften this contradiction by assigning to the businessman the role of mediator among conflicting responsibilities—to stockholders, employees, customers, and the public—and describing the individual business concern as "a family of human beings cooperating in a common purpose." [53] But the strain imposed on the executive suggests that the managerial ideology is not entirely persuasive. Miss Rand finds it preposterous and, because false, immoral. She proposes a bold declaration that economic self-interest, the profit motive, is the basis of ethics not only in business but in all of life.

Miss Rand's emphasis on the problem of guilt suggests that her fictional businessmen may after all have something in common with the protagonists of Hawley and Swiggett. Hank Rearden, as Atlas, presents a visible token of his bad conscience in the blood running down his chest; it is a psychosomatic symptom. The organization man's uneasiness about the profit motive is more deeply buried because he is able to shift some of his burden of guilt to the impersonal corporation. Thus his own conflict can be kept below the level of consciousness, and he experiences it as a diffused anxiety about his status within the system. In either case, the businessman in contemporary fiction offers a striking contrast to Frank Cowperwood, a Titan heroically free from the pangs of conscience.

Twentieth-century American novels about business have identified a number of moral dilemmas inherent in a capitalist system, but they have not produced a character properly described as a capitalist hero. Frank Cowperwood is conceived on a heroic scale, but he cannot enact the role of a hero because he defies the moral standards of his society and is indifferent to its welfare.

[52] Francis X. Sutton, Seymour E. Harris, Carl Kaysen, and James Tobin, *The American Business Creed*, Harvard University Press, Cambridge, Mass., 1956, pp. 354–355.

[53] *Ibid.*, p. 357.

The protagonists of the Swiggetts and the Hawleys fail to perform a significant action; they are controlled by the implausible benevolence of the System. Even Ayn Rand's protagonists are shown suffering rather than acting. Besides, she demands that the reader accept a fictive universe wildly at variance with history or contemporary experience. Serious novelists of our day have not even attempted to consider the possibly heroic traits and accomplishments of the businessman. Virtually all of them create protagonists who are antiheroes—outcasts, pariahs, varying only in the manner and degree of their repudiation of a society portrayed as being coterminous with the business system. The search for a capitalist hero has thus led to no viable results, and there is little indication that it will be more successful in the future. For the stereotypes used by the popular novelists cannot sustain a character of real imaginative substance, and serious writers seem unable to take an interest in a system of values based on economic assumptions.

4

What Happened to the Antitrust Movement?

Notes on the Evolution of an American Creed

Richard Hofstadter

I

The antitrust movement is one of the faded passions of American reform, but historians have neglected to tell us very much about its fate. The writers of general history books deal with the antitrust issue in connection with the rise of the great corporations and the passage of the Sherman Act and then, again, in discussing antitrust sentiment in the Progressive era and the enactment of further regulatory laws. Most of them touch on it briefly once more, when they discuss the New Deal antitrust revival associated with Thurman Arnold and the T.N.E.C. Then, for the most part, they drop the subject. Presumably they drop it not because they imagine that antitrust has lost its role in our society, but rather because it is no longer the object of much public attention.

Although it may seem superficial of historians to be influenced by such a criterion, I have come to realize that in their neglect of this matter there is a certain self-protective wisdom at work. In our time, the issue of the regulation of monopoly and competition has acquired a complexity, both legal and economic, that the historian is ill-equipped to handle. It is much simpler for him to sweep the whole thing under the carpet. And in his willingness to do so lies one key to the disappearance of the antitrust issue from our politics. In this matter the historian too is a layman who shares the general public bafflement. He sympathizes with the common retreat from an issue that has become a maze of technical refinements in which specialists alone can find their way.

Perhaps the essence of the problem can be put this way: once the United States had an antitrust movement without antitrust prosecutions; in our time there have been antitrust prosecutions without an antitrust movement.

Like all such formulas, this one oversimplifies considerably, but it has the merit of putting in stark outline a puzzling episode in the history of reform. In 1890, when Congress passed the Sherman Act, many Congressmen believed that they were responding to an overwhelming public demand; it is the presence of this kind of influential and active sentiment that I mean, when I speak of a social movement. During the mid-nineties, when the depression made other issues more urgent, there was a brief lapse of interest in the "trust problem"; but then a new outburst of business consolidation between 1898 and 1904 quickened it into life again. During the Progressive era, strong public sentiment against big business made itself felt almost everywhere. Often a common hostility to big business was the one link that bound together a variety of interest groups whose views on most other issues diverged widely. The Progressive era, which culminated with the passage of the Clayton Act and the creation of the Federal Trade Commission in 1914, probably marks the high point of anti-big-business sentiment in our history.

But the early accomplishments of antitrust, hampered as it was by the courts and by administrative lassitudes, were slight. Historians have often made sport of the contrast between aspiration and performance, particularly of the reputation of Theodore Roosevelt as a trustbuster, which survived his repeated repudiations of the trustbusting philosophy. They have enjoyed pointing out that under his regime the Antitrust Division of the Justice Department sallied out against the combined might of the great corporations with a staff of five lawyers and four stenographers.

Roosevelt and his contemporaries witnessed the first of three phases in the history of antitrust. In the first, from about 1890 to 1914—the era of the founding fathers of antitrust—the opening steps were taken, in statutes and in the courts, to define what form the antitrust efforts of the federal government might take and to see how they would work. The second phase, lasting from the First World War to about 1937, might be called the era of neglect. Enforcement during the conservative 1920's was almost minimal, and in its opening years the New Deal actually suspended the antitrust laws to accommodate the N.R.A. codes. The present phase, from 1937 onward, is marked by a considerable revival, which stems from the New Deal's reactivation of the Antitrust Division and from the T.N.E.C. investigation. It is characterized by a sharp legal and administrative increase in antitrust activity. But this has taken place without any corresponding revival of public sentiment against big business, indeed in the face of a growing public acceptance of the large corporation. In this phase, antitrust concern has been confined to small groups of legal and economic specialists, who carry on their work without widespread public interest or support.

Whereas the first of these phases was characterized by tentative efforts at enforcement with nearly negligible results, and the second by minimal or token enforcement, the latest turn in antitrust is relatively vigorous. Here prosecutions may serve as a rough index. During all the years from 1891 to 1938, the government instituted an average of nine cases a year. The peak years in this half century were 1912 and 1913, with 29 and 27 prosecutions. For about 30 years after these dates the typical load was about a dozen cases, often considerably fewer, and the objects of prosecution were not often vital points in American industry. In 1940, with the Roosevelt-Arnold revitalization well under way, the number of cases jumped to 85—only two short of the number instituted during the entire first *two decades* of the Sherman Act. After that the number fluctuated, but stayed at a considerably higher level than before 1938.[1] In 1962 the Antitrust Division,

[1] On prosecutions to 1940 see Walton Hamilton and Irene Till, *Antitrust in Action*, T.N.E.C. Monograph No. 16 (Washington, 1940), esp. pp. 135–143; see also *United States versus Economic Concentration and Monopoly*, a Staff

employing 300 lawyers and working with a budget of $6,600,000, instituted 92 cases. Figures, of course, are crude, but a qualitative analysis of the legal victories of the antitrust revival would show that it has won decisions from the courts, particularly since 1940, that have amplified the possibility of enforcement. Despite the collapse of antitrust feeling both in the public at large and among liberal intellectuals, antitrust as a legal-administrative enterprise has been solidly institutionalized in the past quarter of a century. The antitrust enterprise thus appears to be a case of magical levitation, and it seems incumbent upon us to find out what is holding it up.

II

The antitrust movement and its legislation are characteristically and uniquely American. Perhaps this is attributable to the particularly flagrant form that monopoly took in America during the early years of its development. It may also be said that no other people has taken the principle of economic competition so earnestly as to try to underwrite it by statute, although in recent years some European countries have begun to show interest in the American approach to the subject, and we may see more of this in the future. The idea of competition as a means of social regulation—as an economic, political, and moral force—has grown stronger roots in the United States than elsewhere, partly because it has had little to compete with in the way of aristocratic, militaristic, or labor-socialist theories. Founded to some degree in the common-law tradition whose injunctions against restraint of trade proved an inadequate basis for the protection of competition, the antimonopoly tradition rested intellectually upon classical economic theory and upon the pluralism of American democratic thought.

But in America competition was more than a theory: it was a way of life and a creed. From its colonial beginnings through most of the nineteenth century, ours was overwhelmingly a

Report to the Monopoly Subcommittee on Small Business, House of Representatives (Washington, 1946), pp. 276–289.

nation of farmers and small-town entrepreneurs—ambitious, mobile, optimistic, speculative, antiauthoritarian, egalitarian, and competitive. As time went on, Americans came to take it for granted that property would be widely diffused, that economic and political power would be decentralized. The fury with which they could be mobilized against any institution that even appeared to violate these expectations by posing a threat of monopoly was manifest in the irrational assault on the Bank of the United States during Jackson's presidency. Their most respected thinkers habitually assured them that the order of society that they enjoyed was God-ordained or natural, and they probably thought it would last forever.

Then, with extraordinary rapidity as historical time is reckoned, that order was overwhelmed by the giant corporation. In the last three decades of the nineteenth century a wholly new economic order came into being. An American born in 1828, the year of Jackson's election, came of age in a society in which the old small-enterprise economy, however dynamic and expansive, had kept its fundamental pattern more or less intact. But in his mature years he would have watched that economy fast becoming obsolete, and if he lived as late as 1904, he would have seen industry concentrated to a degree unthinkable even during most of his adult life. This economic transformation happened so fast that the mind could not easily absorb it. An entire people could hardly be expected to cease overnight to dream the dream of the small entrepreneur. In 1900 the problem of big business and the threat of monopoly were still so new that it was hard to get one's bearings. Bigness had come with such a rush that its momentum seemed irresistible. No one knew when or how it could be stopped.

It is hardly surprising that the men of the first antitrust generation made some frightening projections into the future. A nation that had gone so fast from competitive small enterprise to corporate giantism might readily develop with equal speed from corporate giantism to a system of monopolistic tyranny. Hence, discussions of big business in the last decades of the nineteenth and the opening decade of the twentieth century are full of anxious prognostications, most of them plausible enough at the time; however, hardly any of them have been realized. In 1890 and even in 1914, bigness had not yet been domesticated either as a force in the economic world or as a factor in the American imagination.

Since it had been widely assumed that competition, being "natural," would be largely self-perpetuating, the classical theory had not reckoned with the possible necessity of underwriting competition by statute. But as soon as it became clear that the common-law tradition against restraints on trade had ceased to have any force and that state laws on the subject were altogether inadequate to the purpose, the demand arose for federal action. George Gunton thought in 1888 that "the public mind has begun to assume a state of apprehension almost amounting to alarm," and that the social atmosphere was "surcharged with an indefinite but almost inexpressible fear of trusts." [2] Senator Sherman warned his colleagues that "the popular mind is agitated with problems that may disturb the social order," singling out inequities of wealth and the formation of combinations of capital so great that they threatened to produce "a trust for every production and a master to fix the price for every necessity of life." Congress must heed the appeal of the voters, he said, "or be ready for the socialist, the communist, and the nihilist. Society is now disturbed by forces never felt before." [3] Historians, like contemporaries, have differed as to how imperative the demand for federal action was. In a careful survey of articulate opinion on the "trust" problem in 1890, Hans B. Thorelli concludes that public demand, though perhaps less than an irresistible tide, was too strong to be ignored by the politicians.

Historians have often doubted that the Congress of 1890 meant the Sherman Act to be a serious threat to trusts and have suggested that it was cynically offering a sop to public sentiment.

[2] Quoted by G. W. Stocking and M. W. Watkins, *Monopoly and Free Enterprise,* Twentieth Century Fund, New York, 1951, p. 257.

[3] *Congressional Record,* 51st Cong., 1st sess. (March 21, 1890), p. 2460. "Although this body is always conservative," Sherman said hopefully, "yet, whatever may be said of it, it has always been ready to preserve not only popular rights in their broad sense, but the rights of individuals as against associated and corporate wealth and power."

The plutocratic character of that Congress lends some credence to this view, as does the observation of Senator Orville Platt, at one point in the debate, that the conduct of the Senate during the previous days was "not in the line of honest preparation of a bill to prohibit and punish trusts" but was merely an effort "to get some bill headed 'A bill to punish trusts' with which to go to the country." [4] These circumstances of its origins have helped to confirm many historians in their suspicion that antitrust was, from beginning to end, only a charade.

But there is also reason to believe, on the contrary, that most Congressmen thought of the competitive order in business as being the cornerstone of the whole democratic way of life and that they thought of themselves as making the first tentative step in formulating a policy for the control of trusts, which, if it could be put on sound constitutional footing, might serve as the basis for litigation and perhaps subsequent statutory changes. Admittedly, they were breaking new ground. Senator Hoar said that Congress was entering a wholly new field of legislation and that "the opinions of Senators themselves, of able and learned and experienced lawmakers, were exceedingly crude in this matter." [5]

It is true, of course, that Congress emerged with a statute written in the most general terms, which for many years was emasculated by judicial decisions and administrative lethargy. But it is very likely that, with its broadly worded prohibition of conspiracies in restraint of trade and of efforts to monopolize, Congress was attempting to lay down a declaration of policy that would serve as a guide to future action in much the same flexible way as the Constitution itself had served the country after 1787. Many Congressmen doubtless believed that the self-enforcing fea-

[4] Hans B. Thorelli, *The Federal Antitrust Policy*, Johns Hopkins, Baltimore, 1955, p. 198. There is a mass of information about the antimonopoly aspects of the American tradition in Arthur P. Dudden's unpublished doctoral dissertation, *Antimonopolism, 1865–1890*, Michigan University, 1950. On contemporary views, see also Sanford D. Gordon, Attitudes towards Trusts prior to the Sherman Act, *Southern Economic Journal*, XXX (October 1963), pp. 156–167.

[5] *Congressional Record*, 51st Cong., 1st sess. (April 8, 1890), p. 3146.

tures of the law would be far more effective than they actually
were—that is, that the triple-damage suits authorized for victims
of restraints of trade would cause businessmen themselves to
carry on a good deal of the policing of the economy. Perhaps
the problem confronting Congress can be reconstructed with
greater sympathy if we try to imagine whether a drastically different law would have been passed by a wholly populistic and
militantly anti-big-business Congress, and whether such a law
could have been expected to receive a more successful implemen-
tation than the Sherman Act in the hands of the subsequent
administrative officers and judges.

One may say with reasonable assurance that the confusion of
Congress over the economic significance of antitrust mirrored a
more general confusion in American society. The goals of antitrust may be classified under three headings. The first were economic. The classical model of competition confirmed the belief
that the maximum of economic efficiency would be prompted by
competition, and at least some members of Congress must have
been under the spell of this intellectually elegant model, insofar
as they were able to formulate their economic intentions in any
abstract terms. The second class of goals was political; the antitrust principle was intended to block private accumulations of
power and protect democratic government. The third was social
and moral; the competitive process was believed to be a kind of
disciplinary machinery for the development of character, and the
competitiveness of the people—the fundamental stimulus to
national morale—was felt to need protection.

Among the three, the economic goal was the most cluttered
with uncertainties, so much so that it seems to be no exaggeration
to regard antitrust as being essentially a political rather than an
economic enterprise.[6]   A fundamental difficulty in economic

[6] Hans B. Thorelli, after examining carefully the Congressional debates
over the Sherman Act, concludes, p. 227, that "The Sherman Act is not to be
viewed exclusively as an expression of economic policy," and that in safe-
guarding the rights of the common man in business it "embodies what is to
be characterized as an eminently 'social' purpose." Thorelli believes that
Sherman and many of his contemporaries in Congress saw the legislation as
"an important means of achieving freedom from corruption and maintaining freedom of independent thinking in political life."

thought, troubling from the very start, arose over the relative claims of combination and competition. The Sherman Act was framed and debated in the preexpert era. Economists as a professional group were not directly consulted by the legislators. But even if they had been, they would have given mixed and uncertain advice. A few years earlier the American Economic Association had been founded by men in revolt against the classical tradition and laissez-faire doctrines, although, of course, many economists of the older school were still ensconced in universities and colleges. Economists were hardly strangers to the argument that the competitive order, far from being fixed in a permanent, beneficent, self-sustaining equilibrium, might have a strong tendency toward self-liquidation. One of the early historicists, E. Benjamin Andrews, argued in 1893 that laissez-faire was no more than a systematized expression of anarchy, and warned, the following year:

> Bills have been brought before half the legislatures of the Union to free competition by making trade syndicates absolutely illegal. To my mind there is no question that such legislation will be vain. The age of competition as we have known it is gone forever. As well try to waken the dead.[7]

The more influential voice of Richard Ely was also raised in protest against the ideal of pure competition. He was among those who insisted that size should not be equated with monopoly, and long before Thurman Arnold he held that antitrust legislation was not only futile but actually encouraging to monopoly, because it caused business leaders to replace "soft" combinations by "hard" combinations in the form of mergers.[8]

No consensus was to be had on the proper line of governmental action on trusts or on the kind of law Congress should pass. Nearly all economists believed that attempts simply to prohibit combinations by law would be futile. There was a growing disposition to consider that both competition and combination needed some measure of control and that neither could be elimi-

[7] Thorelli, *op. cit.*, pp. 112n, 316.
[8] *Ibid.*, pp. 314–315.

nated by law. In this sense, as William Letwin has pointed out, the counsel that was available from the economists, however much attended to or ignored, shared the ambiguity that the legislators themselves could feel as lawyers:

> The economists thought that both competition and combination should play their parts in the economy. The lawyers saw that the common law permitted combination in some instances and prohibited it in others. Congressmen seized on this hidden agreement, and set out to construct a statute which by the use of common law principles would eliminate excesses but allow "healthy" competition and combination to flourish side by side.[9]

If one gives due regard to the uncertainties of the matter and to the improbability that any attempt at a quick solution would be effective, one may arrive at a more charitable judgment of the Congress of 1890. Its members were probably trying to lay down general guidelines by means of which their successors might evolve a policy that would give society the advantages of both competition and combination. As Senator Sherman said, "All that we, as lawmakers, can do is to declare general principles." [10] These principles could hardly have been enunciated in more sweeping language than that used in the Sherman Act. Presumably, many Congressmen hoped that the courts would find a way of striking at the notoriously unfair methods of competition that had already been used to build such companies as Standard Oil and the National Cash Register Company, without barring useful consolidations or even such restrictive agreements as were intended to eliminate intolerably rigorous competition.

This original uncertainty about the economic rationale for antitrust continued to haunt well-intentioned progressives in the years before the First World War. The vagueness and inconsistency so often expressed by intelligent and relatively candid political leaders during this era must be taken as a reflection not

[9] William Letwin, Congress and the Sherman Antitrust Law, 1887–1890, *University of Chicago Law Review*, XXIII (Winter 1956), p. 247.

[10] *Congressional Record*, 51st Cong., 1st sess. (March 21, 1890), p. 2460. Sherman was here conceding the difficulty of defining in law the precise difference between legal and illegal combinations, and expressing a preference for leaving such decisions to the courts in particular cases.

on the calibre of the leadership but rather on the intrinsic difficulty of the problem.

Theodore Roosevelt represents, on this count, a maximum of shrewdness combined with a minimum of anxiety. With the exception of railroad regulation, Roosevelt was not profoundly interested in the economic issues that agitated the American public during his presidency; indeed, he was quite candid in confessing his reluctance to tackle them head-on. When in difficulties, as in 1907, he was disposed to trust to the judgment and the political and financial leadership of the conservatives in the Senate or the economic powers in Wall Street. However, he saw the trust problem as something that must be dealt with on the political level; public concern about it was too urgent to be ignored. He understood how important it was to assure the public that the government of the United States had the will and the power to assert its authority over large corporations. Accordingly, his antitrust prosecutions, although few, were in some cases appropriately spectacular. When he assessed the significance of the Northern Securities Case, he did not say that it would open the way to a general assault on bigness, but rather that it was important for showing that "the most powerful men in this country were held to accountability before the law." His fundamental solution for the problem—that bigness must be accepted as a part of the modern industrial and social order, and that its behavior should be subjected to administrative control under full publicity—comes somewhat closer than the views of most of his political contemporaries to anticipating the future course of antitrust procedure.

Roosevelt was accompanied, or perhaps followed, by a school of liberal publicists—among them Charles R. Van Hise, Herbert Croly, and Walter Lippmann—who accepted his conviction that the Sherman Act philosophy was the product of what he called a "sincere rural Toryism" long since outgrown. Lippmann, in one of the most penetrating attacks on the antitrust philosophy, characterized it as the philosophy of "a nation of villagers." This school of Progressives saw the Western world as entering upon a new era of organization and specialization for which the old competitive philosophy was hopelessly retrograde. Some of them, notably Croly and Van Hise, also saw small-scale business as inadequate to the task of competing in the world's markets, which they believed to be a necessity of the American situation. In retrospect, they appear more sophisticated and prophetic than those who put great stock in the Sherman Act as a force for actual dissolution. They foresaw the decline of antitrust as a movement, and in some instances recognized that if the Sherman Act persisted it would be as a basis for occasional *ad hoc* regulatory suits rather than as an instrument for dismantling the corporate economy.

Woodrow Wilson spoke more feelingly for the "rural Toryism" and the village democracy, which seem to have been at the center of popular antitrust feeling; but by the same token he illustrated more clearly than Roosevelt their intellectual difficulties. Speaking in the campaign of 1912, which afforded a full-dress display of the differences between the two schools of thought on trusts, he asserted that he too was not against size as such. He was all for bigness as an inevitable and natural growth, whenever it was the outcome of superior efficiency. But he was against "the trusts," which had grown out of illicit competition. He was never very successful, however, in explaining why a business that had become large through legitimate methods might not become just as menacing to competition as one that had grown large through illicit competition. His statement, "I am for big business and I am against the trusts," seems hardly more than an attempt to evade the argument that there is a self-liquidating threat inherent in competition.[11]

[11] For Woodrow Wilson's position on monopoly, see *The New Freedom,* Doubleday-Page, New York, 1913, pp. 163–222. William Diamond, in *The Economic Thought of Woodrow Wilson,* Johns Hopkins, Baltimore, 1943, makes it clear that in his earlier years Wilson had been committed to the evolutionist acceptance of size but became more devoted to the competitive principle as he came before the public eye and as he accepted the advice of Brandeis. By 1913 he seems to have been persuaded that dissolution was an essential tactic. "Real dissolution in the case of the trusts is the only thing we can be satisfied with," he wrote privately, and he indicated that this was part of a program necessary "to satisfy the conscience of the country." *Ibid.,* p. 112.

III

The political and social arguments against monopoly were pressed with greater clarity than the economic argument and with hardly less fervor.   Antitrust must be understood as the political judgment of a nation whose leaders had always shown a keen awareness of the economic foundations of politics.   In this respect, the Sherman Act was simply another manifestation of an enduring American suspicion of concentrated power.   From the pre-Revolutionary tracts through the Declaration of Independence and *The Federalist* to the writings of the states' rights advocates, and beyond it into the era of the antimonopoly writers and the Populists, there had been a perennial quest for a way of dividing, diffusing, and checking power and preventing its exercise by a single interest or by a consolidated group of interests at a single center.   Hence, the political impulse behind the Sherman Act was clearer and more articulate than the economic theory.   Men who used the vaguest language when they talked about "the trusts" and monopolies, who had not thought through the distinction between size itself and monopolistic practices, who had found no way of showing how much competition was necessary for efficiency, who could not in every case say what competitive acts they thought were fair or unfair, or who could not state a rational program that reconciled their acceptance of size with their desire for competition, were reasonably clear about what it was that they were trying to avoid: they wanted to keep concentrated private power from destroying democratic government.

One of the glories of the competitive model had been that it purported to solve the question of market power by denying any particular location to it.   The decisions of the market were beautifully impersonal, since they were only the averagings of the decisions of thousands of individuals, none of whom enjoyed any decisive power.   The market mechanism suggested that power was not really exercised by anyone.   With the perfect impersonality of Adam Smith's "invisible hand," the market made decisions that ought not be vested in the hands of any particular man or body of men. Hence, the market mechanism met the desire for the diffusion of power and seemed to be the perfect economic counterpart of American democratic pluralism.

Where power *must* be exercised, it was agreed that it should be located in governmental and not in private hands. But the state governments were inadequate; in sheer mass, business enterprises already overshadowed them. Charles William Eliot pointed out as early as 1888 that the large corporations, considered as units of economic organization, had already begun to tower over the states. A Boston railroad company, for example, employed 18,000 persons and had gross receipts of about $40,000,000 a year, as compared with the Commonwealth of Massachusetts, which employed 6,000 and had receipts of $7,000,000.[12] Even individually, some corporations were big enough to dominate state governments, and if they should combine among themselves, they might come to dominate the federal government as well.

The existence of the industrial combinations and the threat that under one auspice or another—perhaps that of the investment bankers—there would come about someday a combination of the combinations that would be stronger than civil government itself provoked a fear that haunted the minds of the writers of the industrial era, including many whose social views were as conservative as Eliot's. The fundamental fear of private power was well put by William Jennings Bryan, in a speech delivered at the Chicago Conference on Trusts in 1899:

> I do not divide monopolies in private hands into good monopolies and bad monopolies. There is no good monopoly in private hands. There can be no good monopoly in private hands until the Almighty

[12] C. Eliot, The Working of the American Democracy, *American Contributions to Civilization*, Century, New York, 1907, pp. 85–86. Three-quarters of a century later the T.N.E.C. found that, as economic units, only ten states had assets greater than the two largest corporations, and that more than half the states were completely overshadowed in size by private businesses. *Final Report and Recommendations*, pp. 676–677; David Lynch, *The Concentration of Economic Power*, Columbia University Press, New York, 1946, pp. 112–113.

sends us angels to preside over the monopoly. There may be a despot who is better than another despot, but there is no good despotism.[13]

And the general sense that the dire economic and political consequences of monopoly were as one was incorporated in the Democratic platform of 1900:

> Private monopolies are indefensible and intolerable. . . . They are the most efficient means yet devised for appropriating the fruits of industry to the benefit of the few at the expense of the many, and unless their insatiate greed is checked, all wealth will be aggregated in a few hands and the Republic destroyed.[14]

The most articulate expression of the Progressives' case against the political power of monopoly was made by Woodrow Wilson in 1912. It was the burden of his case, as against T. R., that once the existence of large-scale combinations is accepted, their regulation by government becomes impossible, because the political power of business combination will be great enough to nullify all attempts at its control. Wilson played artfully on the fears and suspicions of the small entrepreneurs. Even some very powerful men, he said, knew that "there is a power somewhere so organized, so subtle, so watchful, so interlocked, so complete, so pervasive, that they had better not speak above their breath when they speak in condemnation of it. . . . They know that somewhere, by somebody, the development of industry is being controlled." [15] He pictured concentrated capital as being already in control of the government: "The masters of the government of the United States are the combined capitalists and manufacturers of the United States. . . . The government of the United States at present is a foster-child of the special interests." [16]

This would have to be the state of affairs until the combinations were not only unseated by the people, but were also dissolved—until "this colossal 'community of interest'" was dis-

---

[13] Thorelli, *op. cit.*, p. 336.

[14] Kirk H. Porter and Donald B. Johnson, *National Party Platforms*, University of Illinois Press, Urbana, Ill., 1956, p. 114.

[15] Wilson, *op. cit.*, pp. 14, 62.

[16] *Ibid.*, pp. 57–58.

entangled. It was a thing that the laws must "pull apart, and gently, but firmly and persistently dissect." Otherwise, under Roosevelt's plan for accepting and regulating monopolies, there would only be a union between monopoly and government: "If the government controlled by the monopolies in its turn controls the monopolies, the partnership is finally consummated." "If monopoly persists, monopoly will always sit at the helm of the government. I do not expect to see monopoly restrain itself. If there are men in this country big enough to own the government of the United States, they are going to own it." [17]

The third objective of antitrust action, hardly less important than the others, was psychological and moral. It sprang from the conviction that competition has a disciplinary value for character, quite aside from its strictly economic uses. America was thought to have been made possible by the particular type of character that was forged by competitive individualism, a type that had flourished in the United States because competitive opportunities had been so widespread that alert men could hardly fail to see them, to grasp and use them, and, hence, to be shaped by them. The American male character was believed to have been quickened and given discipline by the sight and pursuit of opportunity. For this process to take place it was important that business be carried on fairly—the sporting vocabulary was never far below the surface—and that newcomers be able to enter the game as entrepreneurs on reasonably open terms.

The significance of this faith that competition could be relied upon to form character can be fully grasped only if we bear in mind the Protestant background of our economic thinking. Economists themselves had not been in the habit of analyzing economic relationships in purely mechanical and secular terms, and what may be said of them on this count can be said with greater force about laymen, when they thought about economic issues. Behind the American way of thinking there lay a long Protestant tradition, which tended to identify economic forces with religious and moral forces and which regarded economic

[17] *Ibid.*, pp. 118, 207, 286. For a later statement of this view see the dissenting opinion of Mr. Justice Douglas in *U. S. v. Columbia Steel Co.*, 334 U. S. 495 (1948).

processes from the standpoint of their contribution to the discipline and development of character.   The economic order was not merely an apparatus for the production of goods and services; it was a set of rules for forging good conduct.   Everyone is familiar, I believe, with the proposition that some of the concepts of classical economics were shaped under the influence of a kind of prudential morality in which savings and abstinence were not merely instruments of economic analysis but moral sanctions.   In our time we have heard conservatives frankly condemn government fiscal policy that deviates from the prudential rules suitable to a family budget by appealing to the Puritan tradition.   Such critics are the legitimate heirs of the men of the nineteenth and early twentieth centuries, who saw the protection of competition and its incentives as a safeguard of national morale, as a means for mobilizing and rewarding the industrious and the prudent and for penalizing those whom William Graham Sumner called "the poor and the weak, the negligent, shiftless, inefficient, silly, and imprudent . . . the idle, intemperate, and vicious." [18]

Here again one looks to Woodrow Wilson for the most articulate expression of this emphasis on the economic foundations of character and especially to the masterful speeches of 1912 in which he expressed his concern for "the beginner," "the man with only a little capital," "the man on the make," upon whose genius he thought the country had always been built.   "The treasury of America," he argued, "lies in those ambitions, those energies, that cannot be restricted to a special favored class."   It rests upon the inventiveness and the energy of "unknown men" and would lose its force, if the economic order ceased to stimulate such inventiveness and energy.   It was possible, he hinted, that under large-scale organization the country would turn its back on its past, which he evoked in poignant terms:

. . . the ancient time when America lay in every hamlet, when America was to be seen in every fair valley, when America displayed her great forces on the broad prairies, ran her fine fires of enterprise up over the mountainsides and down into the bowels of the earth, and eager men

[18] William Graham Sumner, *What Social Classes Owe to Each Other,* 1883 Edition, Yale University Press, New Haven, Conn., 1925, p. 21.

were everywhere captains of industry, not employees; not looking to a distant city to find out what they might do, but looking about among their neighbors, finding credit according to their character, not according to their connections, finding credit in proportion to what was known to be in them and behind them, not in proportion to the securities they held that were approved where they were not known.[19]

The prospect that these "fine fires of enterprise" were about to be quenched suggested that the old kind of character would be destroyed, that the old America was about to die—a reason even more imperative than mere industrial efficiency for seeking out the possibilities of antitrust action.

The inherited belief that small property and small business opportunity have forged the American character, which might well lose its form without the discipline imposed by a particular variety of entrepreneurial competition, is one that has never died out. Near the end of World War II the Small Business Committee of the Senate put this faith clearly when it said that the pursuit of opportunity by the small business owner

. . . has been a great motive force among our people. It stimulates expression of the fundamental virtues of thrift, industry, intelligence, schooling, home ties, and family pride—in short, those fireside virtues which have counted for so much in developing our strength and character.[20]

The preservation of small business opportunities, as a member of the S.E.C. put it in 1945, is more important than any economic goal; it is "a goal which transcends economic and political forms and processes as such, and remains fundamentally concerned with the character of the men and women who comprise the nation." [21]

IV

There are two salient differences between the problem of bigness as it was perceived about sixty years ago and as it is per-

[19] Wilson, *op. cit.*, pp. 18–19.

[20] Quoted in John H. Bunzel, *The American Small Businessman*, Knopf, New York, 1962, p. 84.

[21] Rudolph L. Weissman, *Small Business and Venture Capital*, Harper, New York, 1945, p. 164.

ceived now; the first is that it is no longer a new problem, and the second is that the economy has performed in a way hardly dreamed of before World War II. In 1964 we are as remote in time from the passage of the Sherman Act as the men of 1864 were from the first term of George Washington. The public has had almost three-quarters of a century of experience in living with big business, and analysts of the big business problem no longer make the same frightening projections as to its future dangers that could be made with entire plausibility sixty or seventy years ago. At the same time, the public is hardly unaware that a great rise in mass standards of living has occurred during the period in which the economy has been dominated by the big corporation. Whatever else may be said against bigness, the conception of monopolistic industry as a kind of gigantic, swelling leech on the body of an increasingly deprived and impoverished society has largely disappeared.

About the change in public attitudes from those prevailing sixty years ago we can only make an educated guess. Today we can check our impressions of the public mind against opinion polls; for the earlier era we have impressions alone. But it is very difficult for anyone who reads widely in the political literature of the period 1890–1914 to believe that public concern today over big business has anything like the sense of urgency that it had then. In 1951 the Institute of Social Research of the University of Michigan published the results of an illuminating survey, *Big Business as the People See It.* Its findings show some residues of the old popular suspicion of bigness, but the noteworthy thing is public acceptance. Americans have always had to balance their love of bigness and efficiency against their fear of power and their regard for individualism and competition. The survey indicates that this ambivalence has been largely resolved in favor of the big business organization.

A quarter of the population, as represented in the Institute's national sample, showed some concern over big business and an awareness that it had an important effect on their lives. But a substantial majority reacted favorably to big business. Asked to give a general characterization of its social effects, the respondents answered as follows:

The good things outweigh the bad things   76%
They seem about equal   2%
The bad things outweigh the good things   10%
Don't know   5%
Confused; evaluation not ascertainable   7%
    ——
    100%

Plainly, big business was not a scare word to the public at large. Eighty-four per cent of those polled reacted without apparent emotion to the questions, and only a small minority reacted unfavorably. Questioned on particulars, respondents spoke with especial favor of the productive powers of big business and its ability to give jobs and keep prices down. The most critical responses about big business dealt mainly with its effect on "the little man" and the destruction of competition. Very little concern was expressed about the power of big business over its workers (it is commonly regarded as a good employer), and surprisingly little about its influence on government.

Whereas fifty years before, fear of an indefinitely continued increase in the political power of big business was commonplace, the typical expectation expressed in the poll of 1951 was that the power of big business would decline, and properly so. As in the Progressive era, there was a strong preference for a balance of power and a conviction that wherever there must be a clear preponderance of power it should rest in governmental and not private hands. But the existing state of business power was not widely considered to be dangerous. In fact, big business power was regarded as being third in rank among five forces—behind national government and labor unions and ahead of state governments and smaller business. Stronger feeling was shown against labor unions than against big business. Although there was a fraction of the public that saw big business as more powerful than labor unions and would have liked to see the situation reversed, there was a fraction almost twice as large that saw the unions as more powerful and preferred to see the situation reversed.[22]

[22] Burton R. Fisher and Stephen B. Withey, *Big Business as the People See It,* Survey Research Center, University of Michigan, Ann Arbor, 1951, *passim.*

The findings of the Michigan group were not widely at variance with those of Elmo Roper, who a few years earlier had collated the responses of the public over a span of 15 years to questions about business. Roper found that "the public has mixed feelings about big business. There is pride over the achievements of big business but some apprehension over the possible abuses of power inherent in big business." The public was disposed to want a watchdog set upon the amoral and greedy elements in business, but only about a fourth of the respondents were found to believe that the disadvantages of bigness overshadow whatever advantages there might be.[23]

To what can we attribute this public acceptance of big business? Not much, I believe, to the efforts that big businessmen have made to cultivate a favorable "image" for the large corporation. As the fate of the postwar campaign to sell "free enterprise" suggests, such efforts can miscarry badly when they represent nothing more than an attempt to make the public take seriously the blather with which business sometimes comforts itself.[24] What has really made bigness palatable more than anything else is the remarkable performance of the economy since the beginning of World War II. Something too must be credited to the emergence of countervailing bigness in government and labor, whose effects on public attitudes emerge clearly from the Michigan survey. Moreover, anyone who is aware of the historical circumstances under which hostility to big business flourished must be aware that big business has not lived up to the horrifying billing that it got in the age of the muckrakers. It is not merely that no business today treats competitors as they were treated in the early days of the National Cash Register Company or Standard Oil. What is important is that a whole range of fears, expressed in the Progressive generation and based largely upon preoccupation with an unknown future, has vanished. We now live in that future, and although it has fears of its own—

[23] Elmo Roper, The Public Looks at Business, *Harvard Business Review*, XXVII (March 1949), pp. 165–174.

[24] William H. Whyte, Jr., is eloquent on the failure of one such campaign in *Is Anybody Listening?*, Simon and Schuster, New York, 1952.

nightmarish beyond anything anticipated in the days of Bryan and Wilson—they are of a wholly different origin. Probably the worst of the Populist-Progressive nightmares was the notion, expressed in the Pujo Committee's inquiry, in Brandeis's *Other People's Money,* in Wilson's speeches, and in Jack London's *The Iron Heel,* of the formation, under the auspices of the investment bankers, of a giant syndicate, a combination of the combinations, which would rule the country with a tyrannical grip. The self-financing character of the great corporations, the survival of competition in investment banking, and the failure of investment banking to remain a power of the first order after the crash of 1929 have set this spectre to rest.

If no sinister central syndicate had to be feared, it did at least seem reasonable at the turn of the century to anticipate a steady, growing concentration of industry that would eventually deprive the country of every advantage of competition. And here, insofar as the antitrust enterprise was directed against size itself or against concentration, it was beaten before it ever got started; American industry was already highly concentrated in 1904, when T. R. was boasting about the lessons of the Northern Securities Case. But insofar as the Progressives were worried about what the economists later came to call "workable competition" in industry, they might well have been reassured as time went on. The investigations of such economists as M. A. Adelman, G. Warren Nutter, and George J. Stigler have cast considerable doubt on the idea that either the scope of monopoly or the degree of concentration has, in fact, grown since the beginning of the century. "The extent of concentration," Adelman concluded in an important study, "shows no tendency to grow, and it may possibly be declining. Any tendency either way, if it does exist, must be at the pace of a glacial drift." [25] Measuring monopoly

[25] M. A. Adelman, The Measurement of Industrial Concentration, *Review of Economics and Statistics,* XXXIII (November 1951), pp. 269–296. See also the discussion by Adelman and others, *ibid.,* XXXIV (May 1952), pp. 156 ff.; G. Warren Nutter, *The Extent of Enterprise Monopoly in the United States, 1899–1939,* University of Chicago Press, Chicago, 1951; and George J. Stigler, *Five Lectures on Economic Problems,* Longmans, London, 1949, pp. 46–65.

is an undertaking of considerable complexity, and the issues are controversial. But it is at least safe to say that no one who has due regard for the difficulties of the problem can any longer raise alarmist cries about the rapid growth of monopoly without flying in the face of much formidable testimony.

Another cause of concern, very real to many men in the Progressive era and rather quaint from today's perspective, had to do with the progress of industry. "Monopoly," warned Wilson in 1912, "always checks development, weighs down natural prosperity, pulls against natural advance." In the past, he said, competitive America had produced or developed the steamboat, the cotton gin, the sewing machine, the reaper, the typewriter, the electric light, and other great inventions, but the day was at hand when monopoly might end all this. "Do you know, have you had occasion to learn, that there is no hospitality for invention nowadays? There is no encouragement for you to set your wits at work. . . . The instinct of monopoly is against novelty, the tendency of monopoly is to keep in use the old thing, made in the old way. . . ." Only a restoration of freedom could unleash American inventiveness again: "Who can say what patents now lying, unrealized, in secret drawers and pigeonholes, will come to light, or what new inventions will astonish and bless us, when freedom is restored?" [26] To two generations that since 1912 have been astonished and blessed almost to death by inventions, such rhetoric can no longer be alarming or inspiring; it is merely a curiosity. Today the public needs no persuading that it is the large corporations, with their programs of research, that are technologically progressive. As Galbraith has remarked, the showpieces of American industrial progress are, in the main, those dominated by a handful of large firms, and "the foreign visitor, brought to the United States by the Economic Cooperation Ad-

---

However, on the identity of the largest firms and the mobility of firms into positions of leadership, see Norman R. Collins and Lee E. Preston, The Size Structure of the Largest Industrial Firms, *American Economic Review,* LI (December 1961), pp. 986–1003. Fritz Machlup, *The Political Economy of Monopoly,* Johns Hopkins, Baltimore, 1952, pp. 469–528, is instructive on the difficulties of the subject.

[26] Wilson, *op. cit.,* pp. 265–266, 270.

ministration, visits the same firms as do attorneys of the Department of Justice in their search for monopoly." [27]

Another typical fear expressed in Progressive writing was that the possibility of individual advancement would be frozen out, that the upward social mobility that had refreshed and inspired American development in the past would come to an end, when the business of the country was fully dominated by the large corporation. I know of no very certain information on how the American public regards the prospects for social mobility today, although our concerted scramble for educational position and advantage suggests that the middle-class public and even much of the working-class public are rather well aware that mobility still exists; they are also aware of the mechanisms through which it can be pursued. What can be said with greater confidence is that informed observers no longer speak so glibly of the decline of mobility or opportunity.

Indeed, there is strong evidence that the opportunity of middle- or lower-class men to rise to top positions in business has somewhat increased over what it was fifty or sixty years ago,[28] and there is some reason to believe that the increase, or at least the persistence, of occupational opportunity has, in fact, impressed itself on the public mind. In fact, the modern corporation has proved to be a better medium for social mobility and opportunity than the old system of individual and family entrepreneurship, whose openness in this respect was always much exaggerated. Oddly enough, the concentration of capital and the divorce of ownership from the entrepreneurial function may prove in the long run to be more conducive to the lowering of social tensions and to political stability than diffused ownership.[29] The ways of

[27] John Kenneth Galbraith, *American Capitalism*, Houghton Mifflin, Boston, 1952, p. 96; cf. Joseph A. Schumpeter, *Capitalism, Socialism, and Democracy*, Third Edition, Harper, New York, 1947, pp. 81–82.

[28] For a good review of the relevant findings, see Seymour M. Lipset and Reinhard Bendix, *Social Mobility in Industrial Society*, University of California Press, Berkeley and Los Angeles, 1960, Chapter 3.

[29] For a shrewd and heretical statement on the political and social effects of the large corporation, see M. A. Adelman, Some Aspects of Corporate Enterprise, in Ralph Freeman, ed., *Postwar Economic Trends in the United States*, Harpers, New York, 1960, pp. 289–308.

achieving occupational advancement and economic success have changed; individual entrepreneurship is a much less sure and satisfactory path as compared with bureaucratic careers. The acquisition of specialized skills has become more important, and with it the seizure and exploitation of educational opportunities.

I do not mean to suggest that the old ideal of self-employment or the old confidence in the entrepreneurial path to success has been entirely abandoned in favor of the bureaucratic career. The incidence of self-employment and the population that actually lives by the competitive ideal have shrunk very considerably in the three-quarters of a century since the Sherman Act; but most of this is attributable to the numerical decline of family farmers, who in 1890 still comprised nearly half the population and today comprise about a tenth. The farmers, with their contemporary dependence on subsidies and governmentally administered prices, can hardly be looked upon any more as vigorous exponents of the competitive way of life. But the dream of self-employment that dominated the agrarian-entrepreneurial society of the nineteenth century is still alive. It has been estimated that about 20 to 30 per cent of the American working force has been at some time or another self-employed.[30] The growth of small businesses over the past dozen years or so has roughly kept pace with the growth of the adult population, and the aspirations of small business have been institutionalized in Senate and House committees as well as in some antitrust activities.

But although small business holds its place as a segment of the economy itself, its role as a sector of society committed to the entrepreneurial ideal has declined. Small business can no longer be idealized for its independence and hardihood or its devotion to competitive principles. It, too, looks to government intervention for sustenance, whether in the form of resale price maintenance, anti-chain-store legislation, or the Small Business Administration. Small business, which used to be, as one writer has put it,[31] "a symbol of opportunity, enterprise, innovation, and achievement" and of "an independent way of life," has been

---

[30] Lipset and Bendix, *op. cit.*, pp. 102–103.

[31] Theodore O. Yntema, in the Foreword to A. D. H. Kaplan, *Small Business: Its Place and Problems*, McGraw-Hill, New York, 1948, p. vii.

driven largely into the marginal areas of economic life, where it often tries to maintain itself by waging its own assaults upon the competitive principle. Various segments of small business, in their pressure for support for the Robinson-Patman Act of 1936 and the Miller-Tydings Amendment of 1937, have shown how quickly they can be rallied against competition, when it impinges upon their own interests. Vigorous advocates of the Sherman and Clayton Acts where big business is affected, they turn their backs on competitive virility when it suits their purposes. If there is anything rarer than a small businessman who will question the merits of competition, it is one who can understand and abide competition when it really afflicts him.[32]

Not only can the small businessman not purport, in the eyes of any well-informed observer, to be a vigorous and consistent exemplar of the competitive ideal; he can no longer be idealized by progressive-minded men from other walks of life, as he could, say, in the era when Woodrow Wilson waxed rhapsodical about the new men out of "unknown homes" who really made America. In the United States and elsewhere, liberal intellectuals now cock a suspicious eye at him, if not as a potential stronghold of support for fascist movements, at least as the backbone of the reactionary wing of the Republican party. An occasional big business leader may stand out for his enlightenment and urbanity, as compared with the small businessman, who more often than not proves to be a refractory antiunion employer, a parochial and archaic opponent of liberal ideas, a supporter of vigilante groups and of right-wing cranks.[33] As a figure in our economic society, the small businessman still plays a part of some considerable importance, but as a partner in the American liberal coalition, he has all but disappeared, and with him has gone much of the pristine antibigness feeling of the Progressive tradition.

Still, the conviction that American democracy will survive only if small business enterprise survives to sustain the American char-

[32] For an amusing illustration of this incomprehension of competition, see the testimony before the T.N.E.C. quoted in David Lynch, *op. cit.*, pp. 155–156.

[33] On the politics of small business, which, of course, still has a liberal minority wing, see Bunzel, *op. cit.*, Chapter 5.

acter has not disappeared. It has been inherited from the Progressives of yesterday by the conservatives of today. It appears to be, as we shall see, a conviction that flourishes less among the young than among the old, who are often troubled that they cannot persuade their juniors of its importance. "For the development of self-reliance," say two authors of a manual for small business operation, "for making men as well as money, small business excels." [34] In 1936, when the Robinson-Patman Act was under consideration, this effort to underwrite the middleman was touted by the Chairman of the House Committee on the Judiciary as a potential bulwark of the democratic order: "There are a great many people who feel that if we are to preserve democracy in government, in America, we have got to preserve a democracy in business operation. . . . We must make some effort to *maintain the yeomanry in business.*" [35]

In the 1940's and 1950's there has been much evidence of a widespread uneasy conviction that years of war, depression, and bureaucratic expansion have finally drained away the old regard for entrepreneurship among the young, and that the spirit that animated the old competitive ideal has finally succumbed to the world of the large corporation. The signs and portents are numerous, but a memorable article of 1949 in *Fortune* may be taken as a landmark. Surveying "The Class of '49," *Fortune's* editors pointed out that it was perhaps the most significant college graduating class in our history. It was one of the largest, most mature (with a high proportion of veterans) and responsible; but its distinguishing feature was its aversion to risk, its passion for security. "The class of '49," the editors reported, "wants to work for somebody else—preferably somebody big. No longer is small business the promised land. As for the idea of going into business for oneself, the idea is so seldom expressed as to seem an anachronism." Only in the Southwest, which seems socially and intellectually to lag behind the rest of the country, was there

[34] Pearce C. Kelley and Kenneth Lawyer, *How to Organize and Operate a Small Business,* Prentice-Hall, Englewood Cliffs, N. J., 1949, p. 11.

[35] Quoted in Merle Fainsod, Lincoln Gordon, and Joseph C. Palamountain, Jr., *Government and the American Economy,* Norton, New York, 1959, p. 549; italics added.

any sign of significant exceptions to this generalization. The generation who had been impressionable children during the depression and who had come of age in the shadow of the war rendered a firm verdict in favor of security, service, and the good life (measured in modest income expectations) rather than risk, self-assertion, and the big prizes. The emergent young man, the editors reported, "is not afraid of bigness; where his father of the twenties, fearful of anonymity, was repelled by hugeness in an organization, he is attracted." [36]

This was the response of a generation raised in an economy of giant corporations, educated very often in universities with thousands of students, disciplined by army life, and accustomed to the imperatives of organization, mass, and efficiency. No doubt they often saw in big businesses the promise of laboratories and market research to which the atmosphere of the universities had already accustomed them. Because of its army experiences, the class of 1949 may have been unusually security-minded, but there is no reason to doubt that its acceptance of large organization represented a secular trend. Not long after the *Fortune* piece appeared, the Youth Research Institute Survey put to 4,660 high school and college seniors, recent college graduates, and veterans the question: "Do you feel that you will be able to achieve all of your economic desires by working for someone else?"   61.1 per cent said yes, 20.4 per cent no, and 18.5 per cent were uncertain.[37]   In his essay, "The Found Generation," an analysis of the expressed life ideals of the class of 1955, David Riesman revealed not only a bland acceptance of the large corporation as a place in which to do one's life work but also a depressing complacency about the terms and rewards of the corporate life. The class of 1949 had at least been aware of making a somewhat difficult choice in which their individuality might be at stake. The class of 1955 took the bureaucratic career for granted.[38]

It is this acceptance of the bureaucratic career that, more than

[36] The Class of '49, *Fortune* (June 1949), pp. 84–87.

[37] William H. Whyte, Jr., *The Organization Man*, Anchor Books, New York, 1957, p. 79n.

[38] David Riesman, The Found Generation, in *Abundance for What?*, Doubleday, New York, 1964, pp. 309–323.

anything else, tells us why there is no longer an antitrust movement. It is far more revealing than the law cases or the books on the control of monopoly. It is also a perfect illustration of how the problems of yesterday are not solved but outgrown. Only a few people today are concerned about how to make the large corporations more competitive, but millions are concerned about how they are going to live inside the corporate framework. The existence and the workings of the corporations are largely accepted, and in the main they are assumed to be fundamentally benign. What is questioned, when anything is questioned, are matters of personal style: what can be salvaged, in the way of either individualism or individuality, in an age in which the big corporation has become a way of life? It is this concern that marks the transition from an age in which *The Curse of Bigness* and *Other People's Money* set the tone of the prevailing anxieties to one in which everyone reads *The Lonely Crowd* and *The Organization Man.*

Long-prevailing systems of values do not usually go under without a fight, and along with the new acceptance there is a good deal of uneasiness about the corporate life. The young may be losing the concern of their elders with the virile prerogatives of enterprise. Certainly they are now much more disposed to ask of the economic order not whether it is raising a nation of enterprising and hardy men but more matter-of-factly whether it is maintaining an adequate level of employment and producing a sufficient increase in the Gross National Product. But there is a persistent uneasiness, which has its manifestations both on the left and the right. The left, if it can be called that, rebels in the name of nonconformity and opts out of the whole bourgeois world, and we get the beat and the hip. The right rebels in the name of the older individualism, which believed that economic life should inculcate discipline and character, and we get Barry Goldwater and his enthusiasts. Though they would hate to admit it, they are both bedevilled in different ways by the same problem; each of them is trying to make its variety of nonconformism into a mass creed, which is a contradiction in terms. The beats opt out of corporate uniformity in uniforms and erect themselves into a stereotype. The right-wingers sing their praises of individualism in dreary, regimented choruses and applaud vigilantes who would kill every vestige of genuine dissent.

In politics, of course, it is the right-wingers who really count— it is they who have the numbers, the money, the political leverage. They can also invoke the greater part of the old American pieties and can appeal to the kind of old-fashioned American who believes that federal fiscal policy can be discussed in language suitable to family budgets. Much of our conservative writing echoes with concern over the decline of the older kind of economic morale, which it identifies with small entrepreneurship. But conservatives understandably fear to make the large corporation the object of their criticism; this smacks too much of subversion. They have a safer and more congenial outlet for their animus against the organization of modern life in the form of denunciations of big government. In this way, the large corporation escapes its proper share of odium. But, historically, it was the giant corporation far more than governmental policy that eclipsed the old-fashioned economic morality.

Oddly enough, although it is primarily conservatives who are profoundly disgruntled with the style of contemporary economic life, many liberals complete the paradox by springing to its defense and, in particular, to the defense of bigness. As we have seen, there was always a large number of Progressive intellectuals who preferred to accept corporate organization and to whom the possibilities of rationalization and order were more appealing than the competitive ideal. Today it is men of such views who seem to have inherited what is left of American liberalism. Of course, big business still holds a place as a negative symbol in the liberal creed, and the liberal creed still gives a certain ritualistic compliance to the anti-big-business sentiment that was once very close to the heart of Progressivism. But by and large, as Carl Kaysen has remarked, "today's liberals have abandoned the symbol of competition without much struggle." [39]

Some of the most striking efforts to reconcile us to the business structure have been written in recent years by liberals who derive

[39] Big Business and the Liberals, Then and Now, *New Republic* (November 22, 1954), pp. 118–119.

from the New Deal tradition.   If, in 1953, one read a paean to big business asserting, among other things, that the emotional antagonism to which it was subject was based on "abuses long since corrected"; that the big business leader is "a man with a strong and practical sense of responsibility to the public, and an awareness of the ethics of present-day business competition"; that "big business has performed economic wonders with one hand tied behind its back"; that it has actually increased competition and multiplied small enterprises; that "size is our greatest single functional asset"; that big business nourished diversity; that "we are living in what is probably the most highly competitive society men have ever known"; that big business research has multiplied opportunities for small business enterprise; that ill-considered antitrust prosecutions have "grave implications for national se- curity"; and that "in Bigness we have the material foundation of a society which can further the highest values known to men, values we describe as spiritual," [40]—one no longer expected to find that one had been reading a speech by a General Motors or A. T. and T. director and was not at all surprised to learn that the author was David E. Lilienthal, once one of the most outspoken democratic idealists of the New Deal bureaucracy and a former disciple of Brandeis.

Lilienthal's innocent rhapsodies to big business may perhaps be taken as the effusions of one who had been reshaped by his experiences in giant public enterprises like the T.V.A. and the A.E.C.[41]   But there is also A. A. Berle, Jr., another New Dealer, who held his first job in Brandeis's office and whose public career was marked by friendships with Robert La Follette, George Norris, and Franklin D. Roosevelt.   In his most recent works Berle has been speculating about the possible development of a corporate conscience and arguing that the contemporary business power system is governed by public consensus.   In his *Power*

[40] David E. Lilienthal, *Big Business: A New Era,* Harper, New York, 1953, pp. 5, 7, 27, 33, 36, 47, 190, and *passim.*

[41] For critiques see Lee Loevinger, Antitrust and the New Economics, *Min- nesota Law Review,* XXXVII (June 1953), pp. 505–568, and Edward S. Mason, *Economic Concentration and the Monopoly Problem,* Harvard University Press, Cambridge, Mass., 1957, pp. 371–381.

Without Property he urged liberals to reconsider their former, and historically justified, antipathy to big business and to judge it in the light of its achievements in increasing income and distributing property.[42]   Finally, there is John Kenneth Galbraith, whose book, *American Capitalism,* has probably done as much as any other work to reconcile the contemporary liberal mind to the diminished role of competition as a force in modern economic society by offering, as an alternative account of the mechanism by which market power is controlled in the public interest, the principle of countervailing power.   Of course, neither Berle nor Galbraith advocates doing away with the antitrust laws—Galbraith, in fact, argues that in the main federal antitrust policies have helped to produce countervailing power, where it has not emerged spontaneously [43]—but the net effect of their view of our society is to lower the premium upon competition and to turn attention to other economic and social mechanisms that promise to control excessive market power.

To say all this is not to say that liberal intellectuals have ceased to be critical of business civilization or, on occasion, of big business.   But a variety of other issues—foreign policy, urban development, civil rights, education, and the like—have become more central, and where these issues are concerned, liberals do not always find themselves in a simple antagonistic confrontation with big business, as they so often did in the past.   Their criticisms of business civilization now rest more on cultural than economic grounds.   The last thing they are interested in is the restoration of competition as the solution to the evils that they see.[44] They are not even particularly titillated by such a thing as the General Electric–Westinghouse scandal, although it may confirm their estimation of the kind of behavior to be expected of businessmen.   In short, that "gale of creative destruction" about

[42] *Power Without Property*, Harvest Books, New York, 1959, pp. 11–16.

[43] Galbraith, *op. cit.*, p. 151.

[44] Nor are contemporary radicals.   The most full-throated indictment of the ruling element in big business that has been written in our time, C. Wright Mills's *The Power Elite*, does not concern itself even fleetingly with the problem of market power.   The Sherman and Clayton Acts are not mentioned in its index.

which Joseph Schumpeter wrote so eloquently, when he described the progressive character of capitalist technology, has driven both the liberal and the conservative ideologies before it.

V

It is easier to account for the decline of the antitrust movement as a matter of public sentiment than it is to explain the persistence and growth of the antitrust enterprise as a legal and administrative fact. But the fate of antitrust is an excellent illustration of how a public ideal, vaguely formulated and often hopelessly at odds with stubborn realities, can become embodied in institutions with elaborate, self-preserving rules and procedures, a defensible function, and an equally stubborn capacity for survival.

The antitrust revival originated in the closing phases of the New Deal. It was a response to the recession of 1937–38, which itself brought about a crisis in the thinking and the political strategy of the New Dealers. The recession gave to the Brandeis liberals, who had always been present in New Deal councils, a chance to reassert their competitive ideas and their suspicion of big business. In 1934, long before the cartelization of the N.R.A. was abandoned, the economist Gardiner C. Means, then economic adviser to the Secretary of Agriculture, had prepared a memorandum on administered prices that provided the economic rationale for a new approach to the depression. Early in 1935 this memorandum was published by the Senate.[45] Means contrasted market

45 Gardiner C. Means, *Industrial Prices and Their Relative Inflexibility*, Senate Doc. No. 13, 74th Cong., 1st sess. Parts of this document, along with later papers on the same theme, are reprinted in Means's *The Corporate Revolution in America*, Crowell-Collier, New York, 1962. For a critique and some reflections on later interest in the theory, see Richard Ruggles, The Nature of Price Flexibility and the Determinants of Relative Price Changes in the Economy, in *Business Concentration and Price Policy*, Princeton University Press, Princeton, N. J., 1955, esp. pp. 443–464, and the conflicting views expressed by economists before the Kefauver Committee, *Administered Prices*, Hearings before the Subcommittee on Antitrust and Monopoly of the Committee on the Judiciary, United States Senate (Washington, 1957).

prices, which were made and remade in the market as the result
of interactions between buyers and sellers in the fashion of traditional economic theory, with administered prices, which were
set by administrative action and held constant for a considerable
period of time.   Market prices are flexible and respond readily
to a fall in demand; administered prices are rigid.   Means considered the disparity between flexible and rigid prices to be an
important aggravating force in the depression.   Although he
did not identify administered prices with monopoly, he focused
attention once again on those industries in which market power
was sufficiently concentrated to make administered prices possible.   Some of his contemporaries seized upon the conception
as a rationale for stepping up antitrust activity, and Franklin D.
Roosevelt invoked it in his message of 1938, calling for the creation of the T.N.E.C.   At the same time, other New Deal theorists,
notably Assistant Attorney General Robert Jackson, who was
then head of the Antitrust Division of the Department of Justice, and Secretary of the Interior Harold L. Ickes, became convinced that the organized power of big business was attempting
to sabotage reform through a "strike of capital" and that a new
assault on business power must be undertaken as a basis for
further attempts at recovery.   The old argument that business
power was a threat to democratic government itself thus entered
into Roosevelt's T.N.E.C. message.

   The new attack on business power took two forms; the first was
the elaborate, if inconclusive, T.N.E.C. investigation, which
yielded a mass of factual information, much of it new, but no
programmatic proposals in which the investigators themselves
had any confidence.[46]   The second was the stepping up of anti-

   [46] Early in its *Final Report,* the Committee confessed that its members
"are not rash enough to believe that they can lay down a program which
will solve the great problems that beset the world, but they are convinced
that the information which this committee has assembled, when eventually
properly analyzed and disseminated, will enable the people of America to
know what must be done if human freedom is to be preserved." *Final Report and Recommendations of the Temporary National Economic Committee,*
87th Cong., 1st sess., Sen. Doc. No. 35, p. 4.   In short, the Committee did
not know what precisely to make of its own data but hoped that in due time

trust activity under the leadership of Thurman Arnold, the new chief of the Antitrust Division. Congress doubled appropriations for Arnold's division in 1939 and then doubled them again in 1940. Between 1938 and 1943 its staff grew almost fivefold.

In retrospect it is instructive to see what results came from uncertain and, at times, ill-considered beginnings. Today the Jackson–Ickes view of the recession seems quite partisan and fanciful; the T.N.E.C. investigation, for all the information it gathered, was from a pragmatic point of view a fiasco; the value of Means's emphasis on administered prices is highly controversial among economists; and Thurman Arnold's experiment with antitrust enforcement can be judged, at least from one angle of vision, as a substantial failure. And yet, as in the case of so many of the gropings of the New Deal, there was a valuable outcome, which in this case can best be got at by looking at the core of success wrapped up in Thurman Arnold's frustration.

Arnold's story is replete with ironies. He had written of the antitrust enterprise with a devastating note of mockery, and the appointment of a man with such views, especially by an administration that had only recently resorted to the wholesale cartelization of the N.R.A., was looked at askance by antitrust-minded senators as a possible effort to sabotage the Antitrust Division. But Arnold proceeded to recruit and inspire a splendid staff and to rehabilitate the entire antitrust function. His goal was not to attack bigness or efficient mass production or efficient marketing, but rather to discipline the pricing policies of business at the vital points where abuses seemed most important. Antitrust was thus to become an instrument of social and economic policy, aimed to stop firms from setting prices above reasonable levels, to prevent businesses from holding new processes off the market, and to reduce unemployment. All this was to be achieved not so much by isolated cases or by responding to this or that complaint, but rather by systematic action against whole industries—motion pictures, petroleum, radio broadcasting, drugs, housing.

---

the public would. See the penetrating critique by two members, Isador Lubin and Leon Henderson, *ibid.*, pp. 51–52.

From a short-run point of view, Arnold's regime could be judged a failure. His program for housing was spiked when the Court made it impossible to act effectively against the labor unions, which constituted a lynch-pin of restraint of trade in that industry; his plan for the food industry lost its point during the war; his program for transportation was put off by the War Production Board.[47] He could not wholly reform a single industry, much less bring about important general structural changes in the economy. And yet he succeeded in demonstrating the usefulness of the antitrust laws. In actually *using* the Sherman Act, thanks to the enlarged staff that Congress had given him, he showed for the first time what it could and could not do. Although it could not alter the fundamental character of the economy or make it less liable to cyclical instability (as Arnold had promised in his book, *The Bottlenecks of Business*), it could significantly affect the conduct of business within the framework of the existing structure. Arnold's Division soon won a number of decisions from the courts—particularly in the Alcoa case of 1945 and the American Tobacco case of the following year—that opened new possibilities for enforcement. It won from Congress a permanent reversal of the former policy of niggardly support. And finally, it put the antitrust enterprise on such a footing that it could flourish under both Democratic and Republican regimes; the return of the Republicans under Eisenhower did not bring a remission of efforts to use the Sherman Act or retrenchment of the Antitrust Division. Instead, it set up the Attorney General's National Committee to Study the Antitrust Laws, which in 1955 returned a unanimous judgment in favor of antitrust policy and of the current state of case law, which had tightened enforcement. Although the Committee did not make any dramatic recommendations for more rigorous enforcement, the effect of its work was to reaffirm the bipartisan character of the antitrust commitment by ratifying the achievements of Democratic administrations in the preceding fifteen years.[48]

[47] See Corwin D. Edwards, Thurman Arnold and the Antitrust Laws, *Political Science Quarterly*, LVIII (September 1943), pp. 338–355.

[48] *Report of the Attorney General's National Committee to Study the Antitrust Laws* (Washington, 1955).

What makes it possible to institutionalize antitrust activities at the higher plateau that has been maintained since 1938 is not a consensus among economists as to its utility in enhancing economic efficiency, but a rough consensus in society at large as to its value in curbing the dangers of excessive market power. As in the beginning, it is based on a political and moral judgment rather than the outcome of economic measurement or even distinctively economic criteria. "It must be recognized," says Professor Edward S. Mason, "that there is an element of faith in the proposition that maintaining competition substantially improves the efficiency of resource use." The option for a minimal level of competition to be underwritten by public policy, although it can be backed by substantial economic arguments, "rests basically on a political judgment," write Carl Kaysen and Donald F. Turner in their inquiry into trust policy: "In our democratic, egalitarian society, large areas of uncontrolled private power are not tolerated." "We found," write Dirlam and Kahn in their book, *Fair Competition,* "that the decisions [of courts and commissions] could not be fully understood or fairly appraised by economic standards alone. Hence we concluded that the appropriate question for economists to ask about antitrust policy is not whether this is the most efficient way of structuring or reorganizing the economy, but the inverted one: Does antitrust seriously interfere with the requirements of efficiency?" "The rationale of antitrust," writes A. D. Neale, a British student of the American experience, "is essentially a desire to provide legal checks to restrain economic power and is not a pursuit of efficiency as such." "For most Americans," concludes Professor Galbraith, "free competition, so called, has for long been a political rather than an economic concept." [49]

In any case, the state of antitrust enforcement seems to correspond with a public consensus. Economists and lawyers differ profoundly on how effective the antitrust laws have been and on

[49] Edward S. Mason in the Preface to Carl Kaysen and Donald B. Turner, *Antitrust Policy,* Harvard University Press, Cambridge, Mass., 1960, p. xx; *ibid.,* p. 5; A. D. Neale, *The Antitrust Laws of the U.S.A.,* Cambridge University Press, Cambridge, 1962, p. 487; Galbraith, *op. cit.,* p. 27.

how effective they could be if they were more amply enforced,[50] but there is hardly a major industry that has not seen a significant lawsuit or two, and in most industries in which intervention might be thought desirable, government intervention has had more than negligible effects.[51] It is also one of the strengths of antitrust that neither its effectiveness nor its ineffectiveness can be precisely documented; its consequences rest on events of unknown number and significance that have *not* happened—on proposed mergers that may have died in the offices of corporation counsel, on collusive agreements that have never been consummated, on unfair practices contemplated but never carried out. Liberals can support it because they retain their old suspicion of business behavior, and conservatives support it because they still believe in competition, and they may hope to gain an additional point of leverage in the battle against inflation. No one seems prepared to suggest that the antitrust enterprise be cut back drastically, much less abandoned, and Congress has consistently supported its enlarged staff. The existing state of enforcement conforms to the state of the public mind, which accepts bigness but continues to distrust business morals. Even business itself accords to the principle of antitrust a certain grudging and irritated acceptance. Visitations by the Department of Justice are a nuisance, lawsuits are expensive, and prosecution carries an unpleasant stigma, but the antitrust procedures can be considered an alternative to more obtrusive regulation such as outright controls on prices. At any rate, big business has never found it necessary or expedient to launch a public campaign against antitrust enforcement; the pieties at stake are too deep to risk touching.

A final element in antitrust enforcement rests on the fact that the government itself is now a major consumer, and the points of exposure of industrial prices to official concern and reaction have been multiplied. One of the reasons for the antitrust re-

[50] See, for example, the symposium, Dexter M. Keezer, ed., The Effectiveness of the Federal Antitrust Laws, *American Economic Review,* XXXIX (June 1949), pp. 689–724.

[51] See the industry-by-industry survey in Simon N. Whitney, *Antitrust Policies: American Experience in Twenty Industries,* 2 vols., Twentieth Century Fund, New York, 1958.

vival in 1938 was the irritation of government officials over the prevalence of what seemed to be collusively priced bids. With his book, *The Bottlenecks of Business,* Thurman Arnold hoped to mobilize the consumer behind the new phase of antitrust enforcement—a forlorn hope when one thinks of the historical passivity of American consumers. But the presence of the government as consumer has perhaps supplied some of the leverage he was looking for.

Antitrust reform is not the first reform in American history whose effectiveness rested less upon a broad movement of militant mass sentiment than upon the leadership of a small group of influential and deeply concerned specialists. In passing from a phase in which it was largely an ideology to one in which it has become largely a technique, antitrust has become, like so many other things in our society, differentiated, specialized, and bureaucratized. No layman can any longer concern himself very much with the immense body of case law that has been built up over the decades or with the truly formidable literature of relevant economic analysis and argument that has grown up since the 1930's. Of necessity the potentialities of antitrust action have become the almost exclusive concern of a technical elite of lawyers and economists. Indeed, the business of studying, attacking, defending, and evaluating oligopolistic behavior and its regulation has become one of our small industries, which gives employment to many gifted professional men. The volume of books and articles in this field and the large number of entrants indicate that this industry, at least, is workably competitive.

5

The New Place of Business

Why Managers Cultivate
Social Responsibility

Earl F. Cheit

For the second time in twenty years, American businessmen are engaged in a campaign to justify their autonomy, to fortify their image, and to promote new understanding of their place in society. In the late 1940's, they were preaching Free Enterprise; today, it is the Gospel of Social Responsibility. Although the historical basis for the former is easy to understand, the reasons why corporate managers today are portraying themselves as responsible have been variously explained and, I think, often misinterpreted.

I am convinced that, in general, the significance of this new posture of corporate managers has been underestimated and that (1) it has not arisen from the much discussed attenuation of corporate ownership control; and (2) it is best understood as a response to the changing social and political environment of business. The change is slow and its magnitude difficult to assess, but its direction is clearly toward an increasing assignment of responsibility to the corporation for the uses of its influence, both inside and outside the plant gates. And so American businessmen, long accustomed to creating their own environment, are adapting to a new circumstance, the necessity increasingly to be responsive to the environment in which they find themselves.

There is no single "business view" of this change. Some businessmen are resisting it, and many others can easily restrain their enthusiasm. A few, such as J. Irwin Hiller, Board Chairman of Cummins Engine Company, have developed a cost/benefit rationale for the new concern of business with its environment. But, whatever their personal assessment of the increasing demand for business accountability, most corporate executives are responding to their changing environment by adapting their ideology to their interest.

I

Business and the men who pursue it have almost always enjoyed a secure and honorable place in American life. But never were they more admired than in the good years of the 1920's—a time, Frederick Lewis Allen observed, when one could pay his clergyman high praise by telling him he had delivered his sermon in a businesslike manner. The protests of the depression era and the policies of the New Deal heretically challenged the wisdom of canonizing business and its ideals, but American business was vindicated by its dramatic record of wartime production and rapid peacetime economic recovery.

So, it is often said that American business was put on trial during the 1930's and won its acquittal during the 1940's.

If businessmen found satisfaction with the verdict, they apparently felt the need, typical of successful defendants, to repair the damage by setting the record straight and, in the process, to win some additional satisfaction. In retrospect, it is clear from their response that American businessmen saw it as their task to fill an ideological gap between business and society. They launched a massive campaign to sell Free Enterprise, which became the subject of William H. Whyte, Jr.'s entertaining and somewhat impatient, *Is Anybody Listening?* (1952), a study that revealed that the American phenomenon of selling had taken a new and interesting turn. According to Whyte, during the late 1940's and early 1950's, ". . . businessmen appeared . . . gripped with a single idea. . . . We must *sell* Free Enterprise." [1]

Many, if not most, of the country's largest business corpora-

---

[1] William H. Whyte, Jr., and the Editors of *Fortune, Is Anybody Listening?*, Simon and Schuster, New York, 1952, pp. 4–6.

tions actively, almost frenetically, promoted a great campaign of inspirational speeches, car cards, outdoor posters, radio "listener impressions," in-plant conferences, and institutional advertisements, supported by visual aids ranging from General Motor's full length Hollywood movie on the profit system to the Free Enterprise Comic Books of Procter and Gamble and Republic Steel.

Unlike earlier efforts such as those of the American Liberty League, this campaign, according to Whyte, was one of the greatest and most intensive sales jobs in history, with expenditures for advertising and public relations running at least $100,000,000 a year, not counting the time and energy of many of America's top business executives and their assistants. In short, at the beginning of the 1950's, the campaign to sell Free Enterprise had become a substantial industry in itself.

The series of operations that made up this campaign presented a special message based on the premise that American business had been "outsold" by collectivism. The public was told that if it did not recognize that the good things of life—the American dream—were the result of the Free Enterprise system, it would soon be victimized by the nightmare of state socialism.

The packaging and distribution of this product may have been an exciting endeavor. Certainly the speeches of the campaign reflected a high degree of excitement. At the same time, the campaign itself must have been puzzling, for although it enjoyed the support of the greatest sales apparatus in history, it seemed to fall on deaf ears. Mr. Whyte observed:

> Never before has the businessman had so much paraphernalia with which to communicate to those about him, and never before has he spent so much time using it. And more and more, as he looks about him, he is coming to wonder . . . is anybody really listening? [2]

If the samples of rhetoric collected by Mr. Whyte are typical— "The challenge I am placing before you tonight is to pioneer in reselling the virtues of our American way of life to our own

[2] *Ibid.,* p. 1.

American people"—it is easy to appreciate why the audience was inattentive.

Its graceless prose aside, there are more revealing reasons why the sell-America copy of the great Free Enterprise campaign failed to command attention. Masquerading as a nonpartisan effort, its actual aims—reducing high marginal rates of income taxation and reversing a labor policy favorable to union organization—were frankly political. And they came too late. Americans had not lost faith in their system; rather, they had found enough faith to try to improve it.

The coming to power in 1952 of a conservative government hastened the same realization among businessmen.[3] Faced with the realities of working with New Deal legislation and the obvious public support for it, a responsible government could find no way to divest itself of its economic inheritance. The abortive attempt to abandon the President's Council of Economic Advisors and, thereby, to tamper with the obligations of the Employment Act is a case in point.

Today the Free Enterprise sales campaign seems to be over. To a surprising degree, American businessmen and writers about business have followed Mr. Whyte's advice to stop interpreting our cooperative society as individualistic; to stop concealing our quest for security in phrases like competition and incentive system; to stop trying to resurrect pre-New Deal capitalism and to make legitimate our adoption of the present economic order. In short, not to sell old ideology as the solution for new, practical problems; and not to talk more but rather to listen to the real concerns that Americans and others have about American business today.

Many American businessmen have apparently taken this difficult prescription seriously. Never before have corporate officials so openly acknowledged the responsibilities of business to society, and never before have they spent so much time discussing them.

[3] In his recent book, *The Economy, Liberty and the State,* Twentieth Century Fund, New York, 1959, Calvin Hoover has a brilliant chapter devoted to The Conservative Acquiescence in the Changed American Economic System.

II

The new gospel of business stresses responsibility to shareholders, to customers, to the industry, to the nation, to everyone. Its tone is restrained. Where the Free Enterprise campaign was aggressive and loud, the Gospel of Social Responsibility is self-conscious and subdued.

At the same time that the sell has become softer, however, a good deal of energy and money is now being channeled into more outright political efforts devoted to specific issues, often supporting the proliferating fringe groups of the ultraright.[4] Advertisements such as those of the power and light companies, which

[4] The National Association of Manufacturers, which Whyte calls the "bell-wether of the free enterprise campaign," could claim three of its former presidents among the members of the First Governing Council of the John Birch Society in 1959. It is not always possible to separate the old free enterprise campaign and the present efforts of the radical right. One of the leading supporters of the Schwartz Christian Anti-Communism Crusade has been Joe Crail of the Coast Federal Savings and Loan Association in Los Angeles, the third largest savings and loan group in the country. Crail set up a Free Enterprise Bureau in 1961, has spent over $250,000 annually to promote his views, and has mailed two million pieces of propaganda to depositors, borrowers, and business concerns. Crail claims that 5,000 companies have inquired about the Bureau and no less than 2,000 firms have established similar bureaus.

Harding College in Arkansas Whyte calls "a sort of ideological center for the job of 'reeducating Americans in the American way of life.'" Its National Education Program made the movie "Communism on the Map"; it was produced by Birch member Glenn Green and widely used by radical right groups but is so inaccurate and vulnerable to criticism that even Fred Schwartz of the Anti-Communism Crusade repudiated it. The National Education Program lists on its letterhead executives from Monsanto Chemical, Swift, Mississippi Power Company, U. S. Steel, Lone Star Cement, Olin Matthiesen Chemicals, American Iron and Steel Institute, and General Electric. One General Electric vice president wrote, "It is a pleasure to endorse without reservation this organization. . . ." Although many of these firms were old mainstays of the Free Enterprise campaign, some of them also were simultaneously sounding the Gospel of Social Responsibility (see, for example, the quotations from Ralph Cordiner of General Electric in Chapter 1). For more facts on business support of the radical right, see Alan F. Westin, Anti-Communism in the Corporations, *Commentary* (December 1963), pp. 479–487, and Fred J. Cook, The Ultras, *Nation* (June 30, 1962).

equate the police state with public power, or those of Timken Roller Bearing, which created the "quotation" from Lenin that "we shall force the United States to *spend* itself to destruction," are examples.[5] Yet, these persistent flashes of economic revivalism make the Gospel of Social Responsibility all the more conspicuous by comparison.

Of course, the profession of responsibility is not new. Its roots can be traced back to the Progressive era. In the late 1930's, Wendell Willkie, writes historian William Leuchtenburg, ". . . helped educate the businessman to a new sense of social responsibility." [6] By 1948, the annual Harvard Business School Alumni Association conference was devoted to the same task. With "Business Responsibility" as his theme, the president of the Association introduced that meeting by observing: "Every day we hear more of the need for business and the men who manage business to live up to their responsibilities."

During the past few years, the meeting of middle-ranked corporate managers that did not stress the responsibility of the modern manager would have been very hard to find. In January 1963, at the annual seminar of the National Industrial Conference Board, company presidents "looked at their jobs." As in previous sessions of this series, it was an off-the-record seminar; however, I am sure I will reveal no confidences when I report that the six corporation presidents were, to a man, self-consciously responsible. According to audience members I checked with, the same theme was presented the year before.

To test my impression that this was a recent, but rather general change, I consulted the American Management Association and learned that its leaders had become so interested in the subject that the Association had commissioned a study and published a revealing document entitled *Management Creeds and Philosophies.*[7]

[5] See the instructive and delightful article by David Spitz, The Timken Edition of Lenin, *Harper's* (March 1961), pp. 56–57.

[6] *Franklin D. Roosevelt and the New Deal 1932–1940*, Harper and Row, New York, 1961, p. 322.

[7] Stewart Thompson, *Management Creeds and Philosophies, Top Management Guides in Our Changing Economy*, American Management Association, New York, 1958, Research Study No. 32.

Some 700 companies were queried for documents that each firm regarded as "a managerial creed or statement of basic objectives." One hundred and three firms responded, and a detailed follow-up was made with 51 companies. Three-fourths of these creeds had been formulated in the previous two to five years, about 80 per cent of them since the peak of the free enterprise campaign. More significant, the study found that creeds were developed because executives thought it desirable to ask themselves questions such as: "What are we doing in business?" "What are our responsibilities as managers?"

It was in response to four full days of discussion of these and other questions, the AMA reports, that the Canadian Marconi Company developed a formal statement of its primary responsibilities, which is representative of the views repeatedly expressed by American corporate executives:

PRIMARY RESPONSIBILITIES
of
CANADIAN MARCONI COMPANY:

1

TO THE SHAREHOLDERS,
for successful results.

2

TO OUR CUSTOMERS,
for price, quality and service.

3

TO OUR EMPLOYEES,
for fair dealing and continuing opportunity.

4

TO OUR INDUSTRY AS A WHOLE,
for constructive and ethical action.

5

TO CANADA,
for economic and social advancement.

There is every reason to believe that if the AMA were doing another study of creeds today, it would find even greater concern with social responsibility. Corporate executives seem increasingly possessed by the idea that they must define and formulate their responsibilities to their publics, both inside and outside the firm. Almost every session of the 1964 National Industrial Conference Board Seminar had some overtone of Social Responsibility, and this year the Conference Board's panel of top executives chose to discuss: "Company 'Social Responsibility'—Too Much or Not Enough?"

IBM Board Chairman, Thomas J. Watson, Jr., in his *A Business and Its Beliefs* (1963),[8] records his firm on the roster of the responsible and by prescription advises those who have not yet done so to join it. Even the most casual sampling of recent literature, professional journals, and business advertising produces countless other examples. This goes well beyond the concept of the stewardship of wealth, as Howard Bowen notes in his treatise on the subject. "Only within the past few years," he writes, ". . . have large numbers of business leaders publicly acknowledged and actively preached the doctrine that they are servants of society and that management merely in the interests (narrowly defined) of stockholders is not the sole end of their duties. Indeed, discussion of the 'social responsibilities of business' has become not only acceptable in leading business circles, but even fashionable." [9] Business documents professing responsibilities, he reported, run into the hundreds, perhaps thousands.

In fact, by the mid-1950's professions of responsibility had become so common that Peter Drucker [10] chided American businessmen: "You might wonder, if you were a conscientious newspaper reader, when the managers of American business had any time for business." A study of newspapers for a single month led Mr. Drucker to report that America's well-known businessmen

[8] Thomas J. Watson, Jr., *A Business and Its Beliefs,* McGraw-Hill, New York, 1963.

[9] Howard Bowen, *Social Responsibilities of the Businessman,* Harper, New York, 1953, p. 44.

[10] Peter Drucker, The Responsibilities of Management, *Harper's* (November 1954), pp. 67–72.

felt responsible for (among other things) support of the community chest, employment of the handicapped, research in the social sciences, symphony orchestras, religious tolerance, the United Nations, economic education of the American people, liberal foreign trade policy, intellectual refugees from China, freedom of the press, conservation of forests, and maintenance of private colleges.

This new posture is anything but disagreeable and seems clearly an improvement over the old "public be damned" attitude. But this new attitude, which Wilbert Moore aptly calls "the public be cultivated," [11] poses problems of its own, not the least of which is the need for a deeper understanding, if not a definition, of what it is that is being offered and why.

III

When a corporate executive says his firm is socially responsible, as Mr. B. C. Shaul of Tidewater Oil Company recently told the San Francisco Bay Area Pollution Control Board, he is saying that he realizes that his decisions may have consequences outside his firm and that he will try to make these private decisions so that the consequences accord with generally accepted values (in this case, the desire to keep the arsenic used in a hydrogen generating plant from turning leaves ashen).

There is a close parallel here between the "business responsibility" approach to the social and political environment and the once fashionable "human relations" approach to the work environment. Both imply that before making a decision, the other fellow's feelings and interests should be taken into account.

As with human relations, some students have attempted to enumerate the interests served by the socially responsible business firm.[12] These lists typically include (although not in any particu-

11 Wilbert Moore, *Conduct of the Corporation,* Random House, New York, 1962, p. 282.

12 See Bowen, *op. cit.,* Chapter 2; Harlan Cleveland and Harold D. Lasswell, *Ethics and Bigness,* Harper, New York, 1962, pp. xxiii–xlvi; and Peter L. Bernstein, Can Business Grasp the Future?, *Nation* (January 13, 1964), pp. 49–51.

lar order) such laudable objectives as economic stability, a high level of employment, technical and economic progress, improved living standards, personal freedom, and, more recently, community development and improvement, and, as Mr. Drucker's inventory shows, many others.

But what happens when the critical questions often asked of human relations policies are put to any specific business action or decision: Is it done only where it pays? What are the other fellow's interests, and are they truly being served? Who decides what the other fellow's interests are? Not many of the firms that profess social responsibility are confronted with the rigid performance test faced by Mr. Shaul's plant. Even when they are, most acts, like the six million or so dollars spent on smog control by this Tidewater refinery, can be fully justified in terms of long-term profit maximizing. Moreover, even when exceptional instances can be cited, there is no real test of business responsibility, since, for the most part and regrettably, the definitions of the public interest generally come from businessmen themselves.[13] For this reason alone some scholars argue that the Gospel of Social Responsibility is more rhetoric than reality. But it is the subject of other charges as well.

In the view of the law, for example, there is little evidence that management has been freed from its legal obligation to maximize profits for the benefit of the stockholders. A recent analysis by Mr. Wilber G. Katz [14] shows that corporate gifts, a frequently cited example of corporate action in the broad social interest, do not require new legal justification or doctrine. Like other expenditures that hope to achieve community or customer good will, they come well within the traditional doctrine of managerial duty.

With respect to output and prices, again the legal responsibility of management has not changed. The same is true with

[13] Henry G. Manne, Corporate Responsibility, Business Motivation and Reality, *Annals of the American Academy*, CCCXLIII (September 1962), pp. 55–64.

[14] See Wilber G. Katz, Responsibility and the Modern Corporation, *Journal of Law and Economy*, III (October 1960), pp. 75–85, whose work I have drawn upon in this section.

respect to plant location or relocation. Katz concludes that with the possible (and in his view not highly significant) exception of some gifts, the legal view of managerial responsibility is still that expressed in the famous decision in which the Dodge Brothers won additional dividends from Henry Ford. The court concluded:

. . . a business corporation is organized and carried on primarily for the profit of the stockholders. The powers of directors are to be employed for that end. The discretion of directors is to be exercised in the choice of means to attain that end and does not extend to a change in the end itself, to the reduction of profits or to the non-distribution of profits among stockholders in order to devote them to other purposes.[15]

In actual practice, most large American corporations make decisions and expenditures of funds that might, by some agreed-upon standards, be counted as an act of social responsibility—scholarship programs, research awards, and aid-to-education grants by companies like du Pont are often-cited examples; less publicized are the attempts by firms like Thompson Ramo Wooldridge at leadership in race relations or by Alcoa in rebuilding of decaying urban centers. A recent innovation is the program of Equitable Assurance and others to hire and train school dropouts.

The nation's top money award for creative writing, the $5,000 Roos/Atkins literary award, was established when, according to the Board Chairman of this northern California clothing firm, "it became quite clear to me that business has a responsibility to the culture of the community in which it operates." A collection of Thomas Williams's short stories won the first award in October 1963, the same month that American Export and Isbrandtsen Lines presented New York's Metropolitan Opera with a gift of $135,000 to underwrite the cost of producing "Aida."

It is often pointed out, however, that when profit maximizing is looked at in somewhat longer-run terms, even acts such as these can usually be seen to fit the traditional doctrine of what it is that business managers are supposed to do. Thus, writers like Herrymon Maurer, who have most vigorously defended the

[15] *Ibid.*, p. 82.

greater social role of the modern large corporation, have at the same time provided more evidence that profit maximizing is truly its goal.[16] Admittedly, it has now become a longer-run goal, but this makes good sense and coincides with any organization's long-run major interest—survival.

Dangers of the Gospel

Those most critical of the Gospel of Social Responsibility point out that none of our studies of human and social relations has produced decisive and reliable norms to replace the competitive pricing process and profit maximizing for the benefit of shareholders. No other norm has been found that would allocate and utilize resources as efficiently; nor is there another norm that would be enforcible.

Moreover, if social obligations require concerted action by several companies, there is an implication that antitrust powers, already weak, might be further weakened. And this fear is fed by proposals that the voting rights of shareholders, meaningless as they are, be taken away.

Finally, and most persuasively, these critics assert that for the powerful corporation to extend its sphere of influence into social affairs with approval under the guise of social responsibility could be disastrous both for the corporation and society at large. The most extreme statement of this view comes from Professor Milton Friedman, who contends that the doctrine of management social responsibility is "fundamentally subversive. . . . Few trends could so thoroughly undermine the very foundations of our free society as the acceptance by corporate officials of a social responsibility other than to make as much money for their stockholders as possible." [17]

Since it can be demonstrated that the Gospel of Social Responsibility is not in competition with but is helped along by the profit motive, the awkward possibility that businessmen might

---

[16] Herrymon Maurer, *Great Enterprise*, Macmillan, New York, 1955.

[17] Milton Friedman, *Capitalism and Freedom*, University of Chicago Press, Chicago, 1962, p. 133. For a more elegant statement of this viewpoint see Ben W. Lewis, Economics by Admonition, *American Economic Review Supplement*, XLIX (May 1959), pp. 384–398.

undermine free society by claiming they are responsible to it seems remote. Mere mention of this possibility would dismay those managers for whom the profession of responsibility is little more than a public relations program to fend off critical attacks. Most businessmen would probably agree with a recent speech [18] by Pierre S. du Pont, in which he asserts that a method better than the "mass communications techniques" used in the past is needed to sell Free Enterprise, and that its key point should be performance.

The broad character, the all-pervasiveness, and the timing of this new campaign, however, warrant the claim that something more than profits and public relations is involved. But what?

IV

In recent years many scholars have provided one possible answer in their renewed concern about the social implications of giant corporations and the separation of their control from their ownership. They assert that "social responsibility" is the managers' attempt to seek legitimacy—to gain sovereign approval of an awkward, if bountiful, *de facto* status that is a natural by-product of big corporations with dispersed stock ownership. Basing their work on a hypothesis that emerged from the celebrated study, *The Modern Corporation and Private Property,* by Adolph A. Berle, Jr., and Gardiner C. Means,[19] these scholars have questioned whether the corporation has outgrown the controls designed to keep its managers behaving in the public interest, and, even more fundamentally, whether separation from its property base strips managerial power of its legitimacy.

In his more recent writing, Mr. Berle contends that the managers of large corporations are restrained by a public consensus, which has required the development of a "corporate conscience"

18 Pierre S. du Pont, The Hard Way Is the Only Way, a speech presented before the Annual Meeting of the Manufacturers Association of Connecticut, Inc., September 12, 1963.

19 Adolph A. Berle, Jr., and Gardiner C. Means, *The Modern Corporation and Private Property,* Macmillan, New York, 1932.

that speaks the language of social responsibility. Mr. Berle and his followers contend that although managers are in the embarrassing position of having (in his happy phrase) power without property, they say that they are responsible, because the force of public consensus makes them so.

On the other hand, to Mr. Berle's critics [20] this is a vague, unconvincing "philosophy" that does not succeed in explaining away the embarrassing situation. Bernard Nossiter's recent attack [21] on the concept of "corporate conscience" contends, for example, that it fails in its mission to fill the gap between the lost world of competition where business decisions were constrained and the present one in which managers are able increasingly to act free of restraint.

The public is coming increasingly to realize that classical economic and legal descriptions of our system are inadequate. A business executive who uses these antiquated descriptions in the face of what we now know of corporate size and control is forced, as Eric Goldman has said in another connection, "to act as if his ideological slip was showing." Thus, managers must *say* that they are responsible, because they are *not*.

The ingredient common to these opposing views of business responsibility is an ideological embarrassment that makes the profession of business responsibility necessary in the first place. As in the great Free Enterprise campaign, it appears that businessmen are trying to fill an ideological gap between business and society. They are not, however, trying to reweave a weakened moral fiber or to temper new, reckless thought with older, more secure truths about business; rather the argument is that they are trying to sell changes that have occurred *inside* the world of business. In the following discussion, I shall examine this argument and, at length, disagree with it.

[20] See, for example, Philip Green, A. A. Berle—New Myths for Old, *New Republic* (June 22, 1963); Manne, *op. cit.;* and Robert L. Heilbroner's review of Berle's *The American Economic Republic* in the *New York Review of Books*, I, No. 1 (n.d.).

[21] Bernard Nossiter, The Troubled Conscience of American Business, *Harper's* (September 1963), pp. 37–43.

V

Although no one knows exactly how many business enterprises there are in the United States, the Internal Revenue Service estimates [22] for the accounting year 1960–61 indicated 11,165,875 business enterprises in the nation; four-fifths were sole proprietorships; 9 per cent were partnerships; the remaining 10 per cent were corporations. According to Dun and Bradstreet, about 15,000 new corporate charters are granted each month. Since the number of failures is slightly lower, the number of corporations is increasing—IRS estimates show a 6 per cent increase from accounting year 1959–60 to 1960–61. These one million corporations employ about one-half of the labor force and generate more than one-half of the national income.

Mr. Berle has repeatedly observed that the actual assets owned by about 150 corporations equal about half the assets owned by all of American manufacturing industry. In its annual examination of the 500 largest industrial corporations (ranked by sales), *Fortune* confirms this general picture. These corporations now account for more than one-half of all U. S. manufacturing and mining company sales and more than 70 per cent of profits.

Moreover, as Mr. Berle has pointed out, ". . . in terms of power, without regard to asset position, not only do 500 corporations control two-thirds of the nonfarm economy but within each of that 500 a still smaller group has the ultimate decision-making power." [23] Thus, our search for the causes of ideological embarrassment leads directly to a relatively small number of corporations.

The Control of Power—Corporate Myths

The real facts about this corporate power, we are told by a growing managerial literature,[24] have been dangerously obscured

[22] U. S. Internal Revenue Service, *Statistics on Income 1960–61: U. S. Business Tax Returns,* Washington, D. C., Internal Revenue Service Publication No. 453 (11-62), Preliminary Report.

[23] A. A. Berle, Jr., *Economic Power and the Free Society,* Fund for the Republic, New York, 1957, p. 14.

[24] See, for example, David Bazelon, The Facts and Fictions of U. S. Capitalism, *Reporter* (September 17, 1959), pp. 43–48; Dow Votaw, The Mythology

by a series of widely accepted myths. We are assured that, given the broad, general incorporation acts, the corporation creates itself. It is not an active grant of power from the state and, furthermore, is put to no close or meaningful scrutiny or control by the state. And we are told further that the shareholder in the large corporation is not an owner in any meaningful sense of the concept of ownership. The fact that he can sell, receive, or not receive a dividend, or vote on those issues presented to him by management, can hardly be construed as ownership. Nor does the shareholder have control, another mythical status popularly accorded to him.

We delude ourselves, it is contended, when we automatically regard management as protector of the shareholders or representative of the shareholders' (or somebody else's) will. How is that will determined? Or indeed, does it exist?

We must not suppose that significant, independent checks on managerial power come from consumer sovereignty, product market competition, or the scrutiny of the capital market. These checks, to a considerable extent, have been rendered malleable, if not impotent, by advertising, administered prices, and internal financing.

These myth writings seek to show that textbook descriptions of the controls on corporate power today are more appropriate to the classic period of the corporation, which was already a business fossil in 1932 when Berle and Means published their study. They describe the corporation up to 1835 as:

. . . a group of owners, necessarily delegating certain powers of management, protected in their property rights by a series of fixed rules under which the management had a relatively limited play. The management of the corporation indeed was thought of as a set of agents running a business for a set of owners; and while they could and did have wider powers than most agents, they were strictly accountable and were in a position to be governed in all matters of general policy by their owners. They occupied, in fact, a position analogous to that of captain and officers of a ship at sea; in navigation their authority might

of Corporations, *California Management Review* (Spring 1962), pp. 58–74; and Michael D. Reagan, *The Managed Economy,* Oxford University Press, New York, 1963.

be supreme; but the direction of the voyage, the alteration of the vessel, the character of the cargo, and the distribution of the profits and losses were settled ahead of time and altered only by the persons having the underlying property interest.[25]

Still relatively free of mutations or other evolutionary change, this concept of the corporation corresponds closely to its original form. When Sir Edward Coke expounded the law of corporations as it developed in the fifteenth and sixteenth centuries, it was clear that the members of the corporation ran its internal relations, and that a vote of the majority of members determined the corporate will.[26]

Mutiny of the Managers

It is now widely held (in no small measure because of the original revelations and persuasiveness of Mr. Berle and Mr. Means) that there has been a mutiny of sorts, that the captain and officers of the ship have committed an act of disseisin by extending their authority far beyond mere matters of navigation. It is they, and not the persons having the underlying property interest, who are directing the voyage, altering the vessel, determining the character of the cargo, and distributing the profits and losses. Even if the disseisin was unwitting, the agents now have control; yet, the very law that allowed control of the na-

[25] Berle and Means, *op. cit.*, p. 135.

[26] In his two-volume treatise, *Corporations,* written in 1897, John P. Davis concluded: ". . . the corporation could act only through its organization; consequently, if an integral part of it should be wanting, the activity of the corporation was suspended until the wanting part should be supplied; thus during the vacancy of the headship, if one were a part of the corporation constitution, the corporation could perform no act until it had first elected a head. Nor might the head, in most matters, act without the body." II, Capricorn Giant, New York, 1961, p. 213.

He cites Coke's authority: "A sole body politic that hath the absolute right in them, as an abbot, bishop, and the like, may make a discontinuance; but a corporation aggregate of many, as dean and chapter, warden and chaplains, master and fellows, mayor and commonalty, etc., cannot make any discontinuance; for if they join, the grant is good; and if the dean, warden, master, or mayor makes it alone, where the body is aggregate of many, it is void and worketh a disseisen. . . ."

tion's business to shift to managers denies them legitimate legal status for the exercise of that power.

It is a long and complicated journey from Coke's *Institutes* and *Reports* to the modern business corporation; yet, its direction has been rather consistently and necessarily toward redistributing the power to act to a smaller and smaller group of members—the managers. It is they who dictate the rate of investment, allocate research and development expenditures from retained earnings, decide what products will be introduced, determine, through advertising, what demand will be stimulated, and because of the size of the firms they manage, shape communities and often the lives of their employees. It is no accident that the researches that led Mr. Whyte to *Is Anybody Listening?* took him next to *The Organization Man*.[27] Indeed, "Within its internal world and in its far-reaching relations with its external world, it is not clear" observes George Leland Bach, "that the modern business corporation has much less pervasive influence than, say, the medieval church in its society." [28]

Crisis of Legitimacy

The power of the medieval church was legitimate because it emanated from a coherent body of accepted social thought, but, as we have been told, the modern corporation cannot make a similar claim today. And so it is held that the managers of the modern corporation face a crisis of legitimacy. When pressing issues of public interest arise, Harland Cleveland writes, there is no "agreed-upon *procedure* for facing them . . . the ultimate source of legitimation is the managers' own perpetuating powers, the survival of their own purposes and functions as the managers define them." [29] As this becomes understood, he continues, the likelihood of further restriction on corporate freedom increases. In defense of their freedom, managers are seeking to blur the distinction between public and private interests, in part by "a

[27] William H. Whyte, Jr., *The Organization Man*, Simon and Schuster, New York, 1956.

[28] Melvin Anshen and G. L. Bach, eds., *Management and Corporations 1985*, McGraw-Hill, New York, 1960, p. 3.

[29] Cleveland and Lasswell, *op. cit.*, pp. xxviii, xxxi.

drumfire of public relations, the primary purpose of which is to justify the manager's present and future actions in terms of some concept of the public interest. . . ."

Professor Edward Mason contends that if modern managerial writing cannot supply a substitute for the undermined precepts of classical economics, the cost will be reduction of institutional stability and opportunities for economic growth, for these depend heavily on an ideology acceptable to leaders of thought in the community. "It cannot be too strongly emphasized," he writes, "that the growth of nineteenth-century capitalism depended largely on the general acceptance of a reasoned justification of the system on moral as well as on political and economic grounds." [30] Managerial literature has successfully attacked these justifications, but offers in their place only vague generalizations about managerial conscience and the "transcendental margin."

Need for Accountability

This same brace of problems—government intervention and reduced rate of economic growth—is cited by a second group of writers who view the corporate problem primarily as an internal one—the adverse effects on the behavior of managers of increasing attenuation of ownership.

Ernest Dale, in his recent *The Great Organizers*,[31] attempts to list some of these problems and also to measure their effect on performance. He starts from the premise that since manager and shareholder interests are not the same, the self-perpetuating managers will think first of their own positions, should a conflict arise. Their exalted role tends to remove them from the consequences of their own acts; it inhibits free discussion and enforces conformity in the organization; it is likely to produce expenditures on staff and salaries that are too high. Dale cites the interesting example of a firm that was losing money and was afraid it

---

[30] Edward S. Mason, The Apologetics of "Managerialism," *The Journal of Business*, XXI (January 1958), p. 6. For a somewhat different view see H. J. Habakkuk, *American and British Technology in the 19th Century*, Cambridge University Press, Cambridge, 1962.

[31] Ernest Dale, *The Great Organizers*, McGraw-Hill, New York, 1960, Chapter 6.

would lose its key employees because of poor morale. Its executives decided to reward themselves and the key employees with a reduced option price on shares. It did not occur to them that the bad financial position was their responsibility and that the company might be better off if they resigned.[32]

He concludes that this conflict between the personal goals of the unchecked manager and the goals of the organization can only lead to poorer performance, that the organization will not release the same initiative as if it were proprietor controlled (or at least partially so). Mr. Dale has little faith in the restraining influence of such "inherent checks" as the professionalism of management or its professed social responsibilities.[33]

Mr. Nossiter's plaint is not that managers will lack initiative, but rather that they may have too much. Since, in many industries, the restraining effects of competition are diminished, a few key executives make decisions that may or may not be in the public interest. Thus, ". . . some business theoreticians have invented a new doctrine, the concept of the Corporate Conscience, to assure us that all is well." [34]

In sum, one view holds that since the growth of corporations has created a crisis of legitimacy, we must find an explanation (apologetic) for the new status of corporations that will lead the public to accept them today as it did in the last century. A second view is concerned, not with the behavior of the public, but with the behavior of managers. Here, the concern is to find ways in which managers can be made to behave as if they were owners and to be as responsible as if they were competitive. Offered as

---

[32] Another example comes from the recent revelation that the costly decision by General Dynamics to build ". . . the 990 was signed, sealed, and delivered without board approval." See Richard Austin Smith, *Corporations in Crises,* Doubleday, New York, 1963, p. 83.

[33] In the place of the partial proprietors who are passing from the scene, he advocates professional directors, who will be put on boards by the large financial institutions (who now tend not to vote at all). These men would devote full time to directorial duties, assure an atmosphere of free discussion on boards, and serve as an independent review on an otherwise unchecked management.

[34] Nossiter, *op. cit.,* p. 37.

a solution to these problems, the Gospel of Social Responsibility or the concept of the corporate conscience has few supporters.

VI

Since organizations ranging from the Roman Curia to contemporary worker-managed undertakings in Yugoslavia [35] have been accused of succumbing to the Iron Law of Oligarchy, there is no reason to assume that the large business corporation would be immune. The debate around the Berle thesis is now over one-third of a century old; its still unanswered questions remain fascinating and useful. In the context of this debate, the social responsibility of business has been shown to be a vague and even potentially dangerous concept; the new doctrine has merely restated existing market and profit norms in longer-run terms but is certainly not a substitute for them.

The desire to justify power is a natural impulse, and its chronicles represent much of the political history of nations. The facts of corporate ownership and behavior, however, hardly warrant the assumption that the Gospel of Social Responsibility is designed to justify the power of managers over an ownerless system. I contend that these facts warrant rather different conclusions.

1. It Is Far from Clear that Attenuation of Ownership Control Is as Complete as Is Generally Assumed

The most recent attempt to bring up to date the famous Temporary National Economic Committee reports published in 1940 is Don Villarejo's detailed analysis of stockholdings by directors in the nation's 250 largest industrial firms.[36] His study concludes

---

[35] See Pope Paul Calls for Reform of the Curia, *New York Herald Tribune* (Int. Ed.), September 23, 1963; and *Workers' Management in Yugoslavia,* International Labour Office, Geneva, 1962, p. 277. In the latter case it is called "following the directorial line."

[36] Don Villarejo, Stock Ownership and the Control of Corporations, *New University Thought,* II (Autumn 1961 and Winter 1962), pp. 33–77 and pp. 47–65. The list of the 250 largest firms, as ranked by total assets, was taken from *Fortune* (July 1960). Usable data could be obtained for 232 of the corporations studied.

that in a minimum of 141 corporations out of 232 concentrated ownership on the Board of Directors was sufficient to secure potential working control in the corporation in question. In the case of the other 91 corporations, the evidence available did not indicate highly concentrated holdings by directors or other large stockholders, but the data were inconclusive and centers of control may well exist.[37]

Villarejo generally uses a yardstick of 5 per cent as the amount of stock ownership required to control a corporation where the stock is widely dispersed, although the necessary figure clearly will vary in individual cases. Of course, definitions of "control" differ from student to student, as do the criteria used to separate owner-controlled from management-controlled enterprises.[38] But the Villarejo estimates seem conservative at every point, since in a highly uncertain field he relies only upon data that are known with certainty.

Another recent investigation of this point has been made by Gabriel Kolko, who calculated the voting stock of directors in the top 100 corporations, based on proxy statements for 1957. He includes stock managed by professional representatives sitting on

[37] The data used were from Securities and Exchange Commission reports, which require a complete current listing of securities owned by the officer or director of each corporation. The major shortcoming of this type of data is that there is no guarantee of finding either the largest holding in a given corporation or the control block of stock. Officers and directors need not report holdings of relatives. Where the controlling group is indirectly represented on the board, there is no available information on the overall holding of the group. Trust holdings of banks in a corporation need not be reported, even if a director of the bank is a director of the corporation in question.

[38] The Temporary National Economic Committee Monograph No. 29, p. 99, defines control as "the power of determining the broad policies guiding a corporation and not . . . the actual influence on the day-to-day affairs of an enterprise." Berle and Means use the definition also adopted by R. A. Gordon, "Possession of the power to select or change management." (See footnote 44.) Berle argues (in *Power without Property,* p. 74) that "management control" is the "locus of power over and the norm of control of the bulk of American industry now." Management control is defined to mean that "no large concentrated stockholding exists which maintains a close working relationship with the management or is capable of challenging it" (p. 73).

boards—either for personal trusts or holding companies—and directors' beneficial interests in partnerships, trusts, and estates, including the known holdings of their direct families. Kolko concludes that the minimum percentage of voting stock owned or represented by the directors was, on the average, 9.9 per cent of the corporation's shares. "That figure would probably be increased by several percentage points if it were possible to include the stock ownership in several closely owned giants that do not issue proxy statements. In only 23 of these 100 companies are directors listed as owning more than 10 per cent of the voting stock; in 36, they are listed as owning less than 1 per cent. As in 1937, the vast majority of stock owned by directors is held by no more than 300 men." [39]

These figures are undoubtedly lower than they would be if full information were available, because of the splitting of blocks of stock among family members for tax purposes and the placing of stocks in professionally managed trusts and investment companies, where identities can be obscured. For example, when T.N.E.C. and current stock ownership figures for the same corporations are compared, in board after board the same family names appear but with very much less stock ownership visible in the current figures.

Another weakness of the attenuation of ownership control position is the fact that directors are increasingly synonymous with management. "In 1937–39, 36 per cent of the directors of the top industrials were also key officers in their respective companies. By 1957, that figure was 50 per cent. This meant, taking into account interlocking directorates, that the majority of the 1,477 directors of the 100 top companies were active officers in some of these companies. In 47 of the top 100, officer-directors held absolute majorities." [40]

It is also significant that, as a group, the wealthiest 1 per cent of adults has increased its concentration of stock ownership over the last 30 years.

[39] Gabriel Kolko, *Wealth and Power in America*, Praeger, New York, 1962, pp. 61–62.
[40] *Ibid.*, p. 60.

Percentage of Corporate Stock Held by Wealthiest
One Per Cent of Adults—Selected Years

Year	1922	1929	1939	1945	1949	1953
Amount	61.5	65.6	69.0	61.7	64.9	76.0

Source: Robert J. Lampman, *The Share of Top Wealth-Holders in National Wealth, 1922–1956,* Princeton University Press, Princeton, N. J., 1962, p. 209. (Note that Lampman warns that these figures are very rough and should be used with caution.)

A recent *New York Times* article, "Multi Millionaire Stockholders Still Rule Big Business," reviews a new University of Pennsylvania study that adds further evidence in support of this conclusion.[41] Persons with incomes over $100,000 a year, it reports, own more than 19.5 per cent of all the stock in the country. It would be surprising if the people who hold these substantial ownership rights in corporations did not wield great influence over them.

Villarejo concedes that the issue of management control can only be settled finally "if lists of, say, the largest 150 shareholdings in each corporation of interest became available to the public." He also willingly concedes that there are some cases in which management appears to enjoy a dominant position, but his impressive array of facts leads him to conclude that "a relatively small group of persons, the propertied rich" (whom he names) "both own and, substantially, control the giant enterprises of the nation."

2. Whether or Not Private Ownership Confers Legitimacy to the Extent Just Suggested, It Is Clear that Managers Already Enjoy the Legitimacy Conferred by Public Acceptance

The ironic fact is that at the very time that the great Free Enterprise campaign was at its peak, Americans were beginning to

[41] *New York Times,* September 13, 1963, pp. 35, 42. The study is entitled Characteristics of Stock Ownership by Jean Crockett and Irwin Friend. Preliminary draft (mimeographed), Table 1.5, pp. 1.24–25. Part of a large-scale Study of Stock Ownership and Trading financed by the Ford Foundation and directed by Professor Friend.

lay to rest their traditional economic fears about large-scale enterprise. More important still, many were actively endorsing the very big businesses that, out of fear, were supporting the Free Enterprise campaign. Today, bigness is widely, if not unanimously, accepted as an economic necessity, even a social good.[42]

One measure of this acceptance is the quiet, almost knowing, reception and early assignment to oblivion accorded the writings of Mr. T. K. Quinn, a man whose credentials and writing skill would have won him a secure place in the journals of economics just a few years earlier. As senior vice president of the General Electric Corporation, he had access to a view of the large business corporation available only to the top man and his heir apparent. His views about the dangers of big business organizations led Mr. Quinn out of G.E. and to the writing, in 1953, of *Giant Business: Threat to Democracy* and, in 1956, of *Giant Corporations: Challenge to Freedom* [43]—both now all but forgotten. In 1956, when William H. Whyte, Jr., poked fun at the managers of organizations, we were ready to laugh at them but not to fear them.

A further measure of this acceptance of managerial capitalism is the apparent lack of impression made by the current writings that bemoan it. In fact, this lack of response is sometimes posed as the major issue in the problem itself. David Bazelon complains bitterly at the conclusion of his "Facts and Fictions of U. S. Capitalism" that when the fictions and power concentrations of our system are pointed out, people are unwilling to confront these facts, or even if they do, they respond, "So what? The System works!" Certainly there is no discernible move toward implementing the reforms that have been proposed.[44] Nor, indeed, is there much evidence outside of managerial literature of a serious intellectual involvement with the problem posed.

[42] See, for example, David Lilienthal, *Big Business, A New Era*, Harper, New York, 1953, serialized in *Collier's* in 1952 and later reprinted as a Pocket Book; John Kenneth Galbraith, *American Capitalism*, Houghton Mifflin, Boston, 1952; and Leonard Sayles, *Individualism and Big Business*, McGraw-Hill, New York, 1963.

[43] Both published by Exposition Press, New York.

[44] For example, those of R. A. Gordon in *Business Leadership in the Large Corporation*, University of California Press, Berkeley, 1961, pp. 347–351, or those of Ernest Dale (see footnote 33).

But what of the views of the shareholders, whose involvement is more than an intellectual one? Do they accept increasing managerial independence?

If there is serious shareholder dissatisfaction with this situation, it cannot be very widespread. Twice during the past decade, the American Society of Corporate Secretaries has queried its member firms (which include most U. S. blue-chip companies) on matters of shareowner attendance and representation at meetings. The findings [45] show a uniform increase in both, with a marked increase in shareowner representation. In 1958 nearly two-thirds of the companies responding to the questionnaire showed between 81 and 90 per cent representation at annual meetings.

Shareholders are more anxious than ever for financial reporting, and the company that overlooks its owners runs the risk of feeling their influence in annoying ways.[46] A discussion with Mr. Lewis D. Gilbert, a man whose professional life has been devoted wholly to advancing the cause of shareholder interests, confirms this view. In the 1962 annual report [47] of his activities, Mr. Gilbert, who is no friend of managers, stresses the progress made by shareholders in advancing their interests. His list of needed reforms is long, but no less impressive is his case that shareholder influence is increasing. Thus, the group most directly concerned with managers—the shareholders—not only is not in revolt, it behaves as if shareholder democracy still has meaning. In short, they too accept the managers.

3. Prominent among the Reasons for This Acceptance Is that Managers Behave Like Owners

Where performance is concerned, it is control not ownership that is important. And there is no generally convincing evidence that managers act differently as managers than they would as

[45] American Society of Corporate Secretaries, Inc., *Shareowner Communications and Related Subjects* (March 1960), pp. 3–4.

[46] See Oscar M. Beveridge, *Financial Public Relations,* McGraw-Hill, New York, 1963.

[47] Lewis D. and John J. Gilbert, *Twenty-Third Annual Report of Stockholder Activities at Corporation Meetings 1962,* New York.

owners. There is much evidence, on the other hand, that they share the profit interests of stockholders and conduct themselves accordingly.

Their share of the stock of the corporation for which they work may be an insignificant percentage of that stock, but it is nevertheless exceedingly significant for their own personal fortunes. Kolko points out that in early 1957, 25 General Motors officers owned an average of 11,500 shares each. Even together, they certainly could not have obtained control of GM through their stockholdings. But each of these men had a personal stake of roughly one-half million dollars in the company, plus the tantalizing prospect of the corporation's continued growth.

Top management, in fact, is committed more strongly than ever to the corporation's profit position as a result of the growth of stock option plans, because without profits the options are largely worthless. By 1957 option plans had been instituted by 77 per cent of the manufacturing corporations listed on the New York or American stock exchanges. Of the largest 100 industrials, only 13 did not have option plans in 1959. Of the 87 with option plans, the 83 for which public data were available had granted key officers options on an average of 1.9 per cent of their outstanding voting stock by 1959. And the percentage of outstanding stock reserved for executive options is suggestive. By 1960, for example, Inland Steel had assigned the equivalent of 11 per cent of its outstanding voting stock for options; Ford, 6.7 per cent.

Furthermore, top corporation executives are extraordinarily well-paid men—the median income of 1,674 top executives of the 834 largest corporations in 1957 was $73,583—and they have been buying stock. In fact, the managerial class is the largest single group in the stockholding population, and a far greater proportion of this class (44.8 per cent) owns stock than any other. Thus, their personal fortunes are bound not only to the money-making success of their own companies but also to that of the larger corporate structure in which they have invested.

Managers are part of the culture that counts gain as the main measure of success. If there were nothing else, the tradition of seeking gain alone would remain a strong influence on their behavior. But in addition to the stock option plans and other perquisites clearly linked to profitable return, an even more important factor is that the corporation's internal operating rules are established on a profit-return basis. Profitability becomes the test of investment decisions, the operating rule for corporate divisions. If survival is the first test of the corporation, maximum return is its test of efficient operation. It is the test by which managers survive in the face of competition from their peers and subordinates; it is the way company divisions gain favors from corporate-level executive committees. The profit level provides strength in wage negotiations and leverage in seeking favors from a local community.

Thus, even in the absence of an immediate ownership interest, managers have remained remarkably true to the interests of owners. When one considers a company like A. T. and T. (with 245 million shares and 2.3 million shareholders), ownership is so widely diffused that it becomes meaningless to talk about it in the customary sense. Indeed, one does not wonder that such companies have not done better, but rather that they have enjoyed the financial success they have.

When looked at objectively, the salaries and perquisites of some managers seem inordinately high, higher than would be necessary to attract needed talent by market considerations alone. Wilbert Moore observes that this seems a polite way for managers to have their hands in the till. Although this is probably true, it is also a part of the managerial culture and not primarily a function of the attenuation of ownership. Managers' salaries in large family-controlled firms such as Ford and du Pont are also very high.

By their professions of social responsibility, managers reflect characteristics long associated with ownership. Whereas the stewardship of wealth was formerly a concern for the rich owners of big corporations, the expression of social responsibility by today's managers seems to be a modern affirmation of ownership values rather than a rejection of them.

The motives and values of the men who make the top decisions in large firms have long been the subject of study. Since it is obvious that many decisions cannot be explained by a simple profit-maximizing assumption, since it is clear that there is some freedom of action away from this norm, many attempts have been made to construct models to predict the behavior of managers. Typically, these emphasize longer-run profit goals or a satisfactory combination of several objectives. A very recent model is that of Robin Marris, who contends that managers act primarily out of concern for the growth rate of their firms, subject to concern for their job security.[48]

None of these studies contends that managers reject the values of ownership or the goal of profit maximizing. Some suggest, in fact, that the freedom of the managers enables them more ably to maximize long-run profits. It is clear that managers have not made the bid for power predicted by James Burnham, nor have they abandoned the system under a socialist onslaught as foreseen by Joseph Schumpeter. This test has never come. Instead, managers have assumed the entrepreneurial position primarily as a technical role.

In their study of the process of industrialism, Kerr, Harbison, Dunlop, and Myers contend that this is a world-wide phenomenon:

. . . despite the fact that the ranks of professional management are destined to expand in all industrializing societies, the managerial class has neither the capacity nor the will to become the dominant ruling group. The managers are characteristically the agents of stockholders, of state bureaucracies, or in some cases of workers' councils. Since they are preoccupied with the internal affairs of enterprise, which become ever more complex, the members of the managerial class are prone to become conformists rather than leaders in the larger affairs of society.[49]

4. Although the Big Corporation and Its Managers Enjoy Public Acceptance, More and More Demands Are Being Made of Them

The resident American managers of European firms are working today in a political and social environment that, so they

[48] See Robin Marris, A Model of the "Managerial" Enterprise, *Quarterly Journal of Economics*, LXXVII (May 1963), pp. 185–209.

[49] Clark Kerr, Frederick Harbison, John Dunlop, and Charles A. Myers, *Industrialism and Industrial Man*, *International Labour Review*, LXXXII (September 1960), p. 10. Also their other work cited therein.

report to their home offices, is simply a more advanced stage of changes that they see occurring in the United States. Direct U. S. investment abroad, although small in relative terms, is large enough to attract considerable blame for the balance of payments deficit, and in several industries it is successful enough to cause governments to seek methods of curbing it. It is also large enough to have an impact on managerial thinking. For in Europe, although much enterprise remains securely private and profitable, the public, represented by the political process, is gaining increasing influence in the direction of the corporation.

The forms vary from worker representation on boards of directors, to so-called partnership-in-planning arrangements between the state and various economic interests. Although the Scandinavian countries have pioneered in the latter arrangement, France, because of the size, diversity, and private character of its industry, attracts most current attention with its Plan. By no means is the attention unfavorable, even from American businessmen, for as *Business Week* has pointed out,[50] voluntary planning in France shows that economic freedom and planning can mix.

In broadest terms, the Plan's objective is to bring economic power under political control, a point clearly understood by American executives operating in France. "At home we think about autonomy," one told me. "Over here we look for influence."

In specific terms, the French government, after consultation with economic interest groups, sets a desired growth rate. Policy directives and, eventually, their technical execution are carried on through tripartite planning commissions, which translate general goals into specific targets for each sector. No direct authority is applied to firms, but fiscal and monetary policy are used to provide incentives to private industry, which has been made aware of the general framework of growth and assured of its place therein.

Intrigued by their success with the first four stages of this experiment, the French express enthusiasm for the fifth and for defining more fully the responsibilities of the private corporation.

[50] April 7, 1962, pp. 80–92.

A new book by François Bloch-Laine,[51] which seeks to do just that, has become required reading in the business community. Although some of M. Bloch-Laine's specific programs for assuring corporate accountability might arouse little enthusiasm in the U. S.,[52] he notes that Americans have already made considerable progress toward his main objective—"social integration of the corporation."

Americans have accepted the big corporation, and they expect much of it. The large corporation has come to play an important role in American society and has come to bear responsibility for many areas of the quality and tone of American life. As Abram Chayes writes: "The neglect of basic research, the dilution of the college degree, the organization man, the dullness and superficiality of the mass media, the level of political morality— all these offspring, wanted or unwanted, find their way in the end to the doorstep of the modern corporation." [53]

It is often pointed out in the writings about managerial capitalism that the position of the managers is getting closer and closer to that of the public administrators; their function is increasingly that of reconciling and mediating among the many conflicting interests that lay claim to the corporation and its fruits.

No one understands this better than the managers who are caught between these interests. Shortly after World War II, when large-scale industrial unionism emerged faster than the attitudes accommodating it, a new type of manager emerged— the personnel manager or industrial relations director—who, as he worked with the realities of union power and grievances, found himself spending most of his time convincing top management of the essential merits of the union position. Since this job had to be performed at the same time that the great Free

[51] François Bloch-Laine, *Pour Une Réforme De L'Enterprise,* Éditions du Seuil, Paris, 1963.

[52] Particularly his proposed system of economic courts, which, among other functions, would resolve conflicts about corporate leadership and attest to the accuracy of its accounting.

[53] Edward S. Mason, ed., *The Corporation in Modern Society,* Harvard University Press, Cambridge, Mass., 1959, pp. 26–27.

Enterprise campaign was gaining momentum, its difficulties cannot be overestimated. It was not by choice that many of these managers changed careers and are today public servants or members of college and university faculties.

In recent years the problem of the industrial relations manager is becoming the problem of all managers. Because of its importance to the realization of national objectives, the corporation is becoming an instrument of national policy. This is especially true in Great Britain where, during the period of nationalization, the problem was to appoint managers who would be efficient but at the same time serve the goals of nationalization. In lesser degree it is also true in the United States, where we have begun to look to the corporation to maintain price stability in the face of wage demands, to restrain inflationary pressures by behaving as if it faced competitive markets, to help sustain domestic expansion, and to assist with the balance-of-payments problem. At the request of President Kennedy, C. W. Greenewalt, Board Chairman of du Pont, is seeking $12,700,000 from U. S. business to finance Radio Free Europe. U. S. Steel concedes that its decision to open higher-paying jobs to Negroes in its Fairfield, Alabama, plant was made because of federal government pressure and the leverage of government contracts.

Given these pressures, it is not surprising that, willingly or otherwise, managers are developing a sense of social awareness and that they act (or at least speak) in response to it. Managers of large corporations cannot help but respond to the demand for social responsibility—the same demand that helped to create a tradition of responsibility in medicine and has led many firms, as we have seen, to develop their own oaths and creeds in the tradition of Hippocrates.

Their motives undoubtedly include profit and job security, but basic to all of these is their desire to maintain their autonomy. In a recent full-page ad, the Celanese Corporation announces that it "proudly cherishes its freedom to innovate, and considers that corporate self-discipline, like personal self-discipline, is the chief condition of retaining that freedom."

If this lesson was slowly learned, it was not for lack of evidence. An accommodation with the American labor movement; a somewhat more realistic view of the world position of capitalism; the discovery that within "socialized" nations such as Great Britain and Sweden much private enterprise goes on, that in others the official definition of socialism is one that members of the NAM would not find too unpalatable—all these have helped American businessmen to the realization that their immediate existence was not being threatened. Many of them have come to understand that the way to long-run assurance of getting what they want most—autonomy—is not the old ideology but a new one—an attempt to show that business serves the public interest. General Motors' public relations campaign is certainly geared to this point. The Free Enterprise campaign presented the corporation as the business on the corner of main street. But no more; GM public relations vice president, Anthony De Lorenzo, states: "We don't try to make ourselves look small, but to look good." [54]

When the discussion of the Gospel of Social Responsibility is limited to assertions that it is self-serving or inadequate to prop up an antiquated ideology, however, its importance is underestimated. It has produced not only the most agreeable posture struck by American business to date, but, as we saw earlier, it has produced socially useful results as well. The businessman's new sense of awareness, of being responsible to society in general, has, among other things, produced the Committee for Economic Development, put students through college, helped their professors gain increased income, and through the Business Committee for Tax Reduction (led by the presidents of Ford Motor Company and the Pennsylvania Railroad) helped the U. S. get a badly needed tax cut.

5. The Importance of Corporate Autonomy Should Be Recognized, Its Limits Defined, and the Discussion of Its Terms Not Limited to Ideology

"One may hazard a guess," George Lichtheim wrote recently, "that in a good many, if not all, backward countries . . . to the despairing question 'How can we sell capitalism to the masses?'

[54] Quoted from Irwin Ross, *The Image Merchants,* Weidenfeld and Nicolson, London, 1960, p. 166.

the obvious answer would appear to be: 'By calling it social-ism'!" [55]

And in our country? By calling it social responsibility?

"Such stratagems," Mr. Lichtheim continues, "need not be conscious; they are, indeed, more likely to be successful, if the exponents of the official creed are in good faith. But for obvious reasons they can work only in backward countries and with fairly unsophisticated electorates (if, indeed, there is any intention of consulting the electorate at all). Where democracy and literacy have already had a trial run, most people are likely to see through such conscious or unconscious maneuvers. . . ."

Perhaps this explains the failure of the great Free Enterprise campaign, but if I am correct in assuming that the Gospel of Social Responsibility is selling corporate autonomy, then by Mr. Lichtheim's test it is worthy of our attention.

In law and in practice, we have recognized that if managers are to do their job, they must be given the necessary independ-ence. TWA managers are currently engaged in a lawsuit, the major aim of which is to keep the corporation's largest stock-holder from interfering in their affairs. John K. Galbraith, when he was Ambassador to India, urged developing nations to resist the temptation to interfere with corporate autonomy, noting that the corporation's goals will be best served if it has inde-pendence.[56] As the experience with codetermination in Germany and nationalization in Great Britain and even the Soviet Union have demonstrated, corporate autonomy is a condition to which ideology must adjust, not the other way around.

Corporate autonomy should be viewed pragmatically. In their daily affairs large corporations confront and create a wide range of complex issues, the solution of which requires managerial free-dom. When this freedom has been abused, as, for example, in labor and financial matters in the past, we have enacted codes and created agencies to administer them.

This approach, combined with a viable democracy, can best

[55] See George Lichtheim, Post-Bourgeois Europe, *Commentary* (January 1963), p. 2.

[56] John K. Galbraith, *Economic Development in Perspective*, Harvard Uni-versity Press, Cambridge, Mass., 1962, Chapter 5.

advance such national goals as balanced economic growth, more equitable income distribution, employment opportunities, and freedom.

In each of these areas, however, it cannot be said that business does not live up to its social responsibilities, unless we are prepared to define these responsibilities.[57]

In the literature on managerialism the conflict between the recognized need for autonomous private organizations and the growing concern about the uses of their power is typically resolved by concluding, "If corporations ought to be doing things they are not now doing . . . then it is up to government to tell them so." [58] Although this correctly places the burden on government, it leaves unanswered the more difficult questions of how socially responsible business behavior is to be defined and the role of private organizations in defining that interest. The fields of agriculture, international trade, labor, and conservation, among others, are replete with evidence that the same diffusion of power that has induced social awareness makes more difficult the development of policies reflecting the public interest. A crisis such as the thalidomide scandal may momentarily disperse public apathy and provoke a prompt definition of business responsibility by Congress, but more often, conflicting interests paralyze legislative action. For this reason the use of presidential power is often prescribed. Although President Kennedy won support in April 1962 when he defined for U. S. Steel its social responsibilities, clearly presidential power cannot often be used in this way. An appeal to President Kennedy by many health groups to appoint a commission to determine "the social responsibilities" of business and government led two years later to the surgeon general's report on health and smoking. Whether and how these social responsibilities of government and business are to be defined is yet unknown.

[57] For a parallel argument on the social responsibility of science, see Bernard Barber, *Science and the Social Order,* The Free Press of Glencoe, New York, 1952, pp. 225–232, especially p. 229.

[58] Andrew Hacker, Business Role in Social Reform, *New York Times,* Western Edition, November 22, 1963.

In his essay "Conglomerate Bigness as a Source of Power," Corwin Edwards concludes that as the large corporation comes to typify the organization of the business community, "its general direction would be toward an authoritarian system of business, within which the significant checks and balances would be, not those of the market, but whatever safeguards might be built into the structure of the corporation or into the relationships between the corporations and the state." [59]

In the decade since Professor Edwards's article appeared, most discussion about the dangers of corporate power stresses either the need for citizens to become alert to the dangers of power or the need for some as yet unspecified institutionalized forms of assuring that power is made responsive. In the end, it may be the process of the discussion itself and the factors that stimulate it that produce the most lasting effects.

During the past year businessmen from various parts of the nation were invited by the Religion and Labor Council of America to participate in a conference on "Channeling Corporate Power in the Public Interest," where they may have been reminded that seventy years ago the Standard Oil Company aroused fear in Henry Demarest Lloyd, because the men who ran it lacked the "restraints of culture, experience, pride, inherited caution of class or rank." But today the growing discussion does not emphasize fear so much as the challenge of defining a mission for the corporation. Should its power be confined to that of a limited-purpose organization for the production and distribution of goods and services? Or should business play a larger role in our achievement of widely desired national goals? And if so, how can we create an environment in which business self-interest coincides with doing the right thing?

6. *The Gospel of Social Responsibility Is Important as a Conservative Response to a Changing Environment*

In his classic volume, *The Organizational Revolution*, Professor Kenneth Boulding observes that change can be orderly

[59] Corwin Edwards, *Business Concentration and Price Policy*, Princeton University Press, Princeton, N. J., 1955, p. 351.

and peaceful only when the leadership group can absorb the challengers. Thus, he notes:

The aristocratic class, especially in England, responded to the challenge of the rising business class by marrying its heiresses. The business class is likewise responding to the challenge of the rising labor and farm group, not perhaps quite in the traditional manner of the earlier aristocracy, but by developing a working relationship of industrial government through collective bargaining and by submitting to the economic encroachments of the social-democratic state.[60]

We have already noted some of the current pressures and expectations faced by the corporation. Even if businessmen were not listening to their critics in recent years, it would have been hard to avoid still others. President Kennedy's confrontation of U. S. Steel is the most spectacular instance, but there are many more. For several years now there have been antitrust proposals to split up corporations that have "unreasonable" market power; during the last steel strike legislation was proposed to require firms in basic industries to give public notice of price increases and afford the public a chance for a hearing before an agency without power to decide prices—only to manage the hearings. The impact of the growing literature of managerialism, the significance of the attempt to define wage guideposts, and the dozens of other ways in which political authority influences corporate decisions are increasingly felt by businessmen who frequently ask, "What does it all mean?" Mr. Harold Brayman, Director of Public Relations for du Pont and an elder statesman in corporate public relations, provided an answer at the last annual meeting of the Public Relations Society of America. Advances in education and communication have made public opinion a new dominant power. It is not a hostile government that business must reckon with, he warned. It is the new authority wielded by the public. In my view, the Gospel of Social Responsibility is best understood as part of the process of absorbing the impact of this changing environment. In this essay I have contended that rules internal to the corporation are important in determining the

[60] Kenneth Boulding, *The Organizational Revolution*, Harper, New York, 1953, pp. 132–133.

behavior of managers, and that insofar as corporate goals have become enlarged through the managers' increased sense of social awareness, this is due to influences outside the firm.

The magnitude of these changes should not be overestimated, however. Neither Admiral Rickover's revelations of faulty work on atomic submarines nor the NASA criticisms of defects in the work of missile contractors brought serious new pressures on the private corporation. And when the Russians launched the first satellite into space, it was the educational system, not the business system, that was criticized. Barring another depression or external economic threat, there is no imminent likelihood that American business will again be put on trial as it was in the 1930's.

Nevertheless, the environment has changed, and business with it. Once closed in behind locked gates, the industrial plant of today is coming more and more to resemble the college campus, and its officers behave more like college deans than business moguls. As Stewart Holbrook notes, businessmen during *The Age of the Moguls* [61] could get away with behavior that today would produce 100-year jail terms. The influences producing this changing environment manifest themselves in many ways beyond those discussed in this essay. An example is the debate now in process between some insurance carriers and their policy holders. The carriers are trying to find ways of eliminating "business risk" losses—losses due to poor management rather than to accident or negligence. Why? Because the responsibility of manufacturers and sellers for the risks of injury due to defective products is expanding and, in the view of underwriters, is being carried forward by a "social and economic philosophy" of responsibility that is approaching "the concept of absolute liability regardless of privity or negligence." [62]

The recent action of a grand jury that accused an advertising agency of fraud in its campaign to sell a weight-reducing drug suggests still another form that the changed environment may

---

[61] Stewart Holbrook, *The Age of the Moguls*, Doubleday, Garden City, N. Y., 1953, p. x.

[62] See R. J. Wendorff, The "Business Risk" Problems of Products Liability Insurance, *Wisconsin Bar Bulletin* (October 1962), pp. 29–50.

take; will advertising agencies be held responsible for the goods they promote?

Although these environmental changes have proceeded slowly, their cumulative effects have resulted in something approaching a textbook example of the behavior that organizations need for survival. When the environment changes and the organization no longer fits, its listening devices report the change. If the organization is to survive over a long period, it must make the necessary alterations in its behavior. These changes, in turn, influence the environment and set in motion a continuing chain of adjustments until a satisfactory fit is achieved.

"We, as managers of business and industry," Pierre S. du Pont told his audience of manufacturers, ". . . have got to take a good look at what we do and how we do it in order to make sure that we deserve popular support. And if the facts do not fit our words, I am afraid we must change the facts to bring them into conformity."

VII

Organizations, as Professor Boulding points out, not only adapt to the changing environment, they also defend themselves against change. As we have seen, along with the new campaign of business responsibility in recent years businessmen have renewed their interest in political activity, as they did during the Free Enterprise campaign. The same companies sometimes participate in both. Summer of 1963 saw the formation of a new political group—the Business-Industry Political Action Committee. Its creation set a national precedent, marking the first time that finance and industry leaders have openly joined political forces. Their announced purpose was to help finance candidates "who support the principles of constitutional government."

Every business gathering reflecting a forward look and a willingness to adapt to change can probably be matched by another that sounds all too familiar as it girds itself to resist change. There are sharp variations in business attitudes by region and by industry, as well as differences between spokesmen for the smaller firm and the large corporation. An interesting confirmation that the latter tends to be more concerned with social responsibility comes from a study of annual reports, which found that companies with large assets and with considerable contact with household consumers, the general public, and regulatory commissions are more likely to give attention in their annual reports to "objectives outside of or superior to the profit motive." [63]

It is still too early to tell to what extent this defensive action can offset the changing environment, but there is ample reason to suspect that, barring a depression or some other source of momentum, the defensive efforts will succeed in delaying change. One can safely predict that if a movement to codify autonomy and extend the definitions of corporate responsibility gains momentum, the old ideology will be revived at crucial times. We have two recent examples. In the fall of 1963, an irreconcilable conflict emerged from President Kennedy's Business Committee for Tax Reduction. Pulled forward by the economic need for tax reduction but held back by their views about budgetary deficits, several businessmen urged that a tax cut be conditioned on reduced government spending. When this view failed to gain support of the Committee, they resigned from it.

A few days earlier, after impassioned debate, the British Trades Union Congress enthusiastically endorsed the idea that its leaders join government and employers in planning the national economy. At the same time, it rejected wage restraint as part of planning. A reporter observed that the workers seemed to realize that they were facing both ways, but debate alone would not resolve the clash between "head and heart: an eagerness for a growing role in the conference rooms of Government and industry, and a refusal to let go of the slogan-filled past." [64]

In 1955, Professor Galbraith in his book, *Economics and the Art of Controversy*, spoofed the absurd situation in which labor, management, and other economic interest groups responded to each other's demands in ideological terms, as if survival were constantly at stake. He showed that this behavior has an economic base; people made a living doing it. What was needed in

[63] The Ethical Content of Annual Reports, *Journal of Business*, XXXVI (October 1963), p. 387.

[64] *New York Times*, Int. Edition, September 5, 1963, p. 1.

most instances was not new economic policies, he concluded, but
new clichés.

A recent analysis of comparative European and American
growth rates leads Everett M. Kassalow to conclude that the price
of old ideology is greater than fresh language. He argues that
private enterprise is the dynamic in both systems but that a
pragmatic attitude by European business has permitted innova-
tions stimulating growth that are impossible in this country, because too many American businessmen still have entrenched
views about the role of government.[65]

We should welcome the Gospel of Social Responsibility on
both Mr. Galbraith's and Mr. Kassalow's grounds; at a minimum,
it has replaced the Free Enterprise campaign with a new cliché,
and, depending on our response to it, may provide the basis for
more flexible use of private enterprise in our mixed economy.

[65] Everett M. Kassalow, U. S. Ideology vs. European Pragmatism, *Challenge,*
XI (July 1963), pp. 22–25.

6

Personal Freedoms and Economic Freedoms in the Mixed Economy

Paul A. Samuelson

I

Although businessmen do not constitute a completely homogeneous group, it can be documented that generally they share a particular set of political and economic beliefs. These beliefs overlap in some degree with those of other groupings in the community; but in some degree they differ, and the differences can become quite sharp. That is, the typical view among academic economists and other social scientists on topics such as the proper role of government expenditure and regulation has become increasingly different from that of the typical view among businessmen.

How can we account for business ideology? Much of this discussion will be devoted to this question and to previous attempts to answer it. Since it takes two to make a difference, the business ideology of intellectuals will also be studied.

The second part of the essay attempts to analyze various interrelations among economic and personal freedoms. Agreeing that governments everywhere take a more active role in the conscious direction and regulation of economic life, we may speak loosely of "a decline in business freedoms." At least some people will want to distinguish between the concept of the freedom of a seller to market his product as he wishes and the freedom of a family man to go to the church of his choice; to think and utter the thoughts of his fancy; and to read his evening paper within the four walls of his castle, with the secure feeling that the moat separating it from the outside will not be breached by bailiffs without due process of law. They will be willing to fight to the death to defend these personal freedoms but will not care to risk more than a few scratches and bruises in the cause of business or economic freedoms.

Yet it can be argued—and, hence, has been so argued—that freedom is one and indivisible: that it is as grave a sin to condemn a man's property and take it over (at court-determined cost) for an urban renewal project as it is to whisk his wife into the county jail on arbitrary charges or on no charges at all. Or (and this is by no means the same argument) that the empirical nature of the political process is such that infringement of business freedoms must lead inevitably to infringement of personal freedoms. Beliefs about the relationships between personal freedoms and economic freedoms represent one of the most important tenets in business ideology. Before beginning to analyze these specific beliefs, I will attempt to account for business ideology in general.

The Business Creed as Delusion

Although this discussion purports to be objective, by its very nature it begins with certain preconceptions. When a social scientist speaks of the puzzle of business ideology, he has already committed himself to the view that these beliefs cannot be explained in terms of their self-evident objective merits. But this is not because he has prejudged the issue from the beginning of time, having known already before his ninth-grade civics course that the pretended merits of laissez-faire are all bunk. Rather, the historian of ideas has built upon numerous earlier studies in the field of economics and politics, which suggest strongly that the conservative business ideology overstates the objective merits of its own case.

When most academic discussions of the business creed begin with this viewpoint as an explicit or implicit axiom, they unavoidably irritate the businessman that they are talking about. There is no real harm in that, any more than there is in the case where radicals become irritated when psychologists attempt to explain their behavior on the picket line in terms of jealous resentment over their mother's love for her husband. The danger is all the other way. When Western anthropologists go to live with South Sea islanders, they end up too often with an exaggerated fondness for the quaintness of the sex rituals there, in just the way that an economist working for an aid program in Pakistan finds himself arguing with the Washington office on behalf of his constituency, using the same arguments that he had himself been previously rebutting. What one must hold against a generation of anthropologists is that they were so taken in by the phenomena they were objectively studying that they made bad empirical predictions about the hardness of the cake of custom and its resistance to material change. I need not point out the danger implied in the proverb, "To know all, is to forgive all."

But an opposite warning is also necessary. Most of the literature that I have seen on this subject starts out too blithely with the postulate that the views of the conservative businessman are palpable delusions, which must, therefore, be approached with the tools appropriate to the analysis of odd beliefs. I exaggerate a little, but copious quotation could show that I do so in a good cause.

Let me illustrate with a recent book on American intellectual history edited by Arthur M. Schlesinger, Jr., and Morton D. White.[1] This excellent work represents the joint contributions of able scholars in the diverse areas of history, literature, philosophy, sociology, and economics. Several essays touch upon the development of conservative business thought in the last century. None of them—my own included—can be fairly termed a panegyric to the views under contemplation. Indeed, the following passage by Max Lerner [2] is more typical:

> One of the paradoxes of American social and intellectual history is that laissez-faire reached its height as a system of economic thought and judicial decision at the very time that its doom as a system of economic organization was already clear.

[1] A. M. Schlesinger, Jr., and Morton White: *Paths of American Thought,* Houghton Mifflin, Boston, 1963.

[2] *Ibid.,* p. 147. This is the opening sentence in Max Lerner's essay, The Triumph of Laissez-Faire.

Lerner is referring here to conservative ideology at the turn of the century. Many other writers have pointed out the apparent paradox of the Jacksonian era, when the Jeffersonian idyll of the prosperous and self-sufficient farmer was being replaced by the growth of industrialism and urbanization. Yet, just as the reality was turning to interdependence and away from independence, Emerson and Tocqueville were articulating the great American belief in individualism. How explain the discrepancy between fact and word? Hallucination? Self-deception? Mendacity?

It is a widespread view among academics that conservative sermons about laissez-faire and individualism represent a simple denial of the reality of society. Maybe this is so. Maybe it is patently so, and no danger can come from prejudging the case in advance. But it is certainly a matter of some moment that what is taken for granted not be wrong. I am here stressing, without guile, *the crucial importance of a scientific assessment of the merits of an ideology as a preliminary to understanding its nonrationalistic content and function.* In handling an upset person who claims to have seen a ghost, it is of some moment to know whether he *has* seen a ghost. It is one thing to be told by an individual in a sanitarium near New York City that he is Napoleon Bonaparte and quite another to be told the same thing by a short, swarthy individual who inhabits the island of St. Helena in 1817.

The way that you calibrate the respondent's verbal behavior and the explanation appropriate to account for it is much altered in the two cases. And the way I calibrate *your* rejection of his claiming to be Napoleon is equally affected by the circumstances. What are we to think of A, who knows that B is crazy to claim he is Napoleon for the sufficient reason that all sane men should know that A is the true Napoleon?

At last I have revealed my hand; I intend to play a double game. I shall try not only to understand businessmen's beliefs about economics and business, but also intellectuals' beliefs on these matters as refracted by *their* reactions to business ideology. The mind reels at this prospect of wheels within wheels. But it is all good, clean fun. At bottom I am an intellectual myself, as ready as the next boy to throw a snowball at the top hat of a nearby tycoon (or at the mortarboard of some dear, departing colleague).

The Economist as Go-between

Actually, this is in a genuine sense no frivolous exercise. The economist is in the unique position of being able to assist the historian of thought and social movements. Just as a pathologist can help a psychiatrist appraise the meaning of a patient's assertion that he has a brain tumor, the economist can—alas, imperfectly—help certify what the reasonable facts are, the necessary benchmark against which to measure delusion and rationalization.[3]

Although the thought would spoil digestions at a downtown eating club, the economist has always played the role of interpreter to the academic community of the businessman and of material activity generally. Fifty years ago, conservative advocates would perhaps invoke the authority of the local Ph.D. in political economy; today they are more likely to regard him as an impractical enemy and send for their lawyer to find that needle in the haystack of economists that a sensible man can rely on. But their view of the economist does not refute my point that we are go-betweens.

Historians and political scientists will go on taking seriously the economic doctrines of Henry George or Bernard Shaw long after any quorum of economists will deem them significant. A sociologist well-trained in what is politely called intellectual history will laugh to hear a businessman claiming that *his* investment will benefit the working man in the future. The sociologist knows that this "filter-down" theory was killed off when John Stuart Mill accepted Thornton's refutation of the classical

---

[3] An example is provided by the apparent incompatibility of individualism and a post-Jeffersonian interdependent economy. The historian needs to be told by the economist that a system of ideal pricing in perfectly competitive markets *can* coordinate the activities of quite egotistic individualist atoms through the impersonal market mechanism. (I discuss this in greater detail later.) Hence, the paradox of post-Jacksonian ideological individualism evaporates as a logical self-contradiction. The Lerner problem remains: Is it oligopolists who will be most fervent in the praise of competition and laissez-faire?

wage-fund theory a hundred years ago. What the sociologist does not realize is that, in another form, most modern economists place some credence in that murdered notion while, perhaps, sopping their social consciences by suggesting that workers be given both the increased wages stemming from the new capital *and* the fruit of the capital itself, if it is *their* present sacrifices that are to be involved.

As the general economist is to the other social scientists and the historians, often the business economist is to the general economist. Business school economists will, I think, agree with my observation that in past decades professors in commerce departments voted more conservatively than their colleagues in economics departments. Times have changed a little. Where only two out of the hundreds of professors at the Harvard Business School chose Franklin Roosevelt over Wendell Willkie in 1940, a majority chose Kennedy over Nixon in 1960. The more things change, the less they are the same, as a Frenchman might say. Yet, it is still the case, I believe, that the majority for Kennedy was greater in the Harvard economics department (and liberal arts faculty) than in the Business School. And it is still fairly typical of colleges everywhere that business school professors are more sympathetic toward business than are members of the other faculties (with the possible exception of the engineers).

I am not saying that management school faculty members are "kept" men, apologists for business. In part, their difference in attitude may be traceable to their more detailed research into the complexities of business life; in part, to the evident attitudes of men who have chosen as their lifework the training of accountants, marketing experts, and other business practitioners. Economists who are known to be radical are less likely to be courted by business school deans and are less likely to succumb to available suitors. This may be just as well. The man who adores business is likely to lose objectivity. And the man who hates business is also handicapped in being objective. Neither Casanovas nor misogynists are apt to make cracker-jack obstetricians.

Here, I think my role as an economist can be a useful one. If you "know," as many social scientists know, that the praise of laissez-faire is beside the point, your analysis has to run along different lines than would be the case if, like Professors Frank Knight and Milton Friedman of the University of Chicago or Professors Gottfried Haberler of Harvard and William Fellner of Yale, you "know" there is much objective merit in the viewpoint. To be sure, a rabid business spokesman like Mr. Edgar M. Queeny of the Monsanto Chemical Company [4] does not state with any meticulousness the scientific findings of economists who belong to the secret lodges of the *Mont Pelerin* Society; but, then, neither did Franklin Roosevelt catch correctly the nuances of doctrine of his brain trust in the week in question; and few of the New Frontiersmen who have returned from Washington to their ivory towers would give top grades to their intermediate students for the utterances that they admire in high officials. Samuel Johnson's dictum on walking dogs and preaching women must be invoked here.

Business Ideology on the Defensive?

Before we try to account for business ideology, it may be well to examine its importance. Certainly, one cannot take for granted that its dominance in our society can be measured by its decibel count. Happy is the nation that has no history. And most secure may be the laissez-faire economy that no one bothers to talk about. In the 1920's, when Calvin Coolidge was Chairman of the Board, the business of America was business. As a boy entrepreneur I used to sample my own wares and read in the *Saturday Evening Post* (and in the now-defunct *American Magazine*) the success stories of American businessmen. Although they appeared in the nonfiction columns, they read like fiction. (Only after 1929 did I learn that they actually were part fiction!)

Nevertheless, despite the considerable volume of such panegyrics, there seemed to be less ideological defense of private enterprise in the 1920's than appeared in the mid-1930's, when Roosevelt's New Deal was at the apex of its power and when the rearguard actions of the Liberty League served the function of self-expression more than that of persuasive social propaganda.

---

[4] Edgar M. Queeny, *The Spirit of Enterprise*, Scribner, New York, 1943.

The felt need for articulation of business creed and *apologia* may itself be a sign of inner uncertainty on the part of the business community and conservative leaders. In the vigor of manly growth the motto is "Ask me no questions, and I'll tell you no lies." As the bachelor balds, and perhaps begins to pall, come the better rationalizations for the lively life. Eulogy and obituary are not accidentally related words.

Implicitly, I have been raising the suspicion that the business ideology may no longer have the importance for good or evil that it once had. How can this be reconciled with the common observation that radical reform has become a dead movement in American life? Communism has no following. Socialism has lost even the small appeal it once had. No utopias fire the imaginations of Americans and provide an alternative to the philosophy of business enterprise. In short, business is allegedly now in the saddle.

Now, this is not quite the way I hear it down at the Union League Club. There, they would be astonished to learn that they are in the saddle. The active businessman has not these many years been fearful of utopian socialists; nor of card-carrying communists, as such. He has regarded it as an over-nice distinction to worry about whether an intellectual is a fellow traveler or a lodge member. Since Karl Marx advocated a progressive income tax in the *Communist Manifesto* of 1848, why bother to distinguish between Marxians and progressives who hold such uncomfortable views? I believe it was the retired President Herbert Hoover who introduced into the vocabulary of American political life the compound word Marx-and-Keynes.

To say that people are now merely New Dealers or New Frontiersmen is not even to provide cold comfort to business ideologies. Franklin Roosevelt was the enemy, not Earl Browder or Norman Thomas. The thing to fear is not the full-fledged alternative social system, so much as the hard-to-differentiate "mixed economy." For one thing, Eugene Debs, the I.W.W., and earlier radical movements (including Populism) have, I suggest, an importance in the minds and writings of historians, social scientists, and conservative alarmists out of proportion to their actual historical importance. And although Norman Thomas can claim with some factual accuracy that many of the programs in his platform were adopted by Franklin Roosevelt, it would be politically naive to suppose that the socialist party was the spearhead and wedge for these social changes. The dawn does not pull up the sun, any more than the rear guard pushes the army in front of it.

The Mixed Economy

I question whether business has climbed back into the saddle. The story is much more complicated; history does not consist of one-way trends. History oscillates, backtracks, and spirals. Admittedly, in the twenty years after 1929 the trend seemed to be toward limitations on business, but during the last dozen years of that period, the strength of strong radical dissent was also on the ebb. One forgets how desperate the populace was in 1932. Half of the small-town editors, for example—a group usually about as conservative and reactionary as any that can be found—then favored nationalization of the banks. The success of Roosevelt's New Deal in stemming the tide of collapse acted as a lightning rod in dissipating the forces of fascism and drastic reform.

Since 1950, both in America and the West generally, there has been some comeback of private enterprise and an increasing reliance on markets rather than government controls. But even this movement has been a spotty one; thus, Germany, Japan, France, and Italy—to say nothing of The Netherlands and Great Britain—have, by planning, interfered extensively with laissez-faire. In the United States, the Eisenhower Administration retained most of the post–1933 economic institutions. Although the Kennedy-Johnson Administration has paid less lip service to the business cause and has been regarded by businessmen as a hostile adversary, its performance has been mixed. Labor unions these days regard themselves as being in the descendancy, both in terms of public opinion and government support. It is ironical that the first major step in gutting America's egalitarian structure of taxation should have been taken by a Democratic rather than a

Republican administration. And still, it is this same administration that pushes medical care for the aged, regulation of drugs and security markets, and other programs distasteful to business.

Perhaps the one discernible trend is toward less polarization of ideology; less of laissez-faire versus socialism; of freedom versus totalitarianism. This does not mean that the conflict is over, but rather that it is taking place along other battlelines. It is in this sense that I contend that the "mixed economy" is the enemy and the ever-present effective challenge of the business ideology.

The mixed economy is not a very definite concept. I have purposely left it vague, in part because that is its intrinsic nature and in part because increased precision should come at the end rather than at the beginning of extensive research.

Search for New Goals

The vagueness of the opposing ideology naturally begets a responding vagueness in the business creed itself. The old clear-cut bastions become too vulnerable. Yet, once they are left behind, the new ground to be defended becomes hard to define. This leads to a certain frustration and an urge to find a new formulation of the business creed. Professor Jesse W. Markham of Princeton University in his editor's introduction to R. Joseph Monsen, Jr., *Modern American Capitalism: Ideologies and Issues* [5] asks why capitalism, despite its demonstrated performance in producing highest real incomes, should be seriously challenged in the new uncommitted nations and at home. Markham concludes:

> In this book Professor Monsen provides some meaningful and thoughtful answers to this question, the most plausible of which is the absence of a clearly articulated ideology of private capitalism.

Monsen himself puts the matter bluntly:

> Americans will never be able to persuade other countries to follow an anti-communist route to development if they cannot explain and understand what they themselves are for—and why.[6]

[5] R. Joseph Monsen, Jr., *Modern American Capitalism: Ideologies and Issues*, Houghton Mifflin, Boston, 1963, p. vi.
[6] *Ibid.*, p. ix.

I regard the Monsen study as valuable in demonstrating the differences and the nuances in capitalist ideology. It is debatable that the best defense of a system comes from a thorough understanding of its nature and a self-conscious articulation of its merits and demerits; and, therefore, I should be less sad than Monsen if it turned out that a would-be missionary, starting out to sell the American way of life to the Hottentots, Laotians, and Yankees, were to find his eloquence paralyzed by learning from Monsen that there are at least five versions of capitalistic ideology:

1. Classical Capitalist Ideology (of the N.A.M. and the Chicago economics department).
2. Managerial Ideology of Capitalism (of the C.E.D. and *Fortune* magazine).
3. Countervailing Power Ideology (of J. Kenneth Galbraith, and of whom else?).
4. People's Capitalism (of the New York Stock Exchange's Keith Funston and the American Advertising Council).
5. Enterprise Democracy (associated with the Eisenhower Administration, and particularly with its "semi-official ideologist" Arthur Larson).

Since it is not clear that the best preparation for the soap salesman is a thorough briefing in the scientific laboratory that produces soap, one cannot be sure that Monsen's contribution towards a sixth ideology will restore the aplomb of the American missionary:

It is suggested that the U.S.I.A.'s currently exported American Capitalist Ideology be reoriented toward these basic elements of the American system, particularly pragmatism and compromise, elements not at present included in Enterprise Democracy.[7]

A New Capitalism?

The five versions of capitalism cited from Monsen can be boiled down to two categories: old-fashioned profit maximizing markets that are perfectly or imperfectly competitive; and the

[7] *Ibid.*, p. 128.

newer notion of "managerial capitalism"—that the corporation (and its officials) are responsive to the interests of *all* parties it deals with—employees, customers, shareowners, the public, the federal government. I fancy that most of the big business guinea pigs dissected by Robert Heilbroner lean toward this last view. And so do the well-known writings of A. A. Berle on the separation of ownership and control of the modern corporation and on new roles of property and of corporate bureaucrats.

Many economists have been skeptical about this new capitalism. Edward S. Mason, a judicious scholar of industrial organization, has gently debunked it. A more cavalier rejection is provided by Jack Hirshleifer:

> There are several interesting things about this defense of capitalism —that capitalists are really not selfish after all. The first is that, as a defense, it is a hopeless failure. There are many reasons why this argument must fail, but perhaps the most conspicuous reason is that it is untrue. . . . What does all this prove? Simply that all the world is largely governed by self-interest, and all the world knows it. . . .[8]

Of course, every schoolboy knows that "what everybody knows" is true only about half the time. Although I agree that there is exaggeration in the new view, the matter cannot be carried far by *a priori* reasoning.

My colleague, Morris A. Adelman, in a too-little known essay, "Some Aspects of Corporate Enterprise," [9] has emphasized some of the limits of corporate political power. He has also emphasized that in these days the political power of many small businesses is more potent than that of giant corporations. Congressmen know that. Often a large firm will try to get an association of small firms linked to its cause; and an outsider is amused to see an international oil firm frightened of its domestic subsidiary, when the latter has powerful allies among the small, but numerous, local producers. General Motors would be foolish to risk

[8] Jack Hirshleifer, Capitalist Ethics—Tough or Soft?, *Journal of Law and Business,* II (October 1959), p. 116. E. S. Mason, The Apologetics of "Managerialism," *The Journal of Business,* XXXI (January 1958), pp. 1–11.

[9] In R. E. Freeman, ed., *Postwar Economic Trends in the United States,* Harper, New York, 1960, pp. 291–307, particularly pp. 299–302.

the wrath of Congress by pushing its dealers around, and many a giant has been blackmailed by its numerous pygmies. Although one group may have a controlling vote in a corporation, in politics it is still one vote for one head. (The coefficients of reactionariness and of bigness are certainly *not* correlated in any simple, positive fashion.)

Adelman also has some trenchant remarks on the corporation as a profit maximizer, and I think Earl Cheit and he would form a heroic minority of dissenters against the fashionable interpretation of the Berle–Means thesis concerning dispersed ownership of corporations and its separation from management control. By and large, what is good for General Motors *is* good for Charles E. Wilson, GM president. This does not ignore the existence of some conflicts of interest between ethical and unethical inside officers. Degree of concentration of ownership among different corporations turns out on sober examination to have few predictive consequences for corporate behavior. Standard Oil of New Jersey has employee board members. Some oil companies have family control. What differences in behavior are traceable to this difference? More research would be needed to give a significant answer to this question—a fact that you might not guess from reading the vast literature on this subject.

As Adelman has indicated, simple profit maximizing for owners and exercising trusteeship for pluralistic claimants do not lead to very significant differences in behavior. To be significantly different, a change must make a difference. When it is damnably difficult to make an operationally meaningful experiment (even in principle) in order to detect a difference, why care much? For example, some economist friends work for one of the largest companies in the world. In privacy, they have tried to get top management to admit that it "really acts so as to maximize long-run profits." They have never been able to squeeze out such an admission. Is this surprising? The men at the top are *not* completely free wills. But they have spent most of their 40 years of adulthood with the company; the crises in their lives—the "hard times"—have no more been associated with stockholder pressure than with pressure from government and labor. But suppose that such an admission had been wrung out of them?

What difference would it have made?   Really none at all, since this company acts much like its rivals, which are organized differently.   Economists are like pedants (a redundancy!) in wanting to save the face of their principles even when naught is at stake.

If it is wrong to think that separation of ownership and control makes a great deal of difference, that does not mean that corporations can be regarded as simple conduits for funneling earnings into the hands of owners and for funneling decisions of owners into corporate acts.   Large corporate oligopolies have considerable degrees of freedom in the short run (and to a degree even in the long run), which atomistic competitors lack.   The folkways and mores that these authorities follow are, therefore, somewhat indeterminate and tend to be self-determining by the group.

Corporations act *as if* they were independent entities; ask any fund raiser, and he will tell you that.   Corporations have behavior patterns, personalities, and styles.   It is witchcraft to impute these persistent patterns of behavior back to something antecedent to the corporation called "owners," and Occam's razor can kill off these antecedent spirits.   Corporations have attitudes toward Negroes and Jews, toward wage rates and work conditions, toward research and charity.   To say that the vast differences in behavior between U. S. Gypsum and National Gypsum are merely reflections of the personal tastes of a man called Avery and a man called Baker is either to be saying nothing or to be saying something wrong.   When Sewell Avery died, U. S. Gypsum did not change *its* spots.

Just as we call a spade a spade, we must call a corporation an actor in the scenario of economic life—no different from the rest of us puppets.   This is quite distinct from the normative question whether it would be a bad thing for corporations to exercise independent choices in the pursuit of goals other than simple profit maximization.   Professors Hirshleifer and other writers of the Chicago school have expressed disapproval of any such actions.   There is little that is compelling in such opinions.   Contrary to allegation, economic theory does not tell us that a farmer should first maximize his profits and then satisfy his personal utilities and tastes.   There is no such inherent separation of functions, either in fact or in ideal theory. Similarly, in a diverse corporation there is no basis in economic theory for the assertion that decisions *should* be taken so as to maximize that single thing called "profit." Although it is possible that observing economists could more simply predict the behavior of entities that maximize a simple magnitude called "dollar profit," there is no reason why the world should accommodate itself to our desire for a lazy life.

If it comes to ethical issues of value judgment, I, for one, can as easily imagine a good society in which corporations freely act according to certain patterns as one in which private individuals are given the ostensible power to make decisions about fair employment and other practices. Indeed, one of the few positive arguments for bigness in corporations is that such entities are less able to break the law and resist the social pressures of democracy. The family farmer can and will cheat where the vast corporate farmer will not. Altruism is a scarce good, and corporations may help society economize on its use.

Explaining the Business Creed

By far the most important attempt to describe and explain the business ideology is that of Francis X. Sutton, Seymour E. Harris, Carl Kaysen, and James Tobin in the *American Business Creed*.[10] Although they are friends, I think no one will think me partial when I call them the cream of the elite of American scholarship. Here a leading sociologist, disciple of Talcott Parsons and Ford Foundation administrator, teamed up with three economists of the highest distinction. Without disrespect to my profession, one must admit that here is a case where the three economists seem pretty much won over to the view of the sociologist. (This must be qualified by the recognition that economists have never been happy about the fashionable economic interpretation of history or of events; those who knew little of technical economics have been the ardent boosters of the doctrine that economic interests are dominant in life.)

---

[10] Harvard University Press, Cambridge, Mass., 1956, and Schocken Paperback, New York, 1962, hereafter referred to as Sutton et al.

Their book has received a fair measure of attention but, except among connoisseurs, not nearly the attention it deserves. Its value is great, even though—as will become evident—I think it has essentially failed in its attempt to explain business ideology in terms of a theory of "strain" in the business role. This failure, I cannot help but think, throws some light on the weakness of our present-day best sociology. In the brief space at my disposal and in view of my amateur status in these realms, I make no pretence to giving a convincing proof of the view that I have just expressed. Certainly I shall not pretend to put up a better theory than the one I criticize; but I do not think that criticism is beside the point, if it is not able to be constructive and to provide a superior alternative to what is being criticized. They also serve who merely point out that the emperor has no clothes or that the clothes he does not have fit badly.

It will be economical of space if I first quote at some length from these authors. (In every case, the emphasis is mine.)

> Our aim in this study is to answer the questions: Why does the business ideology say what it does? On what theory can the themes, symbols, arguments, which form the business ideology be explained? . . . To reach the answer to our ultimate question, we first seek to define the general role of ideologies in social life. We find our answer, broadly speaking, in the strains and conflicts inherent in every institutional position in a complex society, whether the position be that of businessman, or university professor, or labor leader. These conflicts are of several kinds: conflicts between the demands of the particular position and the broader values of society; gaps between the demands of social positions and the capabilities of the human beings who hold them to fulfill these demands; inherently conflicting demands built into the social definition of certain positions. This general proposition is applied to an investigation of the particular strains inherent in the business role in the United States, and the major themes of business ideology are shown as verbal and symbolic resolutions of these conflicts. This is our central proposition . . . (page vii).

> We have rejected the "interest" theory, that ideologies simply reflect the economic self-interest, narrowly conceived, of their adherents. Ideology, in this view, is merely an attempt to manipulate symbols and marshal arguments which will persuade others to take actions from which the ideologist stands to profit financially. The ideologist may

or may not believe the things he says. If he does happen to believe them, it is maintained, it is only because he has succeeded by wishful thinking in convincing himself that truth and self-interest coincide.

The "interest theory" contains important elements of truth. It is easy to understand why the ideology of the domestic watch industry, both management and labor, features support of tariff protection and includes all the venerable arguments and symbols which might persuade the Tariff Commission, the Congress, and the public of the protectionist case. Were this the model for all ideology, there would indeed be little problem of explanation and little need for our book. Actually the relationship between specific ideologies and economic interest is seldom so clear. A more typical example is provided by the passionate support a businessman gives to the principle of a *balanced federal budget*. We surely cannot conclude that he has reached this position by sober calculation of his profit prospects *under balanced and unbalanced budgets*. Assessing the ultimate effects of alternative budgetary policies on the profits of a specific business firm is a formidable econometric problem. Yet businessmen speak on the subject with such confidence, emotion, and unanimity that, in the "interest theory" of ideology, we would be forced to conclude that they have no trouble knowing on which side of the issue their economic interests lie, and that varying effects on different groups of businessmen are never to be anticipated.

It is true that with sufficient ingenuity one can construct a chain which reconciles practically any ideological position to the economic interest of its holder. Or one can make the task easier by attributing to the ideologist a mistaken or unduly certain conception of his own interest. One can make the task still easier by widening the notion of self-interest to encompass psychological satisfactions other than economic returns. But these expedients are really the end of the theory they are designed to salvage. They reduce it to a tautology: "Men act in their own interests" becomes "Men act as they are motivated to act" (pages 12–13).

. . . Why do businessmen so fiercely oppose *deficit financing* on the part of the government? Such opposition cannot be the result of a rational calculation of their tangible interests. In the short run many businesses (for example, construction firms) stand to gain from this policy. It is possible that in the long run, business interests may be injured by *deficit financing*, but it is certainly not inevitable. In any particular instance it is exceedingly difficult if not impossible to assess the remote consequences of *deficit financing*. And so there is no rational basis for the simplicity and certainty of business opposition.

If we stick to a theory of rational self-interest we can only dismiss examples such as this as evidence of ignorance or error. But this is obviously unsatisfactory. . . .

The clearest way to give the theory a definite character is to equate
interests with objective, private economic advantage. Formulated in
this way, the interest theory, *as our deficit financing example shows,*
simply cannot account for a considerable part of the business ideology
(pages 303–304).

A Trial Balance

Where do such explanations get us? The simple notion of
strain as nervous collapse, in which the businessman says gib-
berish because he is in a state, is, of course, not what is intended.
This is a pity, in that the vulgarization of a theory usually contains its operationally meaningful content in the sense of logical
positivism and Peirce-James pragmatism.

I do not think that vulgar or sophisticated self-interest theories
have been given a fair shake by the authors. The space spent
on refuting what they point out is the single most popular and
natural theory is, by my count, amazingly small and amazingly
repetitive. You cannot get very far in proving that Americans
are very tall by telling anecdotes about how many tall men you
know. And this is particularly the case, if you keep repeating
the one name of John Kenneth Galbraith. Yet, as my repeated
italicizing of words in the quotations from the Sutton book will
show, about the only case they cite in which businessmen *seem*
to be acting against self-interest is the case of opposition to deficit
spending (and we might add to expansionary monetary policy).
Where are the hundreds of other examples? I believe I could
find half a dozen, and no doubt they could triple this number.
But I suspect that the end product will not be terribly impressive.
Personal views, in fact, rarely contradict personal interest. Read
the papers for a month and count the score.

I agree that it is a terribly interesting question why business
generally has been antiexpansionary in the area of aggregate
demand. I wish the authors had addressed themselves more
specifically to it. Indeed, they cite, but do not really linger on,

the attempt made by Sidney S. Alexander [11] to tackle this very problem. I must report that there is more wisdom *on this specific matter* in the short essay by Alexander than in their whole book (and yet Alexander would be the first to admit that he has not said the last word on the puzzle).[12]

In my limited space I can say but little on this specific subject. Let me stress that macroeconomics is not an easy problem for a businessman or any lay person to understand. Moreover, I am not sure that businessmen are *in the concrete* opposed to expansionary policies. They have trouble in rationalizing their frequent longing for such policies, which seems to me to be natural. But when it counts, the defense producers are eager for increased expenditures. We have had much recent experience that business, if it can save face and get *its* kind of tax cut, is willing to let deficits soar in a good cause. General Motors has repeatedly criticized tight money, when it hurt sales of cars on credit. Bankers, who benefit from tight money, are its most vocal exponents.

To make the point that businessmen believe in what they say publicly, the authors quote a public opinion poll showing that the business ideology on budget balancing is that "of the population at large; a variety of polls indicates that the people as a whole are 'budget balancers,' and it seems safe to infer that the polled sentiments of businessmen would show the same pattern" (page 324). If true—and in a degree this is true—what has become of their one case where a strain theory proves to be the superior one? There is apparently no peculiar business view here that has to be explained by peculiar business-role strain!

[11] S. S. Alexander, Opposition to Deficit Spending for the Prevention of Unemployment, in Alvin H. Hansen et al., eds., *Income, Employment and Public Policy*, Norton, New York, 1948.

[12] Alexander classified business opposition to deficit financing under four headings: misunderstanding of the validity of the mechanism; desire to have slack labor markets to keep worker performance high relative to wages; class antagonism, which associates deficit spending with other liberal programs that are against business; fear of increasing power of the state and of groups other than the business elite. Interestingly, he omits opposition to inflation, even though he wrote during the 1947–48 postwar inflation.

I suspect that the Sutton group somewhat exaggerates the element of unpleasant strain involved in business, perhaps because of the natural tendency of any academic person to suppose that others experience the discomfort that *he* would experience if placed in business life. The great Cambridge physicist, J. J. Thomson (discoverer of the electron), was once asked how he felt about the fact that any broker in the City made three times the income he did as a professor. "But just think of the work they have to do," he replied. Like most academics, he used his preferences to project into the business role strains and unpleasant-nesses that businessmen may not feel. Brokers like being brokers, hard as that is for professors of botany to believe. Business is a great game to many people. It is a relatively well-paid game, as every prospective father-in-law knows. A second-class violinist in the family is a tragedy; a third-class businessman is someone you can lean on in your old age.

In every country the party of business is the more conservative party. In every case, when it comes to marginal decisions that bear on business interests, the party of business acts friendlier to those interests. Why then deny or overlook the obvious? Admittedly, no *explanation* has been provided by this recognition. But that is no reason to reject the fact. We laugh when a Molière character speaks of the power of opium to induce sleep *because* of its "soporific" quality; however, that should never make us overlook the fact that opium does induce sleep.

Rich and (what is not necessarily the same thing) acquisitive men do labor under the strain of being natural objects of dislike and envy. The Bible tells us that and so does a theory of self-interest. It is hard for people to believe that the road to heaven is paved with selfish intentions, even when it is true. That much I grant to the business-strain theory.

In its wider sense, a strain theory that finds associated with each occupation a characteristic strain explaining its ideology comes full circle to a materialistic interpretation of ideology of the Marxian type. To see this, repeat the word "strain" over and over again. It is like repeating "ice-cream cone" over and over again; the words begin to lose meaning. But in the last case, the mind's eye can keep looking at the dripping cone.

However, since strain does not mean anything so concrete as biting one's nails or experiencing facial tics and the shakes,[13] one can replace "strain" by x. A farmer believes in this or that because of the x of the farmer trade; the money lender believes what he believes because of his job's x. Why not cancel out the x and stick to the bare facts of differential ideologies, pending the time when fewer x factors than occupations can be found to provide a mnemonic pattern. On the whole, I am left with the impression that an interests-cum-prestige theory provides more of a simplifying pattern than any proposed alternative.

I could go on giving criticisms; they are not intended to be captious but are merely copied from the margin of my copy of their book. But I have said enough to demonstrate my disappointment with the strain theory of business ideology. Let me repeat that the Sutton group has been led to observe things about business strains that are interesting for their own sake, even where they fail to explain the business creed.[14]

Up to now I have largely discussed the problem of explaining business ideology without giving my evaluation of its intrinsic content. My remaining task is to appraise the specific part of it that relates to freedom and coordination.

II

As a prelude to discussing the empirical and analytical relations between business and personal freedoms (which is roughly the distinction between economic and political freedoms), I might usefully give some reflections on the nature of individualism, liberty, freedom, coercion, and the marketplace.[15]

---

[13] Apparently actuarial statistics do not show relatively more heart attacks and ulcers among business decision makers than among routine workers.

[14] One can derive a superficial explanation of intellectuals' behavior from a retaliating use by a businessman of the Sutton-Parsons strain theory of academic life.

[15] Some of the following thoughts appeared in two recent lectures. Since I do not believe in elegant variations, some of the words that follow will be in the same sequence as is published elsewhere. I own to no sense of self-plagiarism since, as indicated there, many of those words were stolen from the present research investigation.

How Divine the Natural Order?

Adam Smith, our patron saint, was critical of state interference of the prenineteenth-century type. And make no mistake about it; Smith was right. Most of the interventions into economic life by the state were then harmful both to prosperity and freedom. What Smith said needed to be said. In fact, much of what Smith said still needs to be said; good intentions by government are not enough; acts have consequences that must be taken into account, if good is to follow.

One hundred per cent individualists concentrate on the purple passage in Adam Smith, where he discerns an Invisible Hand that leads each selfish individual to contribute to the best public good. Smith had a point; but he could not have earned a passing mark in a Ph.D. oral examination by explaining just what that point was. Until this century, his followers—such as Bastiat—thought that the doctrine of the Invisible Hand meant (1) that it produced maximum feasible total satisfaction, somehow defined; or (2) that it showed that anything resulting from the voluntary agreements of uncoerced individuals must make them better (or best) off in some important sense.

Both of these interpretations, which are still held by many modern libertarians, are wrong. They neglect the axiom concerning the ethical merits of the preexisting distribution of land, property, and genetic and acquired utilities. This is not the place for a technical discussion of economic principles, so I shall be very brief and cryptic in showing this.

First, suppose that some ethical observer, such as Jesus, Buddha, or for that matter, John Dewey or Aldous Huxley, were to examine whether the total of social utility (as that ethical observer scores the deservingness of the poor and rich, saintly and sinning individuals) was actually maximized by 1860 or 1964 laissez-faire. He might decide that a tax placed upon yachts whose proceeds go to cheapen the price of insulin to the needy

---

George J. Stigler and P. A. Samuelson, *A Dialogue on the Proper Economic Role of the State,* Graduate School of Business Selected Papers No. 7, 1963; P. A. Samuelson, Modern Economic Realities and Individualism, *The Texas Quarterly* (Summer 1963).

increased the total of utility. Could Adam Smith prove him wrong? Could Bastiat? I think not.

Of course, they might say that there is no point in trying to compare different individuals' utilities, because they are incommensurable and can no more be added together than can apples and oranges. But if recourse is made to this argument, then the doctrine that the Invisible Hand maximizes total utility of the universe has already been discarded. If they admit that the Invisible Hand will truly maximize total social utility *provided the state intervenes so as to make the initial distribution of dollar votes ethically proper,* then they have abandoned the libertarian's position that individuals are not to be coerced, even by taxation.

In connection with the second interpretation that anything resulting from voluntary agreements is in some sense, *ipso facto,* optimal, we can reply by pointing out that when I make a purchase from a monopolistic octopus, that is a voluntary act; I can always go without Alka Seltzer or aluminum or nylon or whatever product you think is produced by a monopolist. Mere voluntarism, therefore, is not the root merit of the doctrine of the Invisible Hand; [16] what is important about it is the system of

[16] Milton Friedman, *Capitalism and Freedom,* University of Chicago Press, Chicago, 1962, Chapters 1 and 2 seem grossly defective in these matters. In the first chapter, he regards market behavior as optimal merely because it is voluntary, save for the single passage: ". . . perhaps the most difficult problems arise from monopoly—which inhibits effective freedom by denying individuals alternatives to the particular exchange" and promises to discuss this matter in more detail in the next chapter. It turns out there that "Exchange is truly voluntary only when nearly equivalent alternatives exist." Why this new element of alternatives? Because, as I point out, *perfect* competition is efficient in the Pareto-optimality sense, and it is this property that modern economists have *proved* optimal (and interesting) about such competition.

Libertarians, like Hayek and von Mises, would be annoyed to learn that their case stands or falls on its nearness to "perfect competition." Unlike George J. Stigler and Milton Friedman, neither of these two men has remotely the same views on perfect competition as do modern economists generally. What libertarians have in common is the hope that departures from perfect competition are not too extreme in our society; Friedman, himself, has apparently come full circle to the view that public regulation of "monopoly" and state regulation of "monopoly" are greater evils than letting well enough alone. I do not feel competent to report on the algebraic degree checks and balances that prevails under perfect competition, and its measure of validity is at the technocratic level of efficiency, not at the ethical level of freedom and individualism. That this is so can be seen from the fact that such socialists as Oskar Lange and A. P. Lerner have advocated channeling the Invisible Hand to the task of organizing a socialistic society efficiently.

The Cash Nexus

Just as there is a sociology of family life and of politics, there is also a sociology of individualistic competition. It need not be a rich one. Ask not your neighbor's name; enquire only for his numerical schedules of supply and demand. Under perfect competition, no buyer need face a seller. Haggling in a Levantine bazaar is a sign of less-than-perfect competition.

These economic contacts between atomistic individuals may seem a little chilly or, to use the language of wine tasting, "dry." This impersonality has its good side. Negroes in the South learned long ago that their money was welcome in local department stores. Money can be liberating. It corrodes the cake of custom. It does talk. In the West Indies there is a saying, "Money whitens." Sociologists know that replacing the rule of status by the rule of contract loses something in warmth; it also gets rid of some of the bad fire of olden times.

Impersonality of market relations has another advantage, as was brought home to many "liberals" in the McCarthy era of

***

of his agreement with Stigler and others who put considerable emphasis on antitrust action. [There appears to me to be a technical flaw in the view of Friedman and A. P. Lerner that regulated or publicly owned monopolies should always (as a matter of principle as well as pragmatic expediency) be permitted to have competition from free entrants. The mathematics of the increasing-returns situation admits of no such theorem; it is simply false game theory and bilateral monopoly theory, which asserts that letting one more viable person in the game must lead to a "better" result in any of the conventional senses of better. To make the Scottish Airlines keep up unprofitable schedules and at the same time permit a free enterpriser to make a profit partially at the regulated lines' expense can easily result in dead-weight loss to society under the usual feasibility conditions. The crime of legally abolishing the Pony Express because it competed with the Post Office would have to be examined on all its complicated demerits.]

American political life. Suppose it were efficient for the government to be the one big employer. Then if, for good or bad, a
person becomes in bad odor with government, he is dropped
from employment and is put on a black list. He really has no
place to go then. The thought of such a dire fate must in the
course of time discourage that freedom of expression of opinion
that individualists most favor.[17]

Many of the people who were unjustly dropped by the federal
government in that era were able to land jobs in small-scale private industry. I say small-scale industry, because large corporations are likely to be chary of hiring names that appear on anybody's black list. What about people who were justly dropped
as security risks or as members of political organizations now
deemed to be criminally subversive? Many of them also found
jobs in the anonymity of industry.

Many conservative people, who think that such men should not
remain in sensitive government work or in public employ at all,
will still feel that they should not be hounded into starvation.
Few want for this country the equivalent of Czarist Russia's

[17] F. A. Hayek, *The Road to Serfdom,* University of Chicago Press, Chicago,
1944, p. 119, aptly presents the following quotations from Lenin (1917) and
Trotsky (1937):

> The whole of society will have become a single office and a single
> factory with equality of work and equality of pay.
>
> In a country where the sole employer is the State, opposition means
> death by slow starvation. The old principle: who does not work shall
> not eat, has been replaced by a new one: who does not obey shall
> not eat.

M. A. Adelman in Freeman, *op. cit.,* p. 295, says:

> . . . It has probably become clearer in the last ten years that the chief
> objection to socialism is not strictly economics but lies rather in its
> startling resemblance to the oldfashioned mining town where the one
> employer was also the landlord, the government, the school, etc., with
> the vital difference that there was a world outside the town which
> afforded means of escape for a few and, in time, of release for all.

See also the valuable words on this matter in Friedman, *op. cit.,* pp. 20–21.
David McCord Wright, *Democracy and Progress,* Macmillan, New York,
1948, p. 41, has observed: "Main Street creates the very diffusion of authority
which protected them [the intellectuals] from Main Street."

Siberia or Stalin Russia's Siberia either. It is hard to tell on the Chicago Board of Trade the difference between the wheat produced by Republican or Democratic farmers, by teetotalers or drunkards, Theosophists or Logical Positivists. I must confess that this is a feature of a competitive system that I find attractive.

Still, I must not overstress this point. A mixed economy in a society where people are by custom *tolerant* of differences in opinion may provide greater personal freedom and security of expression than does a purer price economy where people are less tolerant. Thus, in Scandinavia and Great Britain civil servants have, in fact, not lost their jobs when parties with a new philosophy come into power. In 1953, the Eisenhower Administration "cleaned house" in many government departments for reasons unconnected with McCarthyism. In 1951, when the Tories came to power, they deliberately recruited Fabian socialists to the civil service! Business freedoms may be fewer in those countries, but an excommunist probably meets with more tolerance from employers there.

This raises a larger question. Why should there be a perverse empirical relation between the degree to which public opinion is, in fact, tolerant and the degree to which it relies on free markets? In our history, the days of most rugged individualism —the Gilded Age and the 1920's—seem to have been the ages least tolerant of dissenting opinion.[18]

Fallacy of Freedom Algebra

I must raise some questions about the notion that absence of government means increase in "freedom." Is freedom simply a

[18] Years ago someone asked me, "Why is it that economists who are most libertarian in economic philosophy tend to be personally more intolerant than the average and less concerned with civil liberties and such matters?" I replied, "Is this true?" He said, "Look at the monolithic character of the three most libertarian departments of economics." I said, "The three departments most radical or anything else can hardly be expected to show average tolerance of differences." Our conversation broke off. However, in the last dozen years I have been alert to observe the attitudes and actions of economic libertarians in connection with nonmarket issues—teachers' oaths, passport squabbles, and the like. I am sorry to have to report that my friend

quantifiable magnitude, as much libertarian discussion seems to presume? Traffic lights coerce me and limit my freedom. Yet in the midst of a traffic jam on the unopen road, was I really "free" before there were lights? And has the algebraic total of freedom, for me or the representative motorist or the group as a whole, been increased or decreased by the introduction of well-engineered stop lights? Stop lights, you know, are also go lights.

Whatever may have been true on Turner's frontier, the modern city is crowded. Individualism and anarchy will lead to friction. We now have to coordinate and cooperate. Where cooperation is not fully forthcoming, we must introduce upon ourselves coercion. When we introduce the traffic light, we have, although the arch individualist may not like the new order, by cooperation and coercion created for ourselves greater freedom.

The principle of unbridled freedom has been abandoned; it is now just a question of haggling about the terms. On the one hand, few will deny that it is a bad thing for one man, or a few men, to impose their wills on the vast majority of mankind, particularly when that involves terrible cruelty and terrible inefficiency. Yet where does one draw the line? At a 51 per cent majority vote? Or, should there be no action taken that cannot command unanimous agreement—a position toward which such modern exponents of libertarian liberalism as Professor Milton Friedman are slowly evolving. Unanimous agreement? Well, virtually unanimous agreement, whatever that will come to mean.

The principle of unanimity is, of course, completely impractical. Aside from its practical inapplicability, the principle of unanimity is theoretically faulty. It leads to contradictory and intransitive decisions. By itself, it argues that just as society should not move from laissez-faire to planning because there will always be at least one objector, so society should never move from planning to freedom because there will always be at least one objector. Like standing friction, it sticks you where you are. It favors the status quo. And the status quo is certainly

---

had a point (although there are one or two persons who are residuals from his regression).

not to the liking of arch individualists. When you have painted yourself into a corner, what can you do? You can redefine the situation, and I predicted some years ago that there would come to be defined a privileged status quo, a set of natural rights involving individual freedoms, which alone requires unanimity before it can be departed from.[19]

At this point the logical game is up. The case for "complete freedom" has been begged, not deduced. So long as full disclosure is made, it is no crime to assume your ethical case. But will your product sell? Can you persuade others to accept your axiom, when it is in conflict with certain other desirable axioms?

Property and Human Rights

Closely related to ethical evaluation of business activity for its own sake are ethical attitudes towards the rights of property. Today, demagogues never tire of emphasizing the primacy of human over property rights; this is not an accident but rather a recognition that such sentiments evoke an increasingly resonant response from modern public opinion.

Today when we defend the rights of property, we often do so in the name of the *individual* rights of those who own property or hope one day to do so. The tides of modern politics pay little regard to the older view that property in all its prerequisites is a natural right and that whenever the democratic action of even $99\frac{44}{100}$ per cent of the electorate limits property rights

---

[19] A friend of mine is a justly famous expert on law. He has participated in world conferences, here and behind the Iron Curtain, dealing with such weighty concepts as "the Rule of Law." Apparently, the Russians do not view the matter in quite his way. I am not sure I do. After listening to his view, an eminent judge asked him, "Was slavery in Virginia in 1859 contrary to your 'Rule of Law'?" My friend squirmed. Finally, he replied, "Yes, really. Because the law permitting slavery was essentially a *bad* law." I congratulated my friend on his good luck: how fortunate that he had happened to be born in just those few years of the globe's history when *the* Rule of Law (about equivalent to that approved by a conservative New-Deal type) happened to be in bloom. Libertarians like Hayek are on the same boat, but they want it to stop at a different port; Gladstone's age turns out to have been the nearest approach to *the* (I mean Hayek's) Rule of Law. F. A. Hayek, *op. cit.*, Chapter 6.

in any degree, then an act of theft has taken place. Instead, the effective defense of property rights consists largely of specifying the inefficiencies that will result at the level of means and mechanisms from their impairment—the paralysis of risk taking, the effects upon saving, efforts and incentives; the certain or uncertain ruin that must follow wherever taxation exceeds 10 (or 90) per cent of national income.

All this may be true enough. But for some people it does not go far enough. It is a little like the saying: "Honesty is the best policy." Or, "The golden rule is good business." Beyond the level of expediency, there can be thought to be human property rights at the ethical level in the sense that the individual's property is to be taxed or affected by state action only in an orderly manner, within the framework of constitutional procedures and with "due process" being legally observed.

As a bulwark to historical property rights, this is not saying very much. To say that the electorate cannot arbitrarily do something to one millionaire without doing the same thing to another (essentially similar) millionaire provides little protection to the class of all millionaires, some of whom may even have amassed their millions at a time when it seemed reasonable *not* to anticipate policies of heavy income or capital taxation. Whether we approve or disapprove, we should face squarely the fact that neoclassical economic-welfare policies—which hold that after the ethically desirable distribution of income has been properly determined by democratic decision, a pricing system is to organize and allocate production in response to individuals' purchases—provide little protection to ancient property rights.

Personal Liberties and Rights

This makes it all the more important to study the question of the relation of property rights and market institutions to essential individual freedoms and liberties. These were enumerated by Lord Beveridge in his *Full Employment in a Free Society* as

. . . freedom of worship, speech, writing, study and teaching; freedom of assembly and association for political and other purposes, including the bringing about of a peaceful change of the governing authority;

freedom of a choice of occupation; and freedom in the management of a personal income . . . including freedom to decide to spend now and save so as to have the power of spending later . . . it being recognized that none of these freedoms can be exercised irresponsibly. . . .

The list of essential liberties given above does not include liberty of a private citizen to own means of production and to employ other citizens in operating them at a wage. Whether private ownership of means of production to be operated by others is a good economic device or not, it must be judged *as a device.* (The italics are mine.) [20]

To Americans this British view is interesting, because the distinction is made clear-cut between (1) human individual civil liberties or freedoms and (2) ethical evaluations of property rights and of business activity for their own sakes. So-called diehard conservatives will not alone be shocked by the distinction. At the extreme left, violent exception will also be taken to the view that "political democracy" can exist in the absence of what is called "economic or industrial democracy." Both extremes seem to argue that the essential human freedoms are inseparable from the institutional framework under which production is carried on. But, of course, they believe this in diametrically opposite senses; the extreme conservatives at the ethical level link human freedoms with relatively unhampered free enterprise, whereas the extreme radicals proclaim that human freedoms are empty and meaningless in the absence of "industrial democracy" (in one or another of the many senses in which the last two words are used).

From the standpoint of pure logic, I believe that the two concepts are conceptually distinct at the purely ethical level of ends. Moreover, whatever its pragmatic wisdom, there appears to be nothing inherently illogical (whatever its wisdom) in the ethical belief that individual human liberties have an ethical primacy over the freedoms associated with property and commercial activity.

However, this brings us to a quite different, but possibly important, question: "Granted that human rights are to be accorded ethical primacy over property rights, is it not true that human rights can only flourish and be preserved in a society that organ-

[20] Norton, New York, 1945, pp. 21–23.

izes its economic activity on the basis of relatively free private enterprise?" Many economic libertarians strongly proclaim an affirmative answer to this question. Friedrich Hayek's *The Road to Serfdom* (1944) is an eloquent attempt to read this same empirical law in the tea leaves of history. Frank Knight and Milton Friedman have enunciated interesting views along the same line. It is ironical, but not incriminating, that this is a conservative's variant of the strong Marxian doctrine that economic relationships allegedly determine political relationships.

As stated, this is not at all a philosophical question. Nor is it very much a question of economics. It is primarily a political, sociological, and anthropological question. Basically, it is an empirical question of inductive extrapolation or forecasting rather than one of consistent logical deduction from universally true *a priori* premises. And unfortunately, the patterns of history have not been optimally designed to perform the controlled experiments that would enable us to make either certainty or probability inferences on the hypothesis in question.

It will be plain that I have little confidence in emphatic generalizations concerning the empirical linkage of human political rights with any one economic system. Evidence—as I understand this term—is not at hand to validate strong inferences; and such evidence as may exist has not, to my knowledge, been carefully brought together anywhere and sifted to bring out the degree of our knowledge and lack of knowledge. In a world where economists cannot even accurately predict national income one year ahead or identify the demand elasticity for a single commodity, I find it somewhat *simpliste* to think that economists can arrive at confident answers to an infinitely more complex and important question, resting primarily on noneconomic data. Certainly the degree of confidence and emphasis with which judgments on this matter are proclaimed seems to weaken rather than strengthen one's trust in their validity. I may add as a digression that I greatly resent the prevailing tendency to regard the broad questions of social development as being too important to be left to mere judicious scholarly investigation and to handle them instead by the transcendental poetic talents of a Toynbee or Spengler.

The Limited Nature of Individual Political Liberties

The above discussion has left civil liberties almost completely emasculated of intrinsic economic content. The doctrine "a man's home is his castle" is to apply to rented as well as self-owned homes. But some of the methods and tools used to analyze theoretical economic concepts do have an application in this field of political theory.

For one thing, basic civil rights of the individual are shot through with "external effects." The ideal frontier community never existed in which freedom for the individual meant that he could live on his acre of land exactly as he wished, leaving others to live as they chose on theirs. Certainly today, the right of one man to speak what he wishes conditions the rights of another man to listen to what he wishes. The right of one man to "fair" consideration for a job has implications for the right of another man to "discriminate" as to whom he shall hire. The right of one group to preach nondemocratic principles has effects on the future existence of democracy itself. In the pursuit of happiness, we all interact.

Once we have recognized these external aspects of individual rights, we must recognize that precious little is being said in the familiar qualification that people are free so long as they do not inhibit the freedom of others. Any degree of limitation on freedoms can be rationalized by this formula.

Dogmatic absolutes being thus ruled out, democratic society is left in the position of pragmatically attempting to choose among partial evils so as to preserve as much as possible of human liberties and freedoms. Nor is it only in time of war and siege that it may become necessary to sacrifice some aspects of democratic freedoms in order to prevent losing more important aspects. Those who abandon the unproved faith that democratic individualism *is by its nature viable under all conditions* must compromise with evil at every turn. And it is not at all unlikely that they will end up killing, in the name of its salvation, much of what they wish to save, perhaps in these "scorched earth" operations killing even more than realistically had to be sacrificed.

Final Questions

Consider the little that is known concerning the interrelations between human rights and the organization of economic activity in the U.S.A. (1870, 1920, 1964) and the U.K.; the German Empire, the Weimar Republic, and the Third Reich; Norway, Sweden, Denmark, Australia, and New Zealand; pre– and post–1917 Russia; Italy, Czechoslovakia, and the Balkans—to say nothing of China, Arabia, Fiji, and non-Western cultures. Then ask ourselves what simple truths can be confidently inferred.

For a quite different appraisal of these same matters consider, in the cited Friedman book, the first chapter, "The Relation Between Economic Freedom and Political Freedom." A few quotations cannot do him justice but can give the flavor of the divergence of his view from mine.

The citizen of Great Britain, who after World War II was not permitted to spend his vacation in the United States because of exchange control, was being deprived of an *essential* freedom no less than the citizen of the United States, who was denied the opportunity to spend his vacation in Russia because of his political views. . . .

The citizen of the United States who is compelled by law to devote something like 10 per cent of *his* income to the purchase of a particular kind of retirement contract, administered by the government, is being deprived of a corresponding part of his personal freedom (page 8). (My italics.)

So is the man who would like to exchange some of his goods with, say, a Swiss for a watch but is prevented from doing so by a quota. . . .

Historical evidence speaks with a single voice on the relation between political freedom and a free market. I know of no example in time or place of a society that has been marked by a large measure of political freedom, and that has not also used something comparable to a free market to organize the bulk of economic activity (page 9).

Economists love diagrams. Figures 1 and 2 plot economic freedom (as if it were measurable as a scalar) on the horizontal axes, and political freedom (as if that too were separately measurable as a scalar) on the vertical axes. What I regard as the grossly oversimplified views are shown in Figure 1. Social reform (moving "west") inevitably plunges society ("southward") into serfdom. Hayek does not tell us what his predicted delay period is, but since he formulated his thesis as early as 1938 (and using the simplifying assumption that we are not unknowingly now in serfdom), the mechanism must involve lags of more than a quarter of a century. Friedman also believes in strong positive correlation between Y and X but indicates that economic freedom is a necessary but not a sufficient condition for political freedom. (Sidney and Beatrice Webb, particularly in their final honeymoon stage of infatuation with Stalin's Russia, would relabel the axes as X = Economic Democracy—whatever that means—and Y = Political Democracy. The U.K. and U.S.A. they would place up in the northwest and, except *in extremis* of infatuation, would put Russia in the southeast. As Fabians, they would maneuver the U.K. eastward.)

Figure 2 represents the more relevant question. Will a little more of the welfare state push the U.S.A. westward and necessarily southward? For years libertarians have been challenged to explain what appears to most observers to be the greater political freedoms and tolerances that prevail in Scandinavia than in America. In Norway, a professor may be a communist; a communist may sit by right on the Board of the Central Bank

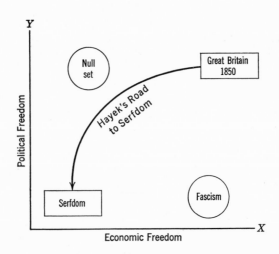

Figure 1

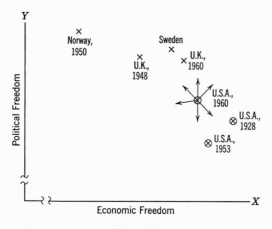

Figure 2

or as an Alternate Board member. The B.B.C. and Scandinavian airwaves seem, if anything, more catholic in their welcome to speakers of divergent views than was true in McCarthy America or is true now. In 1939, I was told that none of this would last; active government economic policy had to result in loss of civil liberties and personal freedoms. One still waits. Figure 2 does not represent my informed evaluation of the facts but merely poses the problem provocatively.

These are subjects that need serious empirical study, not strong *a priori* utterances or casual travelers' anecdotes.

7

The European Business Environment

Business Responsibilities in Europe[1]

Philippe de Woot

Coming from a very pragmatic, down-to-earth, matter-of-fact sort of Continent—I mean young Europe—I feel a bit at a loss among these highbrow, scholarly minded, soul-searching and very distinguished American professors, asking their students who they are and where they are going.

But I will do my best to elevate myself to this level. And I will ask you to excuse me if I do not quite succeed, but we Europeans feel so much younger and less experienced than you, that it should be understandable.

The objective of this short presentation is to show how European business tends to define its role in the present European society. This presentation is a very general and schematic one. Of course, it has to be nuanced for each European country taken separately, but, as a whole, it will give a fairly accurate account of the most recent trend in this field.

One can develop the argument along the following lines:

1. The structural environment of business has changed to a considerable extent.
2. The attitudes of the environmental forces toward business are more or less hostile, suspicious, conflictual.

[1] Transcript of statement presented at Workshop on Social and Political Environment of Business, University of California, Berkeley, January 31, 1964. (See the Preface to this book.)

3. As a response to these changes and attitudes, business has elaborated an ideology that, up to now, has been essentially defensive.

4. A more pragmatic and positive business behavior tends now to appear, based on an analysis of the social function of business and its integration in the society as a whole.

The Structures

The structural environment of business has changed to a considerable extent since the war. And this change is responsible for the change in business behavior. This confirms one of the conclusions of Earl Cheit's paper—that the increased sense of social awareness is not due to changes inside the firm but to influences outside it. What are these changes?

The most significant one is the appearance of *the mixed economy* that Paul Samuelson has referred to. The mixed economy is a reality in Europe, or, at least, in many countries such as France, Holland, Sweden, Belgium. It is there, and we do not consider it as an enemy but as progress in our search of what a good society has to be.

What does this mixed economy mean for business? Among other things, it means (1) the rise of the government as an economic agent, through planning, income policy, price control, larger public spending, aids and subsidies, and initiatives in many fields; (2) a greater political role for labor unions—in many countries they have seized power and they pursue a policy of social welfare; (3) a reduced political influence of business, which has ceased to be the only social force in our society.

Another important change is the *rise of Europe* and the success of the Common Market. This calls for a greater dynamism, a more objective approach to the complex problems of growth and welfare, and, more important, a common effort of all the social forces at work. This has also put a greater emphasis on business as an agent of this economic growth.

The Attitudes

In the field of attitudes, one can say that the business environment is more or less hostile. There are strong antibusiness ide-

ologies—socialism and left-wing Christian Democracy on the one
hand; state technocracy, fairly well represented by M. Bloch-
Laine, on the other.

The basis of these ideologies is that it is not conceivable to let
business define the goals of the society as a whole. Other social
forces must be heard and allowed to defend their own conception
of a good society and their own interests.

The main claim of these other ideologies turns around the idea
of social welfare as a substitute for the profit motive, the idea of
a society oriented towards the good of the many and not the
privileges of the few.

This creates a more or less hostile environment, which is, of
course, neither overwhelming nor overpowering. It is a typical
case of countervailing powers that have neither destroyed nor
defeated the fighting spirit of business. They have merely forced
it to rethink its role in society and to adjust itself to this new
environment.

Business is resisting these pressures fairly well and is devising
new ways of influence. This influence is apparent and even flagrant in many European governments. Everyone knows that the
Prime Minister of one large European country is a former high
executive of a powerful financial group. Business has succeeded
in imposing its own Minister of Finance and its Minister of External Trade on another left-wing government.

A Business Ideology

In this new environment and confronting these more or less
hostile attitudes, business has, of course, put emphasis on certain
themes, which could be considered as an ideology.

This ideology is essentially defensive. It is articulated around
the following themes:

1. *Defense of private property.* The property of the firm is considered by business people as a sacred right given to man by
   the natural law. This is challenged by the other ideologies.
   It has been put into question by the post-war nationalizations.
   At the present time, it is seriously discussed on ideological
   grounds.

2. *Freedom of action and initiative.* This is the great debate on national planning and autonomy of the firm. It has not come to the point of suppressing the right of initiative or the freedom of action but rather of limiting and controlling them. Certain reformers go so far as to recommend the creation of a management license to be delivered only to able people and to be taken back when they cease to be able.

3. *The righteousness of profit.* Public opinion considers the term "profit taker" in a very pejorative sense; it is usually preceded by the adjective "dirty." Business people have to fight to establish the legitimacy of profit and to explain that profit is not a sin but the cornerstone of the whole economic system and the best proof of its efficiency.

4. *A legal status for labor unions,* which have no legal personality and cannot be controlled or sued if they go too far. Business people contend that the dialogue with the labor unions would be greatly facilitated, if they were given this legal status. The unions tend to consider this status as a threat and a limitation to their freedom of action.

5. A vague affirmation that business *contributes to the civilization.* Many words are said to this effect but they do not really define what type of contribution. One gets the impression that business people are vague in this field, because they have no really clear idea on the matter.

The Finality of the Enterprise

In French, the word finality means purpose—an ultimate and fundamental aim; it has a dynamic connotation that it lacks in its English translation. The search for a business finality or fundamental purpose constitutes the most recent trend in this field.

Some business people have understood perfectly that the defensive ideology described is of no use whatsoever. They have realized that every time they have actually influenced the government or the other countervailing powers, it has been through their own power, through pressures of many kinds, through some sort of power politics—and on very pragmatic and concrete questions.

What they are tending to do now is to *integrate* business power with labor power and government power, *provided that their economic role is recognized for what it is.*

That is the reason why business people try to define this role in its specificity. What is the function, in our modern society, that business alone can fulfill? This is their present search, and they are calling it the finality of business enterprise.

The specific functions of business enterprise are not to be defined through an ideology but through an objective analysis of what business is and of what business does. This objectivity will rob the debate of passion and greatly facilitate the dialogue with other social forces.

In this context, business tends to define itself not by profit alone; this does not describe what business is doing. Business defines itself by economic progress.

The main agent of economic progress is the business firm. And self-interest is probably the best motivation to reach this goal. In this perspective profit plays the role of a motor and of an indicator of efficiency. It is the business firm that has enabled society to shift from poverty to affluence, that has taken on its shoulders the weight and the risk of change. This is a social function in itself, and it has to be recognized, protected, and praised as one of the most eminent functions in our society.

At the same time, it is not the only function that society requires in order to be successfully managed. There are other functions, such as the political function, the social function (in the sense of welfare), and many others.

Why not integrate all these functions and put them in a state of dialogue rather than of conflict and suspicion? Each social force will play its specific part in the achievement of a better society to which everyone then will contribute. This is more or less what we mean by a mixed economy.

I had the impression reading these extraordinarily stimulating papers that you in the United States were much ahead of us in the field of individual opportunity and achievement. I also had the impression that we Europeans were perhaps putting greater emphasis in our research on society as a whole and how a good society has to be organized.

Perhaps this could be, in a not too distant future, a field where Europe can contribute to your researches and your studies. We have received so much from you that you must understand that we are longing for the time when we will be able to show you our gratitude in some concrete way.

The French Businessman in His Milieu[1]

Gilbert M. Sauvage

My task is to describe the French businessman in his environment. As these essays have amply demonstrated, I think that we are likely to find business leaders, whatever their trade, ideology, or behavior, influenced to a large extent by their environmental *milieu*. One can paint, therefore, a fairly accurate picture of the businessman merely by pointing out the ties existing between his actual performance and the main features of his environment.

I shall single out four major stages of the businessman's life story: the selection and training of business leaders; the attitudes of the men at the top; business within the planning environment; and industry's reaction to the opening of the European market and the sharpening of potential competition.

I would like to put two conditions, however. First, the businessman I am trying to sketch is the French genus of the species. As an instructor at INSEAD, one of the few European business schools, I would be wary of disregarding national differences too rashly; a European type of businessman is developing nicely, but,

[1] Transcript of statement presented at Workshop on Social and Political Environment of Business, University of California, Berkeley, January 31, 1964. (See the Preface to this book.)

by and large, he is not going to rule over European industry for years to come. Second, a mere profile of the French businessman is what I have in mind; a rough sketch is often more convenient as a practical guide than an encyclopedia.

The Selection and Training of French Business Leaders

While the so-called schools of commerce—*École des Hautes Études Commerciales,* E.S.S.E.C., and other superior schools of commerce, as well as, to a lesser extent, the low schools—continue to provide most of the rank and file of the business community, it is rather typical, I think, that the highest positions in French business have been held over the past fifty years by graduate school alumni. The typical example is the *École Polytechnique*— a sort of French M.I.T. with unusually severe admission standards—whose alumni were once said to hold all the key positions in industry and control France's economy as closely as the Jesuits once ruled Paraguay. Science and engineering graduates were prominent among industry leaders. French industry was largely production-conscious under the rule of the engineers, and marketing, finance, and other management techniques were often given insufficient attention. Thus, there was an exceptionally high degree of reliance on higher education as a means of selection; and the skills of mathematics and the abstract sciences were at a premium (they still are).

The interesting phenomenon of the last thirty years is that the men recruited for the top management posts do not come directly from industry itself. Many of them—an increasing number, in fact—come from government service. For a good many years the Finance Inspection Service, the *Conseil d'État* (Higher Administrative Tribunal), the *Préfets* and *Sous–Préfets* who head French regional and local administration have supplied major French industries with a growing number of higher executives, vice presidents, and presidents. Higher civil service is still regarded as one of the most worthy careers in the country; it also ensures excellent training based on severe selection. Civil servants are appointed as heads of major companies, because they are thought to be the best men for the job, not in order to please the government.

It is easy to see that this man will have, in everyday life, an attitude quite different from that of his American counterpart. His approach to human relations is likely to be more authoritarian. Although his decisions are no longer supported by the full authority of the law, they tend to retain something of this flavor. On the other hand, he will not be afraid of interference by the government, which he is confident that he can channel or control. He will be even more prone to regard his activity as a social task. There will often be no appreciable difference in behavior between him and his colleagues who are managers of nationalized industries and follow very similar careers. The constitution of one single oligarchy of managers or technocrats working in business, public industries, or government may be the consequence of this fact. Are we then justified in speaking of French businessmen as a well-defined social group clearly distinct from other managerial groups?

L'Homme Seul

The second feature of the business leader as he is known in France and in several other countries of Western Europe is that he is a lonely man. The American team, where responsibility is largely shared between the president of the large corporation and his vice presidents, is an exception on the other side of the ocean. The president-director-general does not like to delegate powers. In addition to major policy decisions, which his American colleague might also make by himself, he will want to have minor problems brought to him for decision—everything that he used to see when he was a younger man, and the firm a small entity. He does not want to be just the head of the organization; he wants to be the organization itself. As a consequence, the manager will tend to look outside the firm for the information, support, and technical help that he cannot obtain from the top men around him.

He turns first to the industrial organization to which he belongs. The N.A.M. would appear a very small organization compared to the huge National Council of French Employers (C.N.P.F.) or its powerful Italian counterpart, the *Confindustria*. Their component parts, the industrial federations set up to coordinate and to promote the aims and interests of the various industries, also wield a good deal of power. They can do many things for their members—provide confidential information, help in the promotion of exports, put the point of view of the industry across to the government or the public at large. The lonely man is not alone any more; in fact, he has at his disposal all the resources of several well-equipped clubs—one at the level of the industry, the other at the level of the nation.

If the problems facing the firm are of a more delicate and more technical nature—e.g., matters of organization, product planning, or market research—the businessman will turn to a consultants' agency. This may not be new in the United States, but the interesting thing is that only in France have such consultants' firms reached a similar development. A firm like S.E.M.A. is one of the biggest in the world, and it is by no means the only one in the field. Germany and Italy do not have such large consultants' organizations—at any rate, nowhere near the French level.

Free Business Enterprise within a Planning Framework

It is well known that French businessmen, instead of facing a free market, operate within the framework of the planning mechanism. I would disagree, however, with Earl Cheit's interpretation that the primary purpose of the plan is "to bring economic power under political control." It is rather to help the businessman to expand his economic activity as a contribution to general economic development.

Against the uncertainty and risks of his market, the French businessman of the late 1920's and 1930's used to protect himself by joining cartels and restricting competition as much as he could by concerted practices. Whenever he felt that his position was threatened, redress was sought from the government. The shortages and bottlenecks of the postwar period, combined with an even greater uncertainty about the future of the French economy as a whole and of private enterprise in particular, led businessmen to welcome a tighter form of cooperation. This was found in the Reconstruction and Development Plan, which began in 1947.

If the Plan had had as its sole purpose the optimum allocation of scarce resources on a national basis, it would hardly have awakened the enthusiasm of French private firms. It soon became apparent, however, that the technical programming process, which the Plan Commissioner's Office (*Commissariat au Plan*) and the Bureau of Economic and Financial Studies of the Ministry of Finance have handled so competently for the past fifteen years, was by no means the main feature of the Plan. Everyone would probably agree that the major part of the work is done within the twenty-seven industrial committees that work out the various targets of production, investment, prices, manpower, exports, etc. Business representatives sitting on these commissions with trade union members, government officials, consumer members, and others make up about forty per cent of the commission. Needless to say, they have great weight in the decisions.

To these men, the sets of figures proposed by the *Commissariat au Plan* for their particular industry have no compelling authority in themselves. Their value comes from their economic coherence and from the recognized quality of the expert work involved in their preparation. They represent basically a huge piece of market research combined with analyses of the production apparatus and financial and manpower aspects. Should producers want to change these targets, they are perfectly free to do so to the extent that other committees will be prepared to accept the changes. The iron and steel committee, for instance, will be able to raise its production target by 1.2 million tons only if the building industry will agree to increase its purchases of round steel by 250,000 tons, the automobile industry by 200,000 tons of flat products, and so on until the total increase is absorbed. Otherwise, it will be up to the foreign trade committee to say whether the world market perspectives, the competitiveness of French steel prices, and the anticipated reduction of world tariffs on steel products make it likely that French steel exports can be stepped up by the required amount. After comments have been received on the iron and steel industry's proposals from all the other committees, steel manufacturers sitting on the iron and steel committee will know what they can do and what they should not do. In these circumstances, the limitation to their freedom of action does not come from the Plan Commissioner or the government; it comes from the market itself. Consequently, if it is true to say that the freedom of action of the French businessman is in a certain sense limited by the Plan, one must admit that the Plan primarily gives expression to economic constraints for the benefit of all firms, whereas many of these—mainly the medium-sized or small ones—would have been unable to carry out the complicated calculating in production and programming. Conversely, the elimination of a large part of the risk and uncertainty involved in any new venture is likely to make the businessman bolder in his decisions. This is the key to France's economic recovery and sustained rate of growth since the early 1950's. As a French economist once remarked, "The Monnet plan was designed to limit the economic freedom of the entrepreneur, and, if necessary, to increase it!"

Business and the Opening of the French Market to World Competition

The fourth relevant change that I would like to mention in connection with the businessman is the change in the size and nature of the French market and of industry's attitude toward it. For three-quarters of a century French industrialists have worked behind protective tariff walls about as high as those of the Americans. In both countries, the justification given was that the country should protect itself against low-wage and low-cost competitors abroad, but France, with a quarter of the population and less than half the gross national product of the United States, did not provide her manufacturers with a market big enough for mass production. As for exports, they were the privilege of a few specialized industries, whereas most of the others, unlike their Belgian or German neighbors, regarded selling abroad as an exceptional activity.

The change brought by the Common Market was threefold; first came the certainty that by 1965–66 there would be no customs duties to speak of left between the territories of Benelux, France, Germany, and Italy. Second, no French businessman, however domestic he may wish to be in his outlook, can now decide that he will abstain from invading his three neighbors.

Even if he does not encroach on their market, that will not keep *them* away from his market; his customers may well be enticed away from him by the lure of new products, better service, or better prices, as the tariff wall collapses. Following Clausewitz's principles, he may decide that the best way to defend his own *chasse gardée* may be to carry the commercial war onto his competitors' territory. This is how competition is spreading on the European level. Third, as the common external tariff is being established around the Six as the arithmetical average of the four national tariffs, the highest duties—those of France and Italy—have to go down by as much as the lowest duties—those of Benelux and Germany—must go up. As a result, half the protection that French industry enjoyed in 1957 will be gone by the mid-sixties. The GATT negotiations under the Dillon and Kennedy proposals for tariff cutting on a reciprocal basis are wearing away even further this protection in exchange for further opportunities for French exports on foreign markets.

It is hard to see what can remain of the old French protectionism under such circumstances. Results are, in fact, reflected in the threefold increase of France's imports and exports, whereas the importance of foreign trade as a percentage of the G.N.P. has almost doubled.

For the French businessman as for the French consumer, European and world competition have become an everyday reality, a major change from prewar years.

It would perhaps be tempting, on the basis of the preceding remarks, to draw a profile of the French businessman as an exceptionally well-trained and self-assertive individual working hand in hand with his national federation, the Plan authorities, and the government in order to equip national industry for world competition both within and without the country. Thanks to his newly won dynamism, the country, according to this profile, would be achieving one of the highest long-term rates of growth ever known in a capitalist economy. Should not this man be justifiably proud of himself, of his achievements, and of the whole managerial class to which he belongs?

In painting such an idealized picture, we should not forget the original sin in which our hero was born. However successful he may be, he is still laboring under Adam's curse. He knows that part of the country's interior difficulties were due to the failure of free enterprise to invest enough to provide for depreciation and development of capital equipment. He knows that nationalization and government intervention were performed largely to provide the national economy with adequate supplies of fuel and power, transport, and capital. He knows also that, while fighting for the survival of free enterprise during the great depression, his forebears, in fact, sold their souls to the devil in working out cartels and concerted practices of all kinds designed to control the market mechanism and keep competition to a minimum.

It is doubtful whether this man will ever want to enjoy full, unhampered freedom again. Most likely, he will prefer to rely on a concerted economic system implying a large degree of government cooperation. As the faithful have sought salvation from Adam's curse in the Church, built to bring man nearer to God, the mixed economy is ready to admit the modern entrepreneur, whose main purpose is to fulfill his public tasks, and bring him to closer cooperation with the government. History will say whether this immersion in a complete system of mixed economy will be the fate of the French businessman of tomorrow.

Index